After providing historical perspective and valuable insights into market and sector investment cycles, Pradhuman thoroughly covers small-cap growth/value style investing, and relevant stock selection models. **The book is equally valuable to small-cap investors and anyone considering small-cap stocks in an asset allocation framework.**

—RICHARD J. HOLCOMB
Structured Equity Portfolio Manager
State of Michigan Retirement Systems

Satya's rigorous quantitative work coupled with his perceptive insights into personal investment styles makes **this book relevant and interesting to both professional money managers and individual investors. His history of small-cap performance is excellent, and his work on investment models for companies is first-rate.**

—MARIAN U. PARDO
Managing Director & Head, U.S. Small Cap Group
J.P. Morgan Investment Management, Inc.

Satya Pradhuman's uncommon insight into small-cap stocks is the root of my success, and it could well be the foundation of yours, too. *Small-Cap Dynamics* can benefit the neophyte to the veteran stock picker. It also comes at the perfect time—Wall Street has spent far too long in love with the biggest stocks and ignoring the small fry. In my thinking, that means we may be on the cusp of another period when going small is the way to outperform the market. **I can think of no better guide to the world of small-cap stocks than Satya Pradhuman.**

—MARCUS W. ROBINS, CFA
Founder and Editor-in-Chief
RedChip Review™

Small-Cap Dynamics **combines academic research on small company stocks with real-world knowledge.** While anyone who is interested in small-cap stocks should read this book, there is lots of material that goes beyond this market sector. I especially liked his discussion on value/growth style preference . . . psychology—one's desire to own growth stocks can be measured by a diagnostic test!

—RALPH WANGER
Portfolio Manager
Acorn Fund

Small-Cap
Dynamics

Also available from
Bloomberg Press

Mastering Microcaps:
Strategies, Trends, and Stock Selection
by Daniel P. Coker

Risk:
The New Management Imperative in Finance
by James T. Gleason

Investing in Small-Cap Stocks: Revised Edition
by Christopher Graja and Elizabeth Ungar, Ph.D.

Investing in Hedge Funds:
Strategies for the New Marketplace
by Joseph G. Nicholas

Market-Neutral Investing:
Long/Short Hedge Fund Strategies
by Joseph G. Nicholas

A complete list of our titles is available at
www.bloomberg.com/books

Attention Corporations

Bloomberg Press books are available at quantity discounts with bulk
purchase for sales promotional use and for corporate education or other
business uses. Special editions or book excerpts can also be created. For
information, please call 609-279-4670 or write to: Special Sales Dept.,
Bloomberg Press, P.O. Box 888, Princeton, NJ 08542.

BLOOMBERG PROFESSIONAL LIBRARY

Small-Cap Dynamics

Insights, Analysis, and Models

SATYA DEV PRADHUMAN

Bloomberg Press
Princeton

Library of Congress Cataloging-in-Publication Data

Pradhuman, Satya Dev
    Small-cap dynamics : insights, analysis, and models / Satya Dev Pradhuman.
       p.   cm. — (Bloomberg professional library)
    Includes bibliographical references.
    ISBN 1-57660-029-7 (alk.)
    1. Small capitalization stocks.   I. Title.   II. Series.
HG4971 .P7   2000
332.63'22—dc21

                                    00-030393

Edited by Kathleen Peterson

First edition published 2000

1 3 5 7 9 10 8 6 4 2

To Mary—

You make me want to be a better man.

From As Good As It Gets

CONTENTS

PART II

Navigating in the Small-Cap Universe

ACKNOWLEDGMENTS

T his book would not have been possible without the incredible support I have received from my colleagues. I wish to thank Mohamed Chbani, part of the Merrill Lynch small-cap research team, who has made contributions in all aspects of producing this book. Together we have spent an enormous amount of time discussing, formulating, and stress testing concepts in the small-cap market. He has also been instrumental in pulling together the wealth of exhibits found throughout this text.

I want to thank Kathleen Peterson, my editor, for helping me to crystallize my ideas and for turning a set of research notes into a cohesive body of work. I owe a debt of gratitude to the individuals who have contributed a great deal to my understanding of the financial markets and in particular the secondary marketplace—Phil Appel, Martin Fridson, Alan Gilston, William Kan (also part of the Merrill Lynch small-cap research team), Steve Kim, Jose Rasco, and Nigel Tupper. My ideas and perspective have become more grounded because of their willingness to openly discuss and question financial market concepts. Richard Bernstein belongs in this category as well. But I also wish to express my gratitude to Rich for introducing me to, and sparking my interest in, this complex but truly rewarding field of research.

The book contains a remarkable amount of data and factoids—some terribly hard to find. I wish to acknowledge the remainder of the small-cap team—Laura Barrett and Georgianna Fung—for making this painstaking task possible. I also wish to acknowledge the fine research assistance of Catherine Schneider. I am grateful to Merrill Lynch management, specifically Rosemary Berkery, Andrew Melnick, and Jeff Peek, for nurturing the small-cap research efforts.

I wish to recognize Chris Graja of Bloomberg for encouraging me to take on the task of writing this book on small-cap investing. Others who have contributed and supported me in my efforts include Robert Dolber, Kathy Kelly, Diane Garnick, Silvio Lotufo, Richard Klein, Chris Leupold, Arsen Mrakovcic, Tom White, Dave Webb, Steve Lamon, Joan Christensen, Thatcher Thompson, Tracy Tait, and Sylvia Parker.

Finally, I wish to thank my wife, Mary, for all her support, sacrifice, and encouragement. She has spent countless hours patiently acting as a sounding board for me as I wrote the outline, formulated notes, and wrote the text. She also spent a great deal of time helping me edit the final draft. Thanks also to my children, Jenna Grace and Devon Ross, for the wonderful ways in which they both inspire me.

PREFACE

As we race into the new millennium, smaller stocks in the United States, United Kingdom, Japan, Australia, and Germany have bounced back from a multiyear period of obscurity and have begun to outperform blue chip favorites. Is this a temporary state enticing investors to plunge into one of the riskier components of the equity market or is it the start of a steady, long-term rebound of a hugely undervalued asset? This book attempts to address the age-old issue of whether and when to invest in small stocks for the long run. In doing so, it dissects the small-cap market, defining key drivers and offering tools to maneuver in a challenging investment landscape rich with opportunities.

When I began researching small caps in the early 1990s, I was surprised by the lack of research and analysis surrounding this secondary market. Even the statistical data available on smaller stocks was sketchy. With few metrics to follow, I started from scratch. Ironically, this predicament made me realize that the opportunities for an active investor were perhaps greatest among smaller stocks. Because of the mere trickle of research available on this sector (versus the flood that accompanies large-cap issues), the ability to take advantage of mispricings can be considerably more abundant. Some years later, I also realized that the opportunist findings that had become the core of the small-cap research effort at Merrill Lynch needed to be pulled together into one cohesive body of work—both thorough and accessible to the professional and the private investor alike.

In addressing that need, *Small-Cap Dynamics: Insights, Analysis, and Models* is divided into two parts. The first section, "Fundamentals of the Secondary Market," introduces and defines the distinct characteristics of the small-cap market. This section also addresses dynamic issues that may cause the small-cap market to change. The second section, "Navigating in the Small-Cap Universe," tackles more advanced issues such as asset allocation, drivers of the small-cap cycle, and developing stock selection models that add value in the small-cap market. There is also detailed discussion centered on investment styles—growth and value investing. Also included is a close-up examination of the seasonal bias typically observed among smaller stocks.

Chapter One, "Small Stocks and the Relevance of Size," explains the dramatic swings of the small-cap market. The chapter introduces the concept of the domino principle as it applies to small caps. It argues that the rotation from a large-cap bull market to a small-cap bull market, and vice versa, causes ripples across the entire equity market that affect both small- and large-cap investors. Based on the existence of the domino effect, small- and large-cap investors must take a stance on size. An investor's preference for companies with greater or smaller capitalization levels relates to one's preference for risk.

A section of Chapter One inspects the past cycles of small- and large-cap bull markets for insights into investor preference for risk taking and therefore the ebb and flow between smaller and large companies. Factors such as cyclical growth, credit and cost of capital conditions, profitability, and geopolitical or exogenous shocks have influenced investors' preference for sized investments and have accounted for major shifts in the equity markets.

Chapter Two, "The Small-Cap Backdrop," steps back to discuss the microstructure of equity markets—and answers the question: What are small stocks? This chapter is a primer on the small-cap market, delving into its distinguishing characteristics—factors such as returns and risk levels, economic sensitivity, sector exposures, and information flow—all of which make the small-cap market unique. There is also a complete discussion of benchmarks for the small-cap market.

There have been ten significant turning points for smaller stocks since 1926. Chapter Three, "Major Small-Cap and Large-Cap Cycles," chronicles each of the cycles and these turning points. The focus of this chapter is not only to recount the past, but more importantly, to relate the context that allowed for the shifting change of heart in which the preference for smaller firms in the equity market periodically has emerged and reemerged.

Markets, like all systems, are dynamic, they evolve over time. "A Changing Landscape—Significant Recent Trends Affecting the Small-Cap Market," Chapter Four, closes Part I by addressing the changing investment landscape and how it impacts the small-cap market and the preference of small- versus large-cap investing. Amidst the many factors that affect the relationship between small and large caps, a handful of changes have been truly significant and are most likely to have an ongoing effect. A few of the innovations that have introduced new wrinkles in the small-cap investment process are the evolution of the Internet, smaller firms' increasing access to capital, the expansion of professionally managed assets, a tighter linkage between corporate managers and share-holders, and the use of futures and derivatives. Although many of these changes are generally beneficial for the small-cap market, not all changes necessarily increase the premium that small caps have traditionally received in the market.

The secondary issues and blue chip sector are complementary segments of the equity market, yet factors such as volatility, marketability, and information flow cause small caps to behave quite differently from large caps. The differences between small and large caps support an asset allocation approach to investing in smaller companies. Chapter Five, "Asset Allocation and Small Caps" offers insights into the proper long-term exposure to the small-caps asset class. The chapter tackles the size preference using modern portfolio theory assumptions. Asset class correlations, regional exposures and time diversification are some of the tools utilized to determine and fine tune a solid long-term exposure to smaller stocks.

"Drivers of Secondary Stocks," Chapter Six, formalizes the arguments broached in Chapter 1 regarding the preference for, or the drivers of, the small-cap cycle. Chapter 1 argues that the rotation from small to large stocks, and vice versa, is driven by the changes in investors' appetite for risk taking. Factors such as cyclical growth, credit and cost of capital conditions, and profitability levels significantly affect an investor's acceptance of risk. This chapter rigorously tests such relationships against the small-cap cycle. The chapter also steps through popular myths and misconceptions about what accounts for the rotations between smaller and large firms.

"Market Timing Small Stocks," Chapter Seven, examines four specific risk indicators that allow investors to avoid near-term pitfalls in the small-cap market—volatility, earnings expectations, insider trading, and the issuance market. It explores their impact on the small-cap market and discusses the signals they convey for potential small-cap performance.

Chapter Eight, "Stock Selection Models," gives a detailed examination of stock selection models in the small-cap market. Popular factors such as momentum investing, earnings revision models, and the classic valuation approaches are examined. The discussion not only outlines the process of structuring a quantitative active model, but also discusses the strengths and weaknesses to each approach. The chapter offers guidelines in examining and stress-testing stock selection factors. Finally, there is a solid discussion of structuring a portfolio using a multi-factor approach.

"Style Investing," Chapter Nine, discusses the importance of investment styles, in particular emerging growth versus value investing, in the context of the small-cap market. The small-cap market can be seen as a market that contains severely polarized investments—from the most aggressive growth companies to the terribly under-followed value companies. These extreme worlds come together under one banner called small caps. Attempting to invest successfully in either of these polar styles requires unique goals, discipline, and requisite risk tolerances. The chapter also presents a detailed discussion of measuring investment style returns—an area in the financial markets that is still quite loosely defined. Included as well is an in-depth discussion of the causes of style rotations—which center on three groups of indicators, those based on economic sensitivity, interest rate effects, and market-based signals (e.g., valuations and volatility). The chapter closes with a discussion of personality traits that might cause an individual to have a natural disposition toward investing with an emerging growth or value bent.

Finally, Chapter Ten closes Part II with a discussion of a seasonal anomaly called the January effect. The unusual bounce of returns at the start of the calendar year is positive and pronounced for small stocks. This chapter looks closely at the effects of the seasonal bias, which can be powerful yet fleeting, and discusses its apparent causes. By understanding the potential catalysts for this pricing anomaly, one can better avoid possible pitfalls to the seasonal anomaly and even position holdings to capture or amplify the benefits of the January effect.

The mission of this book is simple: To de-mystify the small-cap market. A great amount of effort and thought has gone into presenting important facts and relationships unique to small-cap investing and explaining their significance to investment. The information and concepts pulled together are meant not only to inform but also to challenge, and hopefully, offer investment wisdom to the reader.

PART I

Fundamentals of the Secondary Market

ONE

Small Stocks and the Relevance of Size

WHY INVESTORS HAVE FAVORED SMALL STOCKS

SMALL STOCKS have outperformed the blue-chip favorites since 1926. The returns of small capitalization stocks—those of companies with a market capitalization under $1.5 billion—have more than doubled those of large companies, or companies with high market capitalization—generally, above $4.5 billion. Figure 1.1 represents the relative performance of small versus large stocks. An investment of $1 in small stocks in 1926 would be worth $3,969 in the year 2000, whereas $1 invested in large stocks appreciated to a value of $1,761 over the identical time frame. On a simple average basis, small stocks have generated 14.7 percent versus 12.3 percent, or 2.4 percent more than large stocks, and on an annualized basis, they have outperformed large stocks by 1.1 percent annually since 1926. This historical premium for smaller stocks has been seen in other markets as well, such as those in the United Kingdom and Japan.

Size, in the terminology of the equity markets, typically refers to market capitalization. A reference to small or large capitalization is a moving target, however, because the market value, or capitalization, of a firm is dynamic. With each tick-up in share price, a corresponding increase occurs in market value or capitalization. Hence, the size of any given small cap (small capitalization firm) changes as the market appreciates.

Historical returns might be the catalyst that has spurred investor interest in small companies, but they cannot fully explain the ongoing interest in small-cap stocks, also referred to as *the secondary market*. Small-cap cycles of underperformance have been equally spectacular.

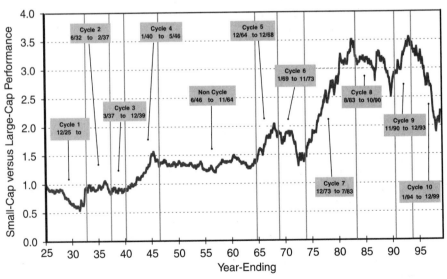

* All figures are represented as annualized total return.

Figure 1.1   Long-Term Small-Cap Cycle (December 1925 to December 1999)

Indeed, the underperformance of smaller companies in the United States and other equity markets in the latter half of the 1990s has caused the arguments in favor of small-stock investing to come under intense scrutiny.

Nonetheless, sparked by their potential, interest in the secondary markets is impressive. Several hundred funds in the United States alone are dedicated to investing in smaller companies, which hold out the promise of being investment jewels because they have not yet been discovered or are not widely followed by the investment community. In fact, there has been a proliferation of size-based products, and numerous choices are available, particularly among midcap funds. Midcap funds offer investors an exposure to middle-sized firms—companies with market capitalization roughly between $1.5 and $4.5 billion.

These investment products have been developed to capture the benefits of smaller caps' performance without all the volatility that accompanies such stocks. Managers have structured portfolios on the basis of small-cap growth, small-cap value, small caps with dividends—and the list goes on. Over the past two decades, the smaller companies' universe has been increasingly parceled along market capitalization lines. Most recently, investors have begun nibbling at the microcap market—companies with under $200 million in market capitalization. In addition, the secondary market has received a noticeable amount of interest at the international level. International funds have begun offering clients exposure to small-cap markets. Many asset management firms—including Merrill Lynch, Lord Abbett, Warburg Pincus, and Bankers Trust—offer numerous international or global small-cap funds.

This interest may partly be due to smaller companies' history of spectacular victories and admittedly painful collapses. These tales of guts and glory, or a chance for a quick killing, may be the sources of continuing investor attraction. Despite the volatility of the small-cap market, investors continue to pursue it in search of the next Microsoft.

CLASSIC SMALL-CAP TYPES

Small stock investments typically take one of three shapes. A rising star is a growth stock that evolves from a microcap to a megacap status, seemingly overnight. Another type of small stock is the fallen angel. Like Icarus, who, in Greek mythology, soared too close to the sun and fell because his wings melted, hyperactive growth can lead to disastrous missteps, which can cause a fall from grace. Small stocks that fall from the large-cap arena into the small or even the microcap world could be considered "damaged goods." The third path of a small stock can be like the rise of the phoenix from ashes. It is a resurgent fallen angel or a stock into which market participants have priced too much risk. All investors want to partake in the first and third stages and avoid at all costs, buying into a falling angel. At one time or another, all stocks fall into one, two, or even all three of these categories.

One can reasonably argue that Oxford Health Plans, the health management organization, has, fortunately and unfortunately, moved through each of the three stages identified—it has been a rising star, a falling angel, and, possibly, a rebounding fallen angel. Cisco Systems, the networking hardware giant, could be seen as a rising star that gained megacap status in just seven years. Cisco has managed to step away from significant threats and nimbly avoid the second stage that rapidly growing companies can encounter. Detailed analyses of these two companies follow.

Oxford Health Plans

A managed care organization that embodied the hopes for a market-based solution to rein in health care costs, this start-up was founded in 1984 and successfully grew into one of the most profitable health management organizations (HMOs). Oxford Health Plans (OXHP) went public in 1991 at $45 million market capitalization and quickly issued an additional 30 million shares, pushing its capitalization to roughly $136 million by September 1991. The stock then rapidly became a star performer by gaining more than 68 percent in market capitalization in just 12 months (see Figure 1.2).

The demand of the market for accelerating growth stocks may have encouraged a more rapid expansion than was foreseen in Oxford's original game plan. The firm had entered the Medicaid and Medicare markets by 1992 and introduced additional plans to broaden its customer base. Aggressive acquisitions in other related fields and regional markets allowed the company to deliver exceptional growth. The stock raced to new highs; by 1993, its market capitalization had shot up to more than $1 billion. Oxford became a midcap stock by late 1994.

Unfortunately, as companies gain growth momentum and become more sizable, the path to continued success becomes narrower. Oxford

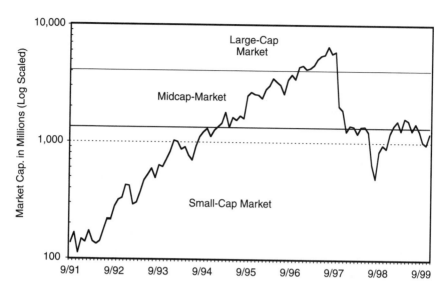

Figure 1.2   Oxford Health Plans (OXHP)—Market Capitalization

became a victim of its success. The rapid growth from which it benefited also made it very difficult to keep tight controls on internal systems. This fault became terribly relevant as expenses in the industry began to rise. Investors then became quite concerned and, in a single October day in 1997, Oxford lost 62 percent of its market value.

    The stock continued to collapse in the subsequent year. From a high of over $6.5 billion, it fell to a mere $500 million by August 1998. In one fleeting year, a very large and successful firm with almost a blue-chip presence fell back into the small-cap market. The company has since attempted to stem the collapse by cutting costs, focusing on core businesses, and placing better internal financial and accounting controls. The stock has rebounded nicely; it almost doubled to over $1 billion by November 1999. For a second time, Oxford has been able to quickly double in size as a small-cap stock. This time, however, its path was not completely new.

Cisco Systems

Cisco Systems (CSCO), the data networking equipment company, is the classic Silicon Valley small-cap success story. The growth of this company lies in its uncanny ability to strategically focus itself on the changing demands of the data networking business. Cisco went public in 1990 with roughly $139 million in market capitalization. The stock subsequently jumped almost one hundredfold in nine years.

Cisco became known for its industrial-strength router equipment. Routers allow separate computing networks to interoperate by sharing data and functionality. With networking traffic beginning to accelerate with the rise of corporate interactivity and the profound increase of e-mail traffic in the late 1980s and early 1990s, Cisco became the dominant player in the router market (see Figure 1.3). In three years, Cisco had grown more than fourteenfold.

With the dramatic increase in the usage of network-based computing, Cisco recognized the need for additional solutions. The company smartly recognized that LAN (local area network) switches were desperately needed to alleviate network congestion. LAN switches allow traffic on a data network to be rerouted to underutilized links. Not being a player in the LAN switching business, Cisco aggressively used its highly valued stock to acquire three key players and enter this market. By 1997, Cisco had captured a dominant market share in the switching business. Since that first acquisition in 1993, technology companies, including Microsoft, Intel, and Oracle, took notice and also began using their rich stock to wield significant influence in the marketplace.

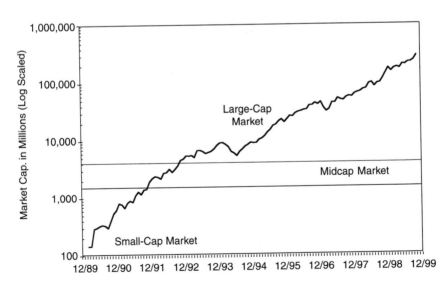

Figure 1.3   Cisco Systems (CSCO)—Market Capitalization

By 1999, Cisco had made several acquisitions and entered into joint ventures to tap into the rapidly growing wireless and Internet market. Cisco has made nearly 30 acquisitions in a mere six years. By 1999, Cisco's capitalization had reached over $200 billion. Is Cisco the next Microsoft? It is certainly off to a good start.

Cisco might be considered a best-case scenario for investors. The stock became recognized, even as a small cap, in a fairly quick fashion, and the investors were rewarded. Cisco is rare because it has been unwavering as a large-cap stock. The company has been quite able to focus on, predict, and satisfy new demands in a rapidly changing technology market.

SMALL-CAP CYCLES TEND TO BE SEVERE

The rapid growth of the Ciscos and Oxfords of the world not only reflected individual success stories, but also was part of a greater rebound of the entire small-cap market in the early 1990s—a rebound that illustrated the type of compelling returns this market can generate. After lagging the large-cap market for seven years, small caps bounded back to the forefront of market attention. The Russell 2000 small-cap index jumped 58.6 percent from the bottom of the cycle in October 1990 to the following year. Small-cap stocks jumped 28.2 percent annually for a gross of 119.7 percent over the entire cycle. Large companies also fared well during this period, but severely lagged the smaller-company market. At least 10 small-cap funds generated returns well over 60 percent during the course of that rebound period.

In the 1970s, the small-cap market had displayed a similar superior performance on a much more extended basis. The small-cap bull market of the 1970s lasted for approximately a full decade. Small stocks generated an astounding 19.4 percent on an annualized basis. By contrast, the blue-chip sector posted a paltry 8.5 percent in this same time frame.

Along the way, small-cap fans have also taken their share of lumps. The latter half of the 1990s perhaps represents one of the most painful chapters in small-cap history. During this time, the global investment village became entranced with mega-size global franchises. Incredible sums of money were diverted from all over the world to capture some of the wealth promised by these titan-size corporations. As a result, the large-cap blue-chip franchises posted spectacular results between 1994 and 1999. In a five-year period, large companies gained a whopping 187 percent, or 23.5 percent annually. Even though small-cap returns were favorable, they posted an annual gain of only 13.9 percent. They lagged the blue-chip sector by a sizable 10 percent annually. Smaller stocks also turned in paltry gains during the 1980s. The fledgling group lagged the large-cap sector as cheap large companies flourished in the then-ensuing disinflationary environment. Between 1983 and 1990, large-cap shares outperformed smaller companies by more than 5.0 percent each year.

The long-term performance figures support the existence of a premium for smaller stocks; conversely, the small caps' periods of underperformance can suggest that a bias toward smaller companies is misguided. Yet it is difficult to accept the contrary argument for large caps—specifically, that safer assets are accompanied by higher expected returns. Ultimately, smaller companies have to carry a higher expected return simply because they are riskier assets. Unless the market is terribly inefficient, the small-stock premium is real. If the outperformance of small stocks over the long term were indeed ephemeral, then small stocks would be unable to come public. Investors would shun this asset class and turn to companies that are indeed likely to generate superior returns. (See Chapter 6 for a detailed discussion of the merits and issues surrounding the small-cap premium.)

SIZE ROTATIONS FROM SMALL CAPS TO LARGE CAPS

Although the size premium debate is perhaps best left to the "believers"—those market participants who can reasonably argue that smaller stocks generally outperform large stocks over the long term—and "nonbelievers"—investors who hold an opposite view—active investors cannot afford to be distracted from the powerful undercurrent of size rotations. Size rotations, or cycles of performance, are powerful shifts within equity markets during which smaller companies significantly outperform large companies. During other periods, large companies thoroughly dominate the market. Even though the issue of whether small stocks outperform large, or vice versa, may remain unresolved with certainty for years to come, one thing is abundantly clear: The cycles of under- and outperformance are dramatic. For example, notice in Figure 1.4 how much the size premium can shift. The small-cap premium, using annualized 10-year returns, can swing from a positive 12 percent annually to a negative 5 percent. Capturing this shift from small to large, and vice versa, may be one of the most relevant and active decisions one needs to make when investing in the equity markets.

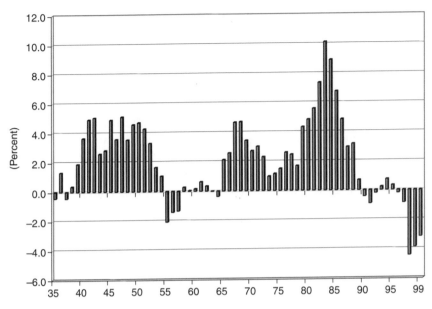

Figure 1.4 Excess Returns—Small-Cap Less Large-Cap Rolling
10-Year Annualized Return (Annual Frequency)

Investors' preference for smaller or larger companies relates to their preference for risk. Risk preferences can sway from one extreme to the other; so also can the overall market trend for smaller companies. Yet the size issue does not simply come down to a debate over whether the large mega-cap franchises or the fledgling start-ups will win the day.

THE DOMINO EFFECT

Size rotations from a small-cap bull market to a large-cap bull market, or vice versa, appear to ripple across the market in an effect known as the domino effect. Size rotations are *monotonic*; the small-cap cycles move in the same direction without variation. Microcaps outperform small stocks, which outperform midcaps, which outperform large caps in a small-cap bull market. Conversely, large stocks outperform midcaps, which outperform small caps, which lead microcaps in a large-cap bull market. In short, as the tide turns in favor of smaller-cap firms, the smaller companies within a large-cap universe also appear to take a similar direction. A bull market for large-cap stocks suggests not only that the largest companies within the large-cap market dominate but also that the largest companies within the small-cap market will perform similarly. As the market moves in favor of small or large caps, it appears that this size rotation has a domino effect[1] on the overall market.

Given this trait of the equity market, the critical issue for active managers is whether to focus on the upper or the lower end of the capitalization segment within their selected investment universe. Because of this size effect, traditional large-cap investors are not only at a disadvantage by having their large-cap "bets" in a small-cap rotation, but are also likely to face a more severe threat: They lag their immediate large-cap peers who are more exposed to lower market capitalization firms within the large-cap domain.

The issue of size rotations runs deeper than simply examining small-cap and large-cap performance cycles. Deciphering the size puzzle is relevant not only to the traditional small-cap investor, but also to the asset allocator; the large-cap, blue-chip investor; and, generally, any active equity investor.

A close look at small- and large-cap returns suggests that size or a rotation in size is not a narrow issue. Small versus large performance cycle data suggest that swings in size have a ripple effect, from the largest to the smallest market capitalization shares. The spectacular periods of past small-cap performance and the utterly overwhelming blue-chip dominance in the market of the 1990s have lulled investors into thinking of large and small stocks as bimodal or as two unrelated sectors. Regarded in this fashion, small stocks outpace large stocks in a small-cap cycle. However, if blue chips rally, large companies dominate the small. In short, if the equity market were only bimodal, one might miss the powerful rotations occurring intramarket or within each universe of stocks. Hence, a rally in blue chips signifies not only that big caps outperform small, but also that the largest-cap stocks are likely to be dominant in both the small- and large-cap markets.

If size rotations operate on the margin and not in bimodal fashion, the implications of the domino effect are more profound. Not only do large caps beat out small caps in a blue-chip bull market, but the largest stocks also dominate within the large-cap market. Conversely, in a small-cap cycle, or one in which small caps outperform large caps, the smallest firms are likely to lead their larger counterparts. As noted previously, this phenomenon is evident not only in the small-cap market, but also in the large-cap market. If the domino effect holds, the smallest stocks in the small-cap market should outperform in a small-cap bull market and recede as the blue chips recover. A small-cap to large-cap rotation should force intramarket rotations within the small-cap and the large-cap markets. As a simple approach to illustrate this effect, examine a size- or market-weighted index versus an equal-weighted proxy. Market-weighted benchmarks emphasize the returns of the most sizable companies; equal-weighted benchmarks represent the simple average of all company returns. The equal-weighted small-cap index should outpace the market-weighted small-cap index in a small-cap cycle if a smaller bias prevails across the equity market. Conversely, the market-weighted small-cap index should outperform the equal-weighted index in a large-cap cycle where large stocks lead the small.

A high correlation between the small-cap cycle and an equal-weighted index versus a market-weighted index supports the operation of the marginal effect or domino effect across the equity market. Figure 1.5 illustrates small-cap cycles over a 74-year period (1926–99) and compares them to the equal-weighted performance of the small-cap index relative to the market-weighted index. The dotted line represents the ratio of performance between the small-cap and large-cap markets. As the dotted line moves upward, it represents a small-cap cycle, a period in which small-cap stocks outperform large caps. Conversely, a declining dotted line represents a large-cap bull market.

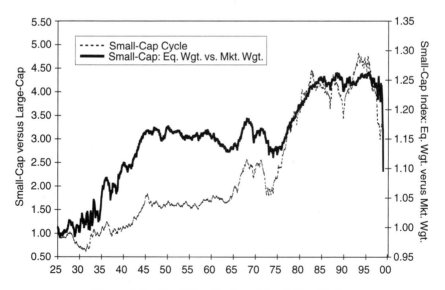

Figure 1.5　Small-Cap Cycle and Small-Cap Market

The solid line in Figure 1.5 represents the ratio of performance between the equal-weighted small-cap benchmark and the market-weighted small-cap benchmark. Note the high correlation between the small-cap cycle (dotted line) and rotations within the small-cap market (solid line). As the bull market for big companies takes hold, the largest issues within the small-cap market similarly begin to dominate. Especially startling, the inflection points, or the turning points, for all size rotations from 1926 to 1999 are concurrent with the turns within the small-cap market.

The small-cap market has lost a considerable amount of ground with respect to large stocks since 1994. The Russell 2000 small-cap index gained a meager 10 percent from 1994 to 1998, whereas the Standard & Poor's (S&P) 500 index rewarded its investors with a staggering 21 percent annualized return. By no coincidence, an equal-weighted index of large-cap companies appreciated by 17 percent compared to the market-weighted S&P 500 return of 21 percent over this time frame. (See Figure 1.6.) Note that the intramarket return spreads do not vary as much as the extreme tails, or small caps versus megacaps, of the market.

The domino effect appears to be present in many international equity markets; among them are the United Kingdom, Japan, Hong Kong, and

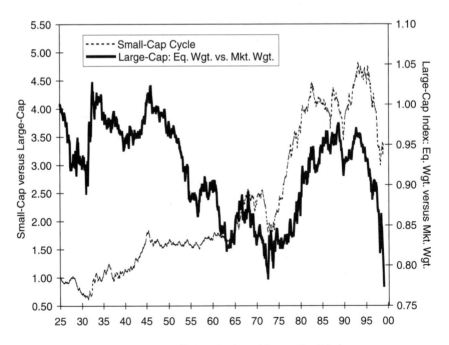

Figure 1.6   Small-Cap Cycle and Large-Cap Market

Australia (see Figures 1.7–1.10). Because the large stocks dominate many major markets throughout the 1990s, the large-cap size bias appears to have permeated most major equity markets globally. Curiously, the effect has not been as strong in Australia (Figure 1.10), primarily because a strong variant trend occurred in 1990–93. During this period, the large stocks appeared to lead the Australian stock market, but the smaller stocks, within the small-stock market, ultimately prevailed.

Investment Implications of the Domino Effect

Because of the existence of the domino effect, small- and large-cap investors need to take a careful stance on size. If a runaway bull market in small stocks is likely to remain in effect over an extended period, one can stem the risk of lagging the market by not holding stocks that emphasize a large capitalization. As illustrated in the preceding section, a bull market for small stocks also implies that holding stocks with a lower market capitalization than one's benchmark or peers offers a significant advantage.

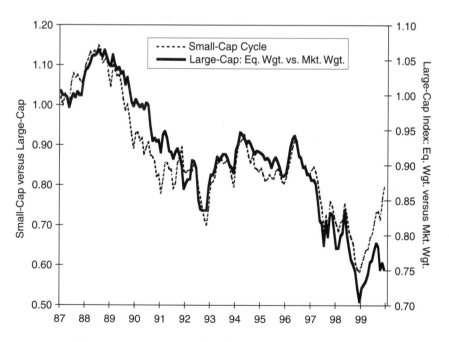

Figure 1.7   U.K.—Small-Cap Cycle and Large-Cap Market

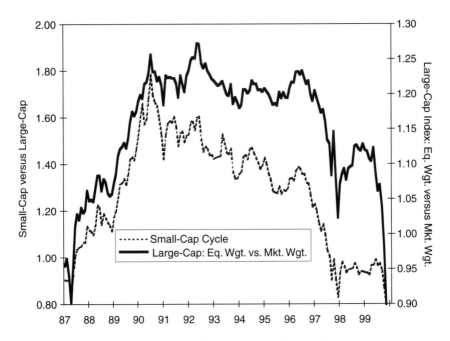

Figure 1.8   Japan—Small-Cap Cycle and Large-Cap Market

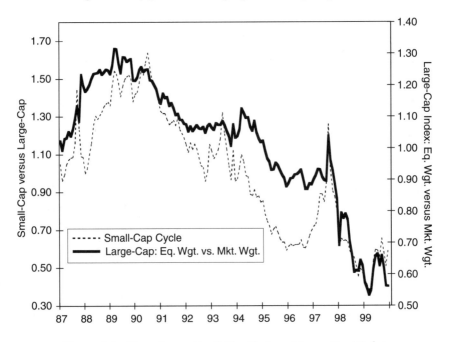

Figure 1.9   Hong Kong—Small-Cap Cycle and Large-Cap Market

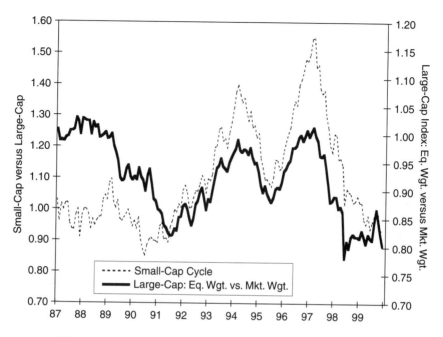

Figure 1.10   Australia—Small-Cap Cycle and Large-Cap Market

Active investors are usually aware of their sector exposures. Because individual stocks tend to reflect broader sector swings, focusing on the appropriate sector increases the chances of finding stocks that outperform. Knowing whether one is holding a large- or a smaller-cap bias in one's portfolio may be subtler than being aware of holding a majority of technology stocks, for instance, but it is just as important.

Whether by accident or design, all portfolios have some size bias. An investor's favoring small caps, or being dedicated to large caps, does not mean that he or she can afford to ignore the size factor. If the market is experiencing a large-cap rally, the domino effect dictates that the largest companies are likely to have a continuing edge. As a result, if a large-cap investor is, by chance, holding a portfolio with a lower market capitalization profile relative to the large-cap universe, that investor is likely to lag his or her peers and the market.

Similarly, a small-cap manager cannot afford to simply hold a portfolio of seemingly choice companies if the market has a large-cap bias. As with the advantages of being overweight in technology stocks in the midst of a bull market for the technology sector, if the market is in the full swing of a megacap rally, the larger stocks within the small-cap framework are likely to offer some reprieve in a shaky small-cap market. Because size rotations tend to cascade across the market, active investors are penalized if they neglect the size bias within their holdings.

Why Markets Exhibit the Domino Effect

Two primary factors support the existence of the domino effect, or the size effect that operates on the margin. The first relates to investors' appetite for risk taking; the second relates to the competitiveness of the investment community.

Investors who assume a high risk-taking posture are led to invest in companies with more aggressive business strategies—generally, firms with lower market capitalization. Conversely, a lower tolerance for risk implies a preference for more secure businesses, which tend to have a large market capitalization. Thus, major changes in attitude toward risk taking are likely to operate on a continuum. For example, risk-averse individuals are likely to consider certificates of deposit (CDs) as safer assets than government bonds at the upper end of their risk spectrum. In contrast, a risk seeker is likely to vacillate between a mature equity market and emerging markets as possible investment choices.

Macroeconomic or primary market factors have a very direct bearing on risk taking. If, for instance, one believes that the economy is stronger than expected, one might increase risk taking. In this instance, investors are more likely to nibble at the lower end of the market capitalization spectrum. However, if the outlook is less certain, investors who reach first for the largest and most liquid stocks will outpace their peers.

A second argument that supports marginal swings in size is that investors compete for returns. The success of a sector or group of stocks forces other investors to investigate the recent market winners. If the reasons for investing are sound, more investors are likely to migrate to these assets. Because performance is paramount, investors cannot afford to have rigidly fixed views toward any asset class.

The trends of increasing assets managed by institutions and more sophistication among individual investors have forced a more sharply delineated equity landscape. Investment managers are no longer simply equity fund managers; instead, they invest in large-cap growth, large-cap value, growth at a reasonable price, and a laundry list of very specific equity investment vehicles that have been carved for a client with more specific needs. Even though the trend in client needs has fragmented the need for investment vehicles, investors are likely to gravitate toward lower market capitalization shares if smaller stocks lead the market. This need to produce exceptional returns can create the drift in funds as investors chase returns.

Managers realize that they are graded with respect to a benchmark, yet they also know that clients are looking for the best absolute returns. As a case in point, consider the difficult state of affairs that small-cap investors have faced in recent years. Even though greater numbers of small-cap managers (compared to large-cap managers) are beating their respective benchmarks, the client-review meetings for small-cap managers are much more difficult than those for their large-cap peers. The simple fact is that the absolute returns for smaller companies dismally lagged those of the blue chips in the 1990s.

A difficult environment forces an investor to search aggressively for the best returns. If a manager's rewards were not performance-based, he or she might be more cavalier in hanging onto an investment approach when economic circumstances cause returns to fade in his or her investment universe. As a result, the competitive financial markets may ultimately explain why large and small caps exhibit more of a domino effect rather than behaving like two mutually exclusive asset classes. If reasonable arguments suggest that a sustained large-cap rally is under way, then the domino effect suggests that small- and large-cap investors need to aggressively lean toward the upper end of their capitalization limits. In other words, the size bias in a market—whether of small stocks edging out large, or vice versa—is an active bet that requires keen oversight of one's portfolio.

PREFERENCE OF LARGE-CAP ACTIVE INVESTORS FOR SMALL-CAP CYCLES

Active manager returns also support the existence of the domino effect. An investor who attempts to outperform a stated benchmark is considered an active investor. In contrast, a passive investor attempts to merely match the benchmark. If the size effect did not operate on the margin across the equity market, then both large- and small-cap active investors might easily outpace their respective benchmarks in a small-cap bull market. Instead, active small-cap and large-cap results tend to operate inversely as size rotations occur. Because small stocks far outnumber large-cap shares, a small-cap rally implies a healthy broad market. In such a market, with more stocks on the rise, active managers are more likely to outperform their benchmarks. Ironically, however, a broader small-cap market improves the odds that large-cap active management will outperform the large-cap benchmark (the S&P 500, for example), yet creates a more challenging environment for small-cap managers seeking to outperform their benchmark—the Russell 2000, the S&P 600, and the like.

Even though this may sound counterintuitive, a ripple toward smaller stocks implies a broadening of the equity market, meaning one in which more stocks are rising. Because smaller stocks represent a majority (in total number of companies) of the equity market, a constructive broad market is synonymous with a small-cap rally. The domino effect suggests that, as small stocks rally, investors in the smallest small stocks (microcap stocks) have the potential to outperform. This also implies that active small-cap managers are likely to face a more difficult time beating their bogey, because many small-cap institutional money managers cannot reach down to the microcap levels that are likely to generate the most spectacular results in a small-cap bull market. As a result, the smallest segment of the small-cap market leads.

As for large-cap managers, it is not by coincidence that they consistently lagged their benchmark, such as the S&P 500, over the latter half of the 1990s. As the rotation toward large companies becomes extreme, fewer stocks participate in the market rally. When fewer stocks generate above-average returns, this reduced number diminishes the probability of success for active managers.

Even though a rotation toward secondary shares is favorable for small-cap investors, a rebound in share prices of thinly traded securities can be problematic for more sizable small-cap funds. Extremely tiny market capitalization stocks—stocks under $50 million in market value, for instance—tend to be illiquid. Hence, as these illiquid shares rise in price, active small-cap managers are less likely to participate and therefore more likely to underperform their benchmarks.

Figure 1.11 charts the percentage of mutual funds that outpaced their respective small-cap and large-cap benchmarks from 1990 to 1999. The dotted line represents the proportion of large-cap funds that outperformed the S&P 500, and the solid line represents the small-cap relationship. The results generally had an inverse trend.

Note that the results for large-cap managers moved inversely with those for small-cap managers. The S&P 500 fell to the second quartile from 1991 to 1993, or led roughly half the active managers in the large-cap sector. It is no surprise that the small-cap market led the large-cap

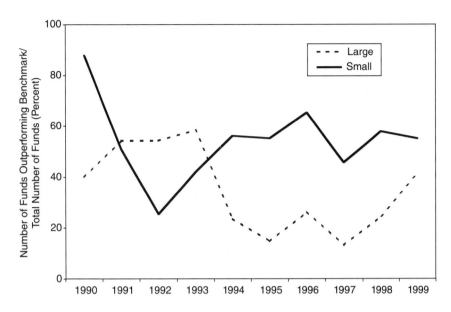

Figure 1.11   Percentage of Funds Outperforming Their Relative Benchmarks Small vs. Large

sector in those years. Yet, as the small-cap market improved, fewer active small-cap managers outperformed the benchmark compared to the prior year. Although 90 percent of small-cap managers outpaced the Russell 2000 in 1990, only 52 percent fared as well in 1991.

The domino effect argues that size rotations have a profound effect on all market participants. By taking an active view on size and adopting a judicious leaning toward larger or smaller stocks, one can mitigate or augment broad market effects. A small-cap investor positioned with an above-average market capitalization compared to his or her peers is more than likely to beat those peers and the benchmark in the face of a large-cap bull market. Likewise, positioning one's holdings below average market capitalization in the midst of a small-cap bull market can accentuate one's smaller stock results. Investors can gain an advantage under those market conditions.

How Much Is the Size Factor Worth, and to Whom?

Table 1.1 summarizes the quartile results of small-cap and large-cap markets from 1990 to 1998. The managers focused on small-cap investing were divided into four equal groups, or quartiles, stratified by one-year performance results. If small-cap managers fell into the first quartile, they were considered in the top 25 percent of the pool of investment managers over that time frame. Similarly, the fourth quartile implied the bottom 25 percent of the universe of investors. Note that a third-quartile large-cap fund manager could have gained 29 percent in 1998 by simply moving to a large-cap overweight. The largest 20 percent of the large-cap market outperformed the smallest-size group by 29 percent. By simply overweighting larger companies, a third-quartile large-cap manager could have generated first-quartile results.

The size rotation effect was not evident in the small-cap market in 1998, but the 1997 results supported the existence of this effect. A middle-of-the-range third-quartile small-cap manager could have shifted into the second quartile by focusing on large-cap ideas. The top fifth by market capitalization outpaced the smallest fifth by 5 percent in 1997 in the small-cap market. The broad universe of small companies, as of 1999, ranged from $200 million to almost $1.5 billion. An investor in this small-cap market has significant opportunities to position a smaller- or larger-cap focus. A portfolio can be pegged to companies with an average market cap of $400 million, or just as easily anchored around companies with $1 billion market capitalization, and still be considered a small-cap portfolio.

Table 1.1   Comparison of Large-Cap and Small-Cap Markets, 1990–99

	Large-Cap		Small-Cap		Percentage of Total	
	S&P 500 Rank*	Total # of Funds	Russell 2000 Rank*	Total # of Funds	Large-Cap	Small-Cap
1990	154	385	123[†]	140	40%	88%
1991	229	422	77	151	54	51
1992	254	468	45	177	54	25
1993	328	561	89	212	58	42
1994	153	649	150	267	24	56
1995	107	727	181	328	15	55
1996	211	804	256	392	26	65
1997	106	804	179	392	13	46
1998	198	804	227	392	25	58
1999	371	900	214	389	41	55

*Ranked within all funds for that year
[†]Example: 122 funds outperformed the Russell 2000 in 1990

The marginal size finding suggests that active managers should utilize specific stocks to manage their size risk, or size-based instruments to control for risk within their portfolios. For instance, a large-cap investor can purchase a relative performance option on smaller stocks, in the event smaller companies begin to significantly outperform larger stocks. This option hedges the size risk that a large-cap fund manager takes on when he or she primarily bets on big stocks.

The size effect argues that index funds are not passive investments. An index fund is a constant bet on large-capitalization stocks. When large stocks outperform small stocks, so too do index funds outperform most active managers. Conversely, when smaller stocks enter a bull market, so too will active fund managers' results. Because the domino effect argues that size rotations are dynamic, when large stocks lag the overall market, so too will index funds.

FOUR PRIMARY FACTORS INFLUENCING SMALL-CAP PERFORMANCE

The domino principle offers some insight into major market rotations—when big stocks are beating small, or vice versa—but fails to offer guidance into the catalysts or drivers of a rotation. Certain factors have influenced investors' preference for small-cap investments and have accounted for major shifts in the equity markets between smaller and larger companies. These factors include cyclical growth, credit and cost of capital conditions, profitability, and geopolitical or exogenous shocks. Even though these four factors have not consistently coincided to drive a preference for smaller stocks in past cycles, they have nonetheless signaled a propensity for investors to migrate toward smaller or larger shares.

Cyclical Growth

Periods in which small caps outperformed large caps have coincided with periods of economic growth. In short, a better economic backdrop encourages increased risk taking among investors. Many episodes of economic rebounds in the past decades have provided a positive setting for smaller firms. Small-stock bull markets have coincided with sharp economic recoveries as far back as the earliest cycles. For instance, secondary stocks, as well as the entire equity market, recovered dramatically from the bear market of the early 1930s when President Franklin D. Roosevelt introduced new fiscal and monetary stimuli packages to stem the collapse in economic growth. The Dow gained 66.7 percent in 1933 and 38.5 percent two years later, and both small and large stocks provided memorable multiyear returns in those years.

As another example, examine the 1990 economic recovery, which signaled a change in market leadership. Large blue-chip firms had dominated the equity market for the seven years dating from 1983. Smaller stocks weakened severely when the economy went sour in the late 1980s. As the economy bottomed and started to recover, the secondary markets similarly bottomed and then entered a three-year period in which they outperformed.

The weakness of smaller stocks in the later 1990s does not fit with the strong cyclical pickup in the economy during this period. Other issues—such as wider relative cost of capital, and slowing profits growth—prevailed over those years, possibly overwhelming the cyclical bias that should have supported a small-cap rebound.

Credit and Cost of Capital

Credit conditions and the cost of capital are exceedingly important for all firms, especially smaller firms. Access to capital and cost of capital could be considered the lifeline to a firm. The cheaper the access to capital, the more likely that a firm can take on more projects and increase its chances of success. Access to capital and therefore to the cost of capital (better access yields lower cost, and poor access implies higher cost) plays a critical role in the potential success of a firm.

Smaller companies are generally at a disadvantage when it comes to financing. After all, a lender is generally more willing to lend to large, well-established franchises. Even though smaller firms face higher capital costs, the higher rates of return of more aggressive projects tend to offset the added financing burdens. Because the cost of capital is not constant, smaller firms can face periods in which financiers are quite willing to participate in financing schemes, and other times in which capital vanishes. Monitoring the willingness of financiers to create transactions with a marginal firm offers a critical insight into the viability of the small-cap investment thesis. In short, the relative cost of capital for small (versus large) firms appears to be a strong determinant of when the market will rotate from small to large firms.[2]

The relative cost of capital can be measured in many ways. Simple measures—the difference between prime rate and Treasury; credit spreads; or the difference in bond yields of higher-quality versus lower-quality bonds—allow investors to establish a pulse on the relative cost of capital. Smaller firms, by definition, carry higher costs of capital. Many of the past cycles have exhibited strong tendencies of a smaller-cap bias when the relative cost of capital was cheap—that is, when the difference between prime rate and Treasury was lower than usual. Conversely, secondary stocks have generally been out of favor when the relative cost spreads were wider than usual. Even though smaller companies are less likely or unable to raise capital in fixed form, the fixed-income spreads offer a healthy proxy for the free flow of risk capital.

The relationship between economic growth and the cost of capital is intertwined. If growth begins to rebound, investors' increased confidence on behalf of the economic outlook is likely to spur easier credit. In difficult times, credit vanishes and only a handful of megacap, blue-chip players are afforded the luxury of capital. As concerns for the economic outlook increase and credit gets tighter, this trend again causes a slowdown in growth. It is difficult to determine whether capital constraints or economic cyclicality has the greater responsibility for the effects on size.

The latter half of the 1990s might have appeared unusual if one had attempted to explain the small-cap market results by simply focusing on economic cyclicality. Although economic growth actually accelerated in the latter half of the 1990s (compared to the early 1990s), smaller firms significantly lagged large megacap firms during this period. One compelling difference of this cycle, compared to previous cycles, was the wide cost-of-capital spreads, as reflected in simple measures such as the difference between prime versus Treasury bonds. The spread between such instruments has averaged over 200 basis points since 1994. Perhaps it was no coincidence that the small-cap bull market came to a close by the end of 1993. The end of this cycle coincided with an increase in interest rates as the Federal Reserve ("the Fed") began taking stringent measures to contain inflationary growth. The absolute and relative cost of capital increased each time the Fed increased interest rates, and the relative cost of capital was high throughout this bull market cycle for large-cap stocks.

In 1998, credit concerns led to one of the most dramatic divergences between large- and small-stock returns in the cycle of the 1990s. Fears that the Asian economic crisis would spread to other markets rippled around the world. Treasury bonds rallied as investors flocked to safer assets. This caused the spread between the prime rate and Treasury bonds to widen by close to 390 basis points by October 1998. To make matters worse, Long Term Capital Management (LTCM), a major hedge fund, defaulted on sizable leveraged positions. This sent, globally, a loud and clear signal that financial contracts were in jeopardy. Quality spreads, or the difference in higher-quality bond and lower-quality yields, also followed suit and widened by over 40 basis points between August and December of 1998. In a span of six months, small stocks lost over 35 percent of their value.

The bankruptcy of the Penn Central Co., in June 1970, had provoked a similar wave of concerns. These concerns rippled across the financial markets and crushed the small-cap market. The economy had already shown signs of deterioration in the late 1960s. By early 1970, companies had become cash-starved. Stock returns had tumbled in the first six months of the year. Based on market-weighted price returns, large stocks lost 21 percent, small stocks lost a whopping 28.4 percent, and microcaps lost 34.7 percent—more than one-third of their value. The case of Penn Central Co., however, brought the concerns of most investors to the surface. In desperate need of cash, the rail operator needed working capital to pay its 90,000 employees and meet its sizable debt obligations. Penn Central was delayed at the opening of the New York Stock Exchange, and, at the afternoon bell, it closed at 6.50, off 4⅝ from its previous close. Trading on a "flat" basis or without an interest payment, the rail unit's bonds lost 11 points, or the equivalent of $110 per $1,000 unit. The news of bankruptcy came after the government refused to sponsor a massive financial aid package of roughly $750 million, which would have allowed the company to meet its obligations. There were signs of an impending cash crunch prior to the Penn Central debacle. For instance, Burlington Northern, formed by the consolidation of the Great Northern and Northern Pacific Railways, withdrew a proposed $60 million issue.

The size/credit relationship echoes as far back as the 1930s. The U.S. economy experienced a dramatic increase in liquidity when the Federal Reserve began increasing the supply of money, which propped up the collapsing economy. This allowed the U.S. economy to start anew and caused credit spreads to dramatically narrow. In a short period, both large and small stocks fiercely rebounded. The Dow bounced back by 66.7 percent in 1933, and small stocks more than doubled with a gain of 104 percent for the year.

Profitability

Corporate profitability can reflect the general riskiness of a company's operating environment. Simply put, more profitable companies signal a more confident environment. Greater profitability increases the willingness of investors to take on more risk.

Curiously, corporate profitability appeared to play a greater role in the size rotations in previous cycles than in the latter half of the 1990s. The profit recovery that companies experienced in the early 1990s was anemic, yet smaller firms significantly outpaced large firms. Profits then grew significantly—roughly 12.5 percent from 1994 to 1999—but a small-cap rebound failed to materialize. This recent disjunction between profitability and the small-cap cycle represents a significant contrast to earlier cycles. For example, in the earliest cycles, dating back to the late 1920s, corporate profits severely weakened in conjunction with the performance of smaller companies. A subsequent rebound in corporate profits in the early 1930s nicely supported a multiyear rebound of smaller company shares.

One possible explanation for the divergent relationship between size and profits may relate to the perceived lack of pricing power that companies have faced since the late 1990s. Pricing power generally refers to the inability of companies to match or raise prices on their final goods and services as input costs rise. This difficult pricing environment has forced firms to operate in a belt-tightening manner. As a result, companies with the most room for cost cutting have generated the most sizable improvements in combating a difficult pricing environment.

In a perfectly competitive economy, all firms would be price takers or would face market-based prices. The reality, however, is that the economy is not perfectly competitive. Smaller firms are likely to be perceived at a greater disadvantage in a difficult pricing environment. If all firms are under pressure, then larger firms are likely to hold some leverage over small firms, which enables them to squeeze their suppliers to contain costs and maintain margins. As a result, profitability, at least on a relative basis, should marginally improve for the large-cap firms.

Market participants have clung to this argument as they have pursued large-cap corporations with a global presence to even higher multiples. Because the market-pricing mechanism is dynamic, however, these valuations are likely to be offset eventually by the perceived size advantages. The cycle or rotation between small and large firms will then start anew. The difficult question is whether current valuation disparities already take into account perceived benefits from size. In the latter half of the 1990s, the market aggressively priced into large companies the significant benefits of a difficult pricing environment. Based on price to cash flow, small stocks sold at a 40 percent premium at the start of the small-cap cycle that began in 1994. As of 1999, they sold at a 30 percent discount to large companies. Large companies enjoyed a far richer valuation multiple than they did in the mid-1990s.

Geopolitical Events and Exogenous Shocks

Geopolitical events or exogenous shocks, such as the collapse of an economy or the outbreak of a war, are other variables that influence investors' appetite for risk taking. In troubled times, investors prefer large-cap shares because they are perceived as being more secure. The collapse of Asian economies in 1997 and 1998 provided a good example of global concerns that led to an adverse ripple effect on secondary stocks. Small stocks lost 3 percent in 1998 compared to a gain of 21 percent by the blue chips—a 24 percent spread in one year's return! Decades earlier, events that led to World War II also caused investors to shy away from risky ventures. The year leading up to the war was an especially uncertain period. Not only did equity returns lag Treasury bills, but the returns of small stocks also lagged those of large caps.

Interestingly, the U.S. equity markets—small stocks in particular—appear to react adversely only when global difficulties spell trouble for domestic interests. For small stocks, this may be partly due to the lower exposure that small-cap stocks have in the foreign markets. Before the United States entered World War II, stocks rallied on the expectation that the United States might benefit from an increased demand for goods. In 1997, U.S. equities continued to appreciate even after investors became aware that Southeast Asian economies were almost certain to enter into a recession. Not until a year later did investors become more concerned about the overseas impact on the domestic economy. At this point, the U.S. equity market, especially small stocks, caught the financial flu that had swept through Asia the previous year. The global concerns overwhelmed the potential benefit of smaller firms' being more domestically based. In particularly troubled times, the issue of size—whether to invest in small caps or large caps—is moot. The real investment choices become limited to either cash in hand or Treasury bills.

Benchmark Definitions

The Merrill Lynch Small Cap Research (MLSCR) International Indexes for the major developed countries (United States, United Kingdom, Japan, Australia, and Hong Kong) are used in illustrations and related studies throughout this book. These indices serve as proxies for the local benchmarks. The cutoff or size delineation of these indices is based on the market capitalization in local market terms. The benchmarks include common stocks domiciled in the country and exclude mutual funds and real estate investment trusts.

Table 1.2 Merrill Lynch Small Cap Research (MLSCR) Index Data as of December 1999

	Number of Companies	Average Market Cap in $Millions	Median Market Cap in $Millions	Market Cap Ranges in $Millions
United States				
MLSCR Large-Cap Index	425	31,333	12,529	5,624–601,029
MLSCR Midcap Index	606	2,949	2,663	1,598–5,605
MLSCR Small-Cap Index	1,758	677	569	253–1,597
MLSCR Microcap Index	1,941	123	108	51–253
MLSCR Nanocap Index	1,333	28	27	10–51
United Kingdom				
MLSCR Large-Cap Index	281	8,601	2,468	673–195,068
MLSCR Small-Cap Index	560	228	176	52–671
MLSCR Microcap Index	560	21	17	0–52
Japan				
MLSCR Large-Cap Index	466	9,064	2,613	922–367,305
MLSCR Small-Cap Index	931	330	250	113–919
MLSCR Microcap Index	931	54	51	1–112
Australia				
MLSCR Large-Cap Index	130	3,172	628	151–69,586
MLSCR Small-Cap Index	86	54	49	1–137
Hong Kong				
MLSCR Large-Cap Index	64	87	83	61–140
MLSCR Small-Cap Index	127	28	27	3–60

Table 1.2 on page 29 supplies the number of companies in each index and the market cap ranges as of December 1999. Note that these benchmarks offer some insights into the size rotation of the market; however, they are not developed with any liquidity constraints. For cross-comparison among all the markets, the data are stated in U.S. dollars.

TWO

The Small-Cap Backdrop

MICROSTRUCTURE OF EQUITY MARKETS

THE BREADTH of secondary stocks, or smaller stocks, in the U.S. equity market is daunting. Over 6,000 companies with sizable equity stakes trade in the U.S. equity market, and this figure does not include the thousands of tiny public firms that trade almost by appointment. Because of the breadth of the market, if a business or industry exists in the United States, it is likely that an investor can obtain some equity exposure to that business.

Public companies range from megacaps or global franchises with capitalization levels above $4 billion, to nanocaps or tiny companies

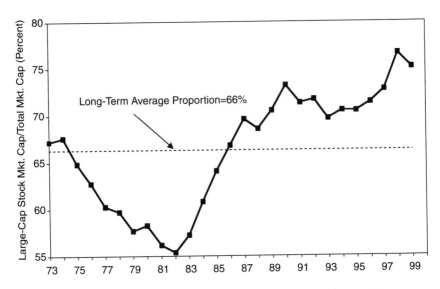

Figure 2.1   Large-Cap Stocks as a Percentage of U.S. Market Capitalization

below $50 million. For example, behemoths such as General Electric and Microsoft have a market capitalization of well over $100 billion and dominate the U.S. stock market. Microsoft, as of April 2000, was worth as much as $460 billion.

The large-cap market accounts for more than 75 percent of aggregate U.S. equity market value. Ironically, these mega-size firms account for less than 10 percent of the number of securities (not counting penny stocks) traded in the United States. The concentration level of large companies has fallen to levels as low as 55 percent of the U.S. equity market, and has risen to very concentrated levels above 75 percent. The U.S. market concentration of 75 percent in 1999 appeared to be at the high end of the U.S. equity market concentration during the 1980s and 1990s. Figure 2.1 represents the large-stock portion of the U.S. equity market as a percentage of total equity outstanding.

DEFINING A COMPANY'S SIZE BY ITS MARKET CAPITALIZATION

A company's size in the financial markets is defined by its market capitalization, or the price of its shares times the total number of shares outstanding. Smaller companies, in the equity markets, are not synonymous with companies with few employees, low revenues, or little in plant, equipment, or hard assets. In the investment community, market capitalization has become the de facto standard for defining small firms.

In other words, the worth of a firm—more specifically, the firm's equity value—is representative of its size. By stratifying the equity market by capitalization, the long-run statistics suggest that smaller capitalized firms have a performance edge over larger firms. Other variables that could be used as proxies for size—such as number of employees, or amount of sales—do not exhibit excess returns. Consequently, market capitalization has become the standard for defining a company's size in the financial markets.

Market capitalization appears to correct many of the pitfalls associated with attempts to distinguish large from small stocks. Furthermore, the marking-to-market effect of closing prices allows for a much more dynamic definition of small and large companies. The number of employees in a firm may remain constant, but market capitalization is always reflecting the current, often shifting, worth of a firm. Simple cutoffs based on earnings, in large or small companies, fail to generate significant results because of the potential variability and cyclical nature of earnings. In addition, similar-size companies may appear substantially different, depending on the accounting or investment decisions that each company makes. Issues such as write-offs can significantly shrink current earnings, further clouding the size of a firm. Revenues may also be inappropriate, given industry-specific pricing and margin issues. Automobile revenues, for instance, may always appear large because of the total revenues of the industry. Yet the thin margins that typify that industry provide a considerably muted bottom line. Another possible factor in determining company size may be the number of employees, but only if the industries are similarly labor-intensive.

IMPLICATIONS OF UNEVENLY DISTRIBUTED MARKET

Not surprisingly, the distribution of public companies by market capitalization is uneven. There are ten to fifteen small stocks for every megacap. This phenomenon applies not only to the U.S. equity market but also to all international equity markets. Figure 2.2 represents a ranking of stocks by market capitalization for the United States, the United Kingdom, and the Japanese equity markets. The uneven or clustered distribution of shares is understandable, given that wealth, like most resources, is limited. Not all firms are successful at catching the attention of equity investors or speculators. As a result, only a limited number of companies can dominate the megacap space. Conversely, the number of smaller firms can appear unending.

An unevenly distributed equity market has several critical implications for small-cap investors. Compared to their large-cap counterparts, small-cap managers are more likely to struggle to understand their

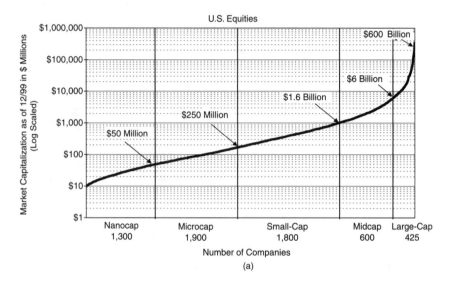

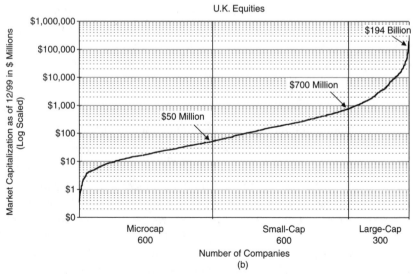

Figure 2.2 International Equities Ranked by Market Value

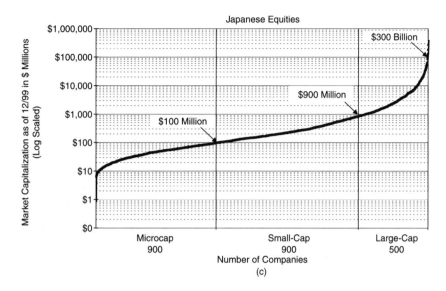

Figure 2.2 (Continued)

competitive environment. The numerous issues that trade in the secondary markets present investors with more opportunities, yet constantly challenge them to understand new concepts, business models, and competitors. Small-cap investors are faced with managing the mountains of data and issues that arise in this dynamic investment environment.

Compared to the extensive research on megacaps (legions of analysts study them in excruciating detail), the breadth of research available on small companies is relatively limited. Because of the sheer number of companies trading in the small-cap market, these second-tier stocks are unlikely to be as well followed as the megacaps. Thus, the information bias between small and large firms is likely to be persistent.

For example, Microsoft is covered by approximately 20 sell-side or Wall Street analysts willing to offer their expert opinions, whereas the average small stock is covered by approximately four analysts. Analysts may have prepared as many as five or six research opinions, or as few as one or none, on some of the companies in the small-cap universe. Figure 2.3 shows the differential in analyst coverage, based on company size.

The lack of coverage for secondary shares presents a real difficulty for those investing in the smaller companies. Without easy access to research, investors' decision making becomes more problematic. A confirming or counter-opinion on a potential investment allows prudent

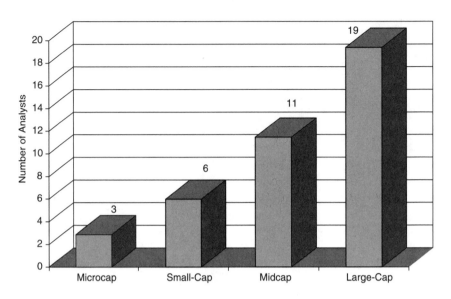

Figure 2.3   Analyst Coverage by Size

investors to have more confidence in their final decision. With fewer analysts covering the average small stock, however, ferreting out advice on the proper course of action becomes more difficult.

Although the lack of coverage for small stocks presents a practical impediment for investors, this coverage bias ultimately provides a true investment opportunity. If secondary stocks are indeed under-followed by the investment community, then their shares are less efficiently priced than their large-cap counterparts.

The simple premise that the markets are less than efficient underlies a fund manager's investment efforts. If the markets were perfectly efficient, then all information—public and private—would already be reflected in share prices. An active investor benefits when a change in the outlook for a company has not been effectively reflected in the price of a security. The investor can quickly acquire shares in this company and then patiently wait for the market to recognize the company's value.

Although the efficiency of the market is still an issue of debate among academicians, one can reasonably argue that the flow of information is far less concentrated in the secondary markets than it is for the megacaps. If, for example, 25 sell-side analysts are generally responsible for covering each megacap, then 25 different institutional equity sales teams, traders, and other personnel are focused on the most minute changes in outlook for that particular security. Thanks to the electronic age, integrated data networks can instantly transmit a change of market opinion to thousands of concerned investors. If this electronic calling card is too subtle, a direct call from an analyst, salesperson, or trader can certainly catch an investor's attention.

Companies have also joined the information flow through hundreds of newly formed investor relations firms. These firms allow the companies to create a direct and extensive link to investors. As information flow increases, share prices become more and more efficient.

Because smaller companies are less followed than large companies, however, active investors have a better chance at reaping benefits when they obtain new insight into a particular company. The difference in pricing efficiency for smaller firms is a powerful argument for active participation in the secondary markets. More important, the uneven distribution of securities dictates that the current information bias between small- and large-cap firms will more or less remain constant.

CHARACTERISTICS OF THE SMALL-CAP MARKET

Anecdotal evidence suggests that the small-cap market is risky. A look at the current environment produces plenty of evidence. Secondary firms that miss consensus profit estimates by a penny are cruelly punished.

Even though the disparity in the market-pricing mechanism for smaller firms appears unfair, the general uncertainty that surrounds the secondary market perhaps justifies the uneasiness of investors when a small company makes a misstep or when its actions come under question. From a qualitative viewpoint, smaller firms are arguably more risky because, compared to their large, better capitalized counterparts, they typically are ill-equipped to handle the vagaries of the economic cycle. Moreover, it could be argued that large companies' many layers of management expertise enable them to tackle sudden shifts in the operating environment.

The perception of safety associated with large-cap firms is further enhanced by the investor relations department that exists in most such firms. The investor relations role has been integrated within corporate management, a move fueled by the increasingly close ties between corporate managers and shareholders. Although most firms offer some form of an "investor support line" that investors may contact for assistance, large-cap blue-chip firms dedicate significant resources to offer guidance to investors. By contrast, at many smaller firms, the investor relations role tends to be one of many hats worn by the chief financial officer. Although these varying approaches to investor relations appear to reflect a marginal difference in corporate focus, it is terribly important to manage investor expectations. If a small firm cannot expertly manage the investment community's expectations, investors become concerned about the company's status. As concerns mount, the company's shares are more likely to reflect greater volatility, which tends to shorten investment horizons. The less certain the investment community, the less likely that investors will retain a buy-and-hold strategy. Management can pay a dear price when corporate strategy efforts appear less than seamless to the investment community. In short, compared to larger companies, smaller companies are more likely to be at a disadvantage when they communicate information to the investment community.

Sources of Risk

A hard look at the performance statistics suggests that small stocks outperform large stocks because they are indeed riskier than their large-cap counterparts. Factors such as stock price volatility, trading liquidity, and earnings consistency bear out this risk profile. Consider, for example, the performance of small-cap stocks within the context of overall market performance.

Although the returns in the U.S. equity market have been dramatic during the past 70 years, the incredibly robust performance of U.S. equities has been accompanied by a great deal of turbulence. For their part, secondary stocks have proved to be a more amplified version of the overall market. Secondary stocks have tended to weaken more than the large-cap market in a downturn, but they have significantly outperformed large-cap stocks in an upturn. The October 1987 market correction was no exception. Large stocks collapsed 19.9 percent that month, but small stocks weakened an additional 5 percent. Conversely, a dramatic 139 percent bounce for large stocks in 1933 generated a whopping 252 percent gain in the secondary market that year. Although these figures appear partly overstated because of the agonizing bear market that occurred prior to 1933, they nonetheless illustrate the point that small-cap stocks react in a more volatile manner than large-cap stocks.

Table 2.1 reflects the best and worst months in terms of small-cap performance over the past eleven cycles. Notice that small stocks outperform large caps when the market rallies, and they lose far greater ground in a correcting market.

Price Volatility

The concerns and opportunities for any asset can be reduced into one single figure—the price—which reflects a great deal of information about that asset. Prices change as the market struggles with new information and concerns. The swings of smaller stock prices, as depicted in Table 2.1, can be much more dramatic than those of large stocks. A

Table 2.1 Small-Cap Performance: Best and Worst Months

			Large		**Small**
Best Month Performance					
Cycle					
1	12/25 to 5/32	11/28	12.93%	06/31	16.49%
2	6/32 to 2/37	04/33	34.23	04/33	54.24
3	3/37 to 12/39	06/38	21.34	06/38	28.50
4	1/40 to 5/46	04/45	7.08	11/45	10.21
Noncycle	6/46 to 11/64	11/62	9.94	11/62	12.81
5	12/64 to 12/68	04/68	8.04	01/67	11.67
6	1/69 to 11/73	12/71	8.00	09/73	10.79
7	12/73 to 7/83	10/74	17.43	01/75	23.09
8	8/83 to 10/90	01/87	13.45	01/87	12.94
9	11/90 to 12/93	12/91	11.78	12/91	10.97
10	1/94 to 2/00	07/97	8.14	01/00	12.23
Worst Month Performance					
Cycle					
1	12/25 to 5/32	09/31	−27.47%	09/31	−30.99%
2	6/32 to 2/37	02/33	−13.19	10/32	−16.79
3	3/37 to 12/39	03/38	−22.31	03/38	−27.34
4	1/40 to 5/46	05/40	−20.47	05/40	−26.62
Noncycle	6/46 to 11/64	09/46	−8.60	09/46	−12.85
5	12/64 to 12/68	08/66	−6.71	08/66	−8.55
6	1/69 to 11/73	11/73	−9.92	11/73	−16.27
7	12/73 to 7/83	09/74	−12.46	10/78	−13.86
8	8/83 to 10/90	10/87	−19.91	10/87	−25.13
9	11/90 to 12/93	06/91	−4.18	06/91	−4.67
10	1/94 to 2/00	08/98	−14.42	08/98	−18.30

simple look at share price volatility suggests that small stocks exhibit approximately 22 percent greater volatility than large caps. Figure 2.4 compares market volatility for microcap, small-cap, midcap, and large-cap stocks, from 1926 to 1999. Size and volatility appear to move in tandem. Put another way, volatility increases as one gravitates to smaller firms.

The annualized volatility for large stocks is 17.8 percent. Midcaps increase to 21.0 percent, small caps to 23.0 percent, and microcaps jump to 27.0 percent. The volatility figure offers some insight into the range of returns an asset can generate and the inherent risks associated with the asset. For instance, a volatility of 10 percent implies that, two-thirds of the time, the range of returns over a one-year period falls between −10 percent and +10 percent of the average rate of return. Assuming that an asset carries an average rate of return of 10 percent and an annualized volatility level of 7 percent, the statistics suggest that such an asset is likely to offer investors a range of returns between 3 percent and 17 percent two-thirds of the time. In other words, riskier assets tend to reflect greater volatility.

Even though volatility measures offer a convenient means for comparing the riskiness of various assets, it is difficult to grasp the implications of an asset class that offers 20 percent volatility. Figure 2.5 examines the risk levels of small stocks in terms of loss or downside risk.

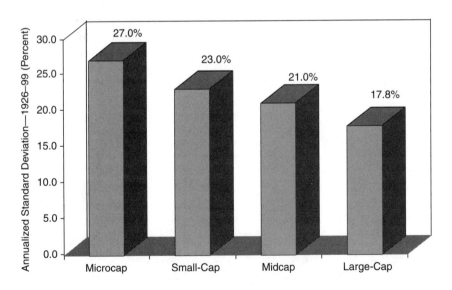

Figure 2.4 Volatility by Size Group

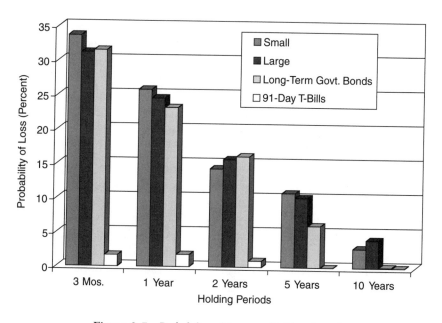

Figure 2.5 Probability of Loss per Holding Period

After all, volatility measures rise if prices change suddenly by either appreciating or depreciating. Investors understand that even if an asset is said to be risky or exhibits high volatility levels, if the price moves are favorable, then such volatility might be considered to be "good." Conversely, increased volatility combined with a price moving downward is always labeled "bad volatility."

Figure 2.5 examines the chances of losing money in the small and large stock market. Over a short-term horizon, the chances of losing money tend to be much greater for smaller stocks. An investor with a short investment horizon of three months has a 31.3 percent chance of losing money in the blue chips, compared to 33.6 percent in the small caps. Note that small caps become more compelling as the holding period is extended—a five-year holding period points to only a 10.8 percent chance of generating a loss. The message in this simple example is: The riskier the asset class, the longer the investment horizon required.

Trading Liquidity

A less traditional, but nonetheless effective, measure of risk is liquidity. In this instance, liquidity represents an investor's ability to exit or enter

an asset with minimal friction. The issue of liquidity is incredibly important for traders in small stocks. In general, small stocks tend to be much
less liquid than their large-cap counterparts. Smaller firms have fewer
shares outstanding. The total assets traded in the large-cap sector are
many multiples of those traded in the small-cap sector.

Figure 2.6 summarizes the simple bid–ask spreads, or the difference
between the price a buyer (bid) is willing to pay and a seller (ask) is willing to accept for stocks of various sizes. A spread of more than 1 percent
suggests that the total cost of entering and exiting an idea is roughly two
times the spread estimate, or 2 percent of the price. Note that large
stocks are approximately four times as liquid as small stocks—the average bid–ask spread of a large company is approximately 0.26 percent,
compared to 0.93 percent for the average small stock. In short, the cost
of trading smaller firms has an impact on the tradability of the shares.
The more expensive the transaction, the less trading occurs.

Figure 2.7 shows the average dollar volume—the shares traded
times the price of a given security—of the equity market by "size." Not
surprisingly, the average dollar volume of smaller stocks is far below that
of the blue chips. This comparison offers some insight into the size, or
the amount of money, an investor is able to trade. Because the dollar
volume is much lower for smaller firms, the market impact of trades can
be dramatically increased. The market impact, if significant, can act as a

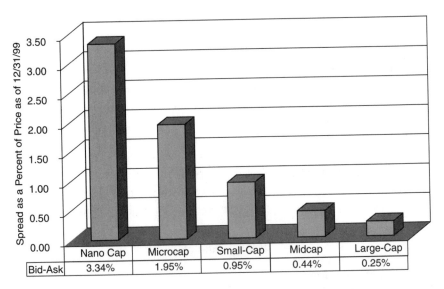

	Nano Cap	Microcap	Small-Cap	Midcap	Large-Cap
Bid-Ask	3.34%	1.95%	0.95%	0.44%	0.25%

Figure 2.6 Liquidity by Size, Using Bid–Ask Spreads

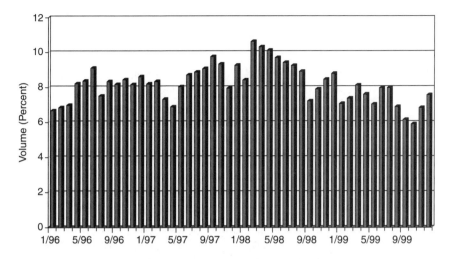

Figure 2.7   Relative Small to Large Liquidity—Median Dollar Volume

deterrent to small-cap investing. Not only is the initial spread prohibitive because it costs roughly four times the amount to trade a small stock, but the cost dramatically increases as an investor attempts to buy a sizable number of shares. This effect is dynamic and difficult to measure. If the simple bid–ask spreads for an asset are wide and the dollar volume is thin, an investor can estimate that the asset will be fairly illiquid.

Risk levels increase dramatically for illiquid stocks. If the market declines, the bid–ask spreads on all stocks are likely to widen. Given an uncertain market, fewer market makers wish to take on sizable positions, especially in the case of smaller, less liquid stocks. A dramatic gap in the blue-chip sector is thus likely to have an amplified effect on the secondary markets.

The relative lack of trading liquidity for small-cap stocks is a unique source of their risk. Because thin trading causes prices to act in a discontinuous fashion, simple volatility measures are likely to portray smaller stocks as being volatile. Note that liquidity and volatility factors are interrelated; more volatility yields less trading, and less liquidity yields more volatility.

Earnings Prospects

The relative certainty of earnings or profitability also influences investors' perceptions of risk. Smaller firms, by nature, have greater business risks and therefore offer less certain earnings. This is partly based on the evolving nature of companies in the start-up or early stages of development. The cyclical nature of the small-cap universe also accounts for the less than stable earnings associated with smaller companies.[1] Figure 2.8 compares the earnings of small-cap and large-cap companies. Although the median earnings growth rate appears to be higher for secondary stocks than it is for large stocks, the smaller stocks exhibit a much wider range of results, as shown in Figure 2.9. The message is simple: Smaller firms appear to grow earnings faster, yet they offer little visibility in earnings compared to the blue-chip segment.

Young growth companies tend to have a less than developed understanding of their potential customer base—and, therefore, the potential demand. As their customer base matures and broadens, however, management can capture a better sense of demand. Competition represents yet another challenge for the management teams of smaller firms. The competitive dynamics may be less clear in developing industries than in mature industries. Likewise, well-entrenched companies can have a clear advantage over a start-up. Imagine a start-up attempting to break into the automobile industry. The sizable start-up costs, the need to forge relationships with original equipment manufacturers (OEM), and the ability to create a sales channel are only a few of the incredible hurdles a start-up might face when it attempts to tackle one of the big three automakers.

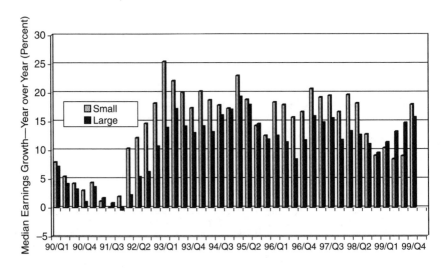

Figure 2.8   Median Earnings Growth—Small-Cap vs. Large-Cap

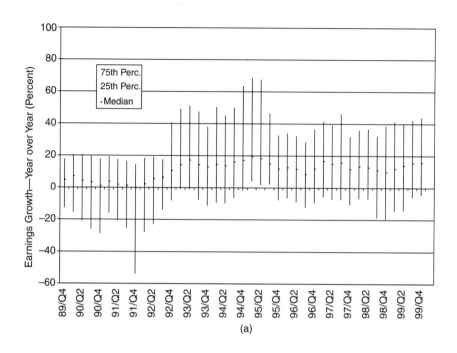

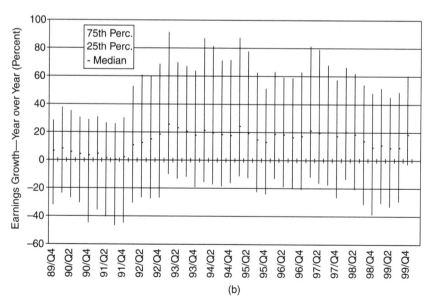

Figure 2.9 Earnings Growth: (a) Large-Cap; (b) Small-Cap

Moreover, emerging growth companies, by nature, tend to offer spectacular growth expectations. Eye-popping expectations may be required for catching the attention of a skeptical investment community, but they make the yardstick of success especially challenging. Management teams with a mature understanding of demand and competition can better manage the bottom line, offer practical guidance, and set realistic expectations for the investment community. This difference in operational experience allows the large, well-entrenched blue-chip franchises to offer a much more consistent stream of earnings.

Greater Economic Sensitivity

Smaller stocks also appear to exhibit greater economic sensitivity than their large-cap counterparts. This more sensitive footing among the secondary stocks also accounts for more erratic earnings. Groups such as retailers and regional banks, which tend to be more economically sensitive, generally proliferate in the secondary markets. Figure 2.10 illustrates the economically sensitive overweight that exists in smaller stocks. In addition, the large-cap market appears to display a greater bias toward the defensive and stable sectors. The bias that small and large firms have for differing sectors is one reason for the more variable earnings displayed by smaller stocks.

The small-stock universe exhibits a greater exposure to the following sectors: (1) transportation; (2) basic industrials (specialty chemicals, metals, and paper and forest products; (3) consumer cyclicals (retailing, appliances and furnishings, textiles, and auto-related businesses); and (4) credit cyclicals (building materials, hardware and tools, and home building). The heftier financial-sector exposure of the small-cap universe may also account for its more cyclical nature. Over the past 20 years, money-center banks may have appeared to be less economically sensitive because their business has become more diversified and less dependent on traditional borrowing and lending. Smaller banks have a more cyclical profile, however. They remain linked to the traditional sources of profitability: loan growth and the slope of the yield curve. Conversely, secondary stocks are also underweighted in consumer staples (food, cosmetics, household products), health care and drugs, and utilities. As a result of the sector underweight, large companies are more likely to reflect a less economically sensitive bent than their smaller-cap counterparts.

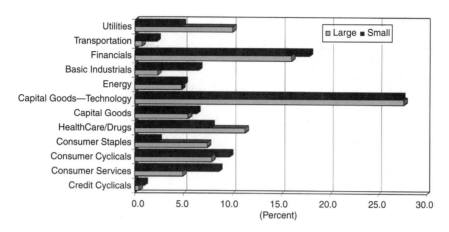

Figure 2.10 Sector Exposure by Size

SMALL-CAP BENCHMARKS

The business of performance measurement, or benchmarking, returns has grown significantly since the early 1980s. As a result, investors are more likely to find a wealth of indices based on the secondary market.

Prior to the 1970s, small-cap benchmarks were unheard of. The dramatic outperformance of the secondary market in the 1970s led to two important research papers on the "size effect," published in 1981 and arguing that smaller stocks generally outperform large stocks. The papers, by Rolf W. Banz[2] and Marc R. Reinganum,[3] generated considerable interest in smaller stocks and in benchmarking their results. Evidence to support the size effect was supplied in a paper by Ibbotson and Senqfeld in 1982. Prior to this period, there were few proxies for measuring the performance of smaller-companies' shares. The introduction of the Ibbotson Small Stock Index in 1982 allowed a more focused look at size results. The index is an outgrowth of results documenting the effects of the small-cap premium in the 1982 paper. Even though the Ibbotson Small Stock Index is popularly quoted as a small stock proxy, it effectively measures a microcap universe of the smallest 20 percent of companies on the New York Stock Exchange and in the National Association of Securities Dealers Automated Quotation System (Nasdaq).

Before the introduction of small-cap indices, close observers of the market were able to approximate the health of the secondary markets by looking at the Nasdaq over-the-counter (OTC) market. One could surmise that if the OTC sector was faring well, then smaller companies, by extension, were performing similarly. The start-up years for Nasdaq, which opened in 1971, represented a good proxy for the health of smaller stocks. However, when successful technology ideas, such as those originating at Microsoft and Intel, became megacaps by the late 1980s, the Nasdaq quote became more representative of the big few. Although a majority of the stocks trading on Nasdaq are smaller stocks, the weighted-average or market weight results, by definition, reflect the dominant large few. Small stocks can trade lower, but if a handful of large caps manage to trade up for the day, the Nasdaq composite is more likely to register a positive day.

In 1979, Wilshire Associates developed the Wilshire Next 1750, the first benchmark to formally track the smaller stock market. Five years later, in 1984, Frank Russell & Co. introduced the Russell 1000, measuring the performance of large stocks, and the Russell 2000, representing the small-cap market. In the Wilshire 5000 and the Russell 3000, both companies have generated very broad-based benchmarks focused on the U.S. equity market. One of the best known benchmarks for secondary stocks, the Russell 2000 comprises the lower two-thirds (2,000 companies) of the largest 3,000 securities in the U.S. equity market, as ranked by market capitalization. The Russell 2000 was launched to formally measure secondary market results.

The Wilshire Associates proxy for small stock performance is called the Wilshire Next 1750. It captures the performance of the bottom 1,750 issues of the largest 2,500 public U.S. companies. This benchmark was developed in 1979. Both Russell and Wilshire offer benchmarks for mid-cap sectors as well. It is also common to find investment-style benchmarks—measuring growth and value, for example—for the small-cap markets.

The Value Line index, which was developed in 1961, is a well-known measure that covers a broad sampling of value stocks. Although the index is not designed to be a smaller-company benchmark, it inadvertently tends to have a lower market capitalization bias because of its focus on value.

In 1996, the Standard & Poor's small-cap index (the S&P 600) was introduced as the small-cap counterpart to the S&P 500 index for large stocks and the S&P midcap index. This index takes a critically different approach from other small-cap indices. It is a managed list that attempts to model the small-cap market by a sampling process. Instead of aggregating the performance of all small-cap stocks, the S&P 600 limits the listing to 600 companies. By using a sampling process, the index can approximate the performance of the entire small-cap market with only one-third of the names. Other popular measures, such as Russell's or Wilshire's, aggregate *all* stocks that are listed in the small-cap market. These benchmarks are passively defined by market capitalization and are reconstituted annually. By contrast, the S&P 600 identifies potential candidates for entry or exit on a case-by-case basis. Figure 2.11 presents an array of popular benchmarks by size.

Structure and Mechanics of Size Benchmarks

Although identifying the small-cap universe by market capitalization appears to be an elementary process, the actual rules for defining small-cap firms can be somewhat detailed. As noted previously, smaller companies far outnumber large firms by an order of at least ten to one. Hence, the number of stocks that appear in a small-cap benchmark is likely to exceed significantly the issues that appear in a large-cap proxy. Benchmarks such as the Russell 2000 or the Wilshire 1750 are prime examples of

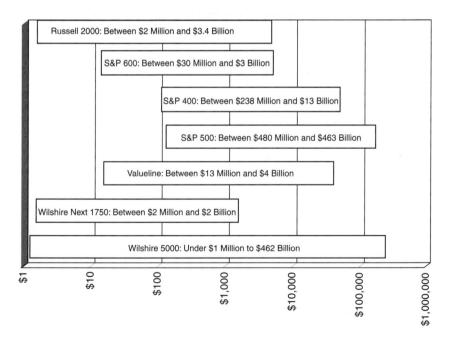

Figure 2.11   Popular Benchmarks by Size

small-cap benchmarks that hold hundreds of securities in an attempt to model small-cap prices. Conversely, large-cap benchmarks, such as the Dow Jones Industrial Average, can be very concentrated. A good example of a blue-chip index, this long-standing index comprises 30 stocks—not 300 or 3,000.

Simply dividing all securities in the equity market into two equal parts, one large and the other small, does not lead to an adequate definition of size because of the wide gaps or "jumps" in market capitalization. The large stocks have displayed a significant jump in size, from approximately $5 billion to $500 billion, as of early 2000. This is a tremendous range in size for approximately 450 companies. Conversely, it takes approximately 2,000 companies to span the small-cap market capitalization range of $250 million to $1.5 billion as of early 2000.

Because of the lopsided distribution in market capitalization, segmenting the equity market in two (small and large), three (small, mid, and large), or four (micro, small, mid, and large) equal parts can similarly yield ill-defined size groups. The rule of thumb for defining size-based benchmarks is: Divide the equity market into fractiles. Using percentiles, instead of quartiles or quintiles, is a common approach. The uneven distribution of securities implies an uneven grouping by percentiles. In general, as of this writing, the large-cap market consists of companies with market capitalization above $4 billion. These 450 or so companies lie between the largest 90th percentile and the 100th percentile. Midcap firms lie between the market capitalization range of $1.2 billion to $4 billion. This maps roughly 700 companies into the 75th to 90th percentiles. Small stocks are generally represented within the 50th to 75th percentiles or the range of $200 million to $1.2 billion. Approximately 1,700 public companies lie in this range. The remainder of the U.S. equity market, short of counting penny stocks, is represented by micro- and nanocaps, or stocks with market capitalization below the 50th percentile. Over 4,000 companies are in this capitalization space. (See Figure 2.2 for the distribution.) Once the cutoff ranges or percentiles are identified, benchmarks can easily be defined for periods going forward or for past years (by rebuilding historical performance data). Many popular benchmarks, especially those that focus on small stocks, are typically rebalanced annually; that is, stocks are added or subtracted, depending on whether they meet capitalization criteria. The Frank Russell benchmarks, for instance, are reconstituted annually at midyear.

The question, then, is: Why not simply "tag" or identify some specific market capitalization range? After all, dealing with fractiles and rebalancing can appear quite cumbersome. Remember, however, that size is a moving target. Shifts in capitalization are dynamic, and assumptions cannot remain fixed. As noted previously, market capitalization is based on shares outstanding × price. Although shares outstanding can remain fairly constant, changes in price can be almost random and unpredictable. As a result, distinguishing small-cap stocks from large-cap stocks in current terms can be misleading. If a small company is successful, its market capitalization can jump dramatically. The sudden shift in value can cause a small or microcap firm to become sizable overnight. Internet shares are a good example of this phenomenon. America Online (AOL) started as a microcap with a market capitalization of approximately $83 million in 1992. By January 2000, it had a market capitalization of approximately $131 billion, a dramatic jump in eight years.

Not only can companies shift from microcap to megacap status, and vice versa, but markets can also reflect significant drifts in market capitalization. In a bull market, the upward drift in share prices can be dramatic. Smaller shares can remain smaller within the market context, yet their absolute level can radically change. In the early 1990s, small companies were defined as companies with market capitalization under $500 million. In 1999, that figure was closer to the lower end of the small-cap range. The upper end of the small-cap range was $1.2 billion, or more than double the size of small companies at the start of the 1990s. In difficult times, or a bear market, these dynamics operate in reverse.

The equity market rotations can present a practical impediment to investing in a universe called small stocks. After all, if a significant portion of the universe can migrate to the midcap or microcap world from one year to the next, it makes identifying one's target so much more difficult. Fortunately, the universe of smaller stocks is quite broad, and most smaller companies remain in the small-cap market for years. The Internet phenomenon of stocks moving from the microcap landscape to megacap overnight is a unique situation that may be an exception rather than the rule. Investors, however, can only hope to be "cursed" with most of their portfolios migrating to megacaps overnight.

Managing the Reconstitution of Benchmarks— A Case Study of the Russell 2000

It is common and necessary for index rebalancing or reconstitution to occur in all size-based benchmarks, including small-cap benchmarks.

Because market capitalization is dynamic, the constituents to small-cap benchmarks need to be reshuffled at regular intervals. Unfortunately, the changes that occur in a reconstitution tend to be dramatic. Depending on the swing of the overall market, 20 to 30 percent of the constituents of small-cap indices such as the Russell 2000 can change on the rebalancing date. These changes can have a material impact on the underlying benchmark.

A second, more recent, phenomenon relates to the increased activity among index funds or funds that track major equity benchmarks. An estimated $146 billion in assets, as of 1998, was indexed to the domestic Russell benchmarks—most notably, the Russell 3000 and its subcomponents, the Russell 1000 and Russell 2000. The sheer bulk of assets currently benchmarked has caused a seemingly maintenance-type activity (the rebalancing or reconstitution of the benchmarks) to become very relevant to the investment community. This event is especially meaningful to both passive and active small-cap investors. Of the $146 billion, an estimated $26 billion is indexed directly to the Russell 2000 or indirectly through the Russell 3000.

The impact of passive funds has added a new dimension of risk to reconstitution. On the trade date or day of rebalancing, liquidity can appear or disappear for no apparent reason on hundreds of smaller stocks. As shares migrate out of the Russell 2000, index fund managers need to account for the rotation seamlessly—they need to sell all exiting candidates and concurrently purchase the new entries on the date of rebalancing. After all, passive or index fund managers are rewarded for their perfect tracking on an index. Their need for "instant" exposure to the newly constructed benchmark can create sizable dislocations among smaller stocks.

In a short amount of time, several billion dollars need to be reallocated from exiting stocks into new candidates. The drive of passive managers to perfectly replicate their bogey or benchmark adds to congestion and trading bottlenecks in the involved securities. There is added confusion because little of the underlying activity is related to "information traders" or active investors. Much of the activity is primarily based on liquidity-driven concerns. The small-cap investor will feel this liquidity squeeze in many ways. As managers aggressively move into stocks, the least liquid smaller-cap names reflect the most significant market impact.

Although many arbitrage opportunities come to mind, active small-cap fund managers can be severely affected by these seemingly mundane changes. The sudden change in liquidity can create opportunities and/or pitfalls for active investors. Laggard stocks that are about to exit the Russell 2000 are likely to exhibit a sharp drop-off in liquidity. After all, if the stocks are outside the index, fewer dollars are likely to chase these shares. These stocks can be further affected as index fund managers sell out of these shares on the rebalancing date. The information trader or active manager who owns such shares is likely to face a plummeting stock without any fundamental change in the company. Conversely, a potential candidate for entry to a benchmark is likely to spur a sudden appreciation and exhibit increased liquidity.

Even though benchmark rotations can wreak havoc within one's investment framework, active fund managers should approach these shifts in an opportunistic manner. A stock that is a potential candidate for addition to a benchmark can represent an investment opportunity if the outlook for the stock is sound. Active investors' awareness that an issue is a benchmark candidate for passive investors creates a window of liquidity that may not otherwise exist. Finding liquidity to create sizable positions in the small-cap market can be fleeting. Similarly, it may be timely to sell select holdings prior to the reconstitution date if the fundamentals of the holdings are in question and the holdings are potential targets for deletion from a benchmark.

Potential Shifts in the Russell 2000

As stocks drift during the year, the Russell 2000 benchmark becomes more polarized along the lines of size, liquidity, valuations, information flow, and the like. To adjust for this polarization, reconstitution removes the clustering effect that typically occurs throughout the year. The underlying premise of annual rebalancing or reconstitution is to realign size groups—that is, to reclassify stocks ranked by market capitalization. This annual event generates numerous, somewhat predictable, effects on the underlying benchmark or index. A new and reconstituted Russell 2000 index is likely to become more evenly distributed in terms of price trend, market capitalization, liquidity, valuations, and information flow.

Because the primary rule for benchmark inclusion is based on market capitalization ranges, the most successful stocks, or stocks with strong price momentum in the Russell 2000, are most likely to migrate out of the Russell 2000 and into the Russell 1000. Conversely, the weakest performing stocks are most likely to drift out of the Russell 2000 benchmark. The newly formed small-cap index is therefore more likely to be evenly distributed by price momentum. The stocks with the most extreme positive price momentum enter the large-cap benchmark to be replaced by less successful stocks. The opposite occurs on the weaker side; the weakest stocks in the small-cap benchmark are more likely to be replaced by stocks of formerly smaller companies exhibiting more positive gains.

Figure 2.12 compares the distribution of a current Russell 2000 by relative strength or price momentum, and a projected rebalanced proxy only months before a reconstitution. Note that the top fifth of the Russell 2000 with the most significant price strength also has the heaviest weighting—almost 40 percent. The quintile with the weakest price trend has the lowest weight—approximately 10 percent. Compared to the current Russell 2000 distribution, the projected version has a much less clustered distribution. The relative weight of each quintile is more or less equal, regardless of its price momentum. For example, the stocks with the strongest price trends are projected to have an approximate 20 percent weight versus a current weighting of 40 percent.

As a result of the Russell 2000's polarization by price trend, similar clustering can be found with respect to market capitalization. As stocks become more successful, their respective market capitalizations similarly follow. As shown in Figure 2.13, the newly formed Russell 2000 is likely to have more weight in the largest fifth of the index, but less so compared to the existing Russell 2000.

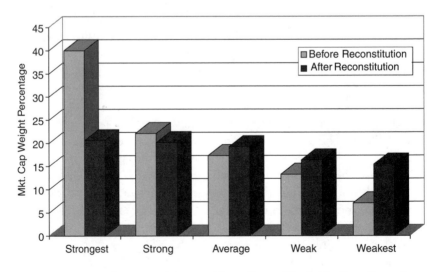

Figure 2.12   Current and Projected Russell 2000 Weights by Price Strength

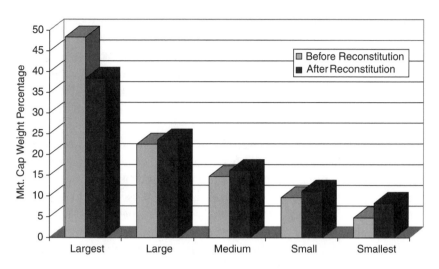

Figure 2.13 Current and Projected Russell 2000 Weights by Size

Upon reconstruction, the less liquid names in a benchmark are more likely to have more significant weight. As the Russell 2000 becomes more stratified by success, or price strength, the benchmark also becomes more polarized in terms of liquidity (see Figure 2.14); that is, the top tier of the most liquid names also has the most significant weight.

These findings confirm the evidence found in the Kim and Lotufo[4] report, which suggested that returns are positively correlated with the

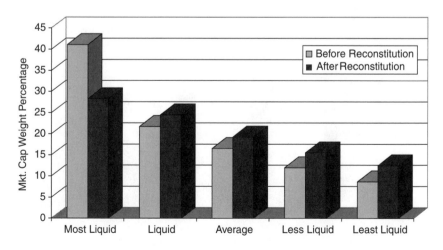

Figure 2.14 Current and Projected Russell 2000 Weights by Dollar Volume (Liquidity)

most thinly traded securities. Although the aggregate measure of liquidity is likely to appear similar both pre- and post-rebalancing, changes within the index are likely to be quite severe. This makes sense because more successful stocks are likely to be more liquid. These stocks have an enormous following and consequently are more likely to be traded. Similarly, the stocks that have weakened most are also most likely to be forgotten and, as a result, are illiquid.

The aggregate valuation level of the projected Russell index appears to be quite similar to the existing benchmark. However, the valuation data suggest that a significant gap in weighting is found between the most expensive fifth of the Russell 2000 and the next most expensive quintile. The projected Russell 2000, to no one's surprise, suggests a more evenly balanced benchmark on a valuation basis. Figure 2.15 shows the weighting of the Russell 2000 as stratified by price-to-earnings ratio valuations. The most expensive group within the projected Russell 2000 appears to hold approximately 5.0 percent less weight than the existing benchmark. The cheapest group in the projected Russell 2000 has an increase in weight of almost 3 percent, compared to the current benchmark.

An interesting side effect of rebalancing is that the newly formed Russell 2000 contains companies subject to less information flow. Very successful, more liquid, and larger stocks are more likely to have more sell-side coverage compared to less successful, less liquid, and smaller

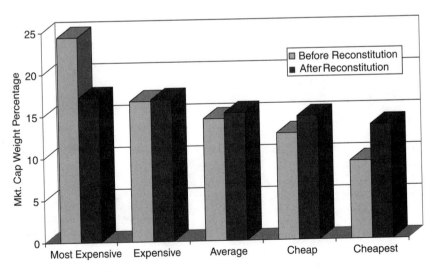

Figure 2.15   Current and Projected Russell 2000 Weights by Price to Earnings

stocks. Figure 2.16 shows the difference in analyst coverage for a current Russell 2000 and a projected version. Note that in the reconstituted benchmark, fewer analysts are covering a greater proportion of companies.

Investors who compete in the small-cap market need to be especially aware of the side effects of an index reconstitution. The renewed proxy for small stocks can undergo considerable change. The impact is evident not only in the considerable turnover in holdings but also at a fundamental level. Basic characteristics of the index can change—a "growthy" or higher multiple index can change into a value or lower multiple proxy. A terribly liquid top-heavy index can lose its most liquid constituents. These changes can appear subtle but nonetheless can significantly affect the manner in which an index sways.

More important, active small-cap investors need to be aware of the index reconstitution of major benchmarks. Simply put, stock prices can escalate without a trace of fundamental change in the company. If a smaller company is earmarked for a benchmark, the sizable influx of index dollars chasing an undiscovered stock can propel its share price to inexplicable new highs. Similarly, a laggard stock that has been marked to

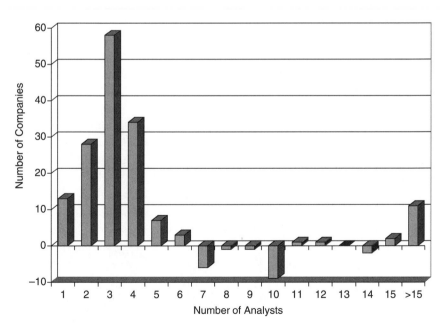

Figure 2.16 Number of Companies by Analyst Coverage—Reconstituted Russell 2000 Less Current Index

be removed from a popular benchmark can fall into a chasm of illiquid and untradable securities without any fundamental change.

Four Conditions Supporting Small-Cap Asset Class

Although equity markets around the world have companies listed with high and low market capitalization, a small-cap asset class may not necessarily be evident. Simply focusing on the lower rank-order market capitalization of companies in any market does not necessarily force the existence of the asset class. Several conditions need to exist in order to support an asset class argument. The four basic requirements are: (1) a mature equity market, (2) reasonable access to the capital markets, (3) reasonable evidence of excess returns to compensate for added risks, and (4) some degree of diversification benefit. Each is discussed in detail below.

1. *Mature equity markets are more likely to contain a small-cap asset class than emerging markets.* Markets such as Brazil or Indonesia, which are subject to concerns over economic and inflationary outlooks and political and regulatory stability, are less likely to present distinct size effects. Although these factors are relevant in every market, they tend to be more benign in mature, developed capital markets. In emerging markets, however, macroeconomic and political concerns have significant ripple effects on all existing shares, both small and large, thereby rendering size less relevant. An especially "young" equity market forces investors to deal with issues more severe than size. Because of these overriding factors, investors are more likely to look to emerging markets for country exposure rather than opportunities that might accrue from small-cap stocks.

Large stocks are likely to be as equally unseasoned or undiscovered as small stocks in a developing market. If investors have the choice of investing in unseasoned firms for any market, they generally prefer more liquid assets. In most markets, the more liquid segments tend to have larger capitalization. As an emerging market stabilizes and matures, and as investors scale the learning curve of investing in these markets, then more subtle market concerns such as size might become more relevant.

2. *Access to the capital markets is critical for smaller firms and for a small-cap asset class.* If smaller firms have limited access to the capital markets, they are less likely to experience fast growth. Without the prospect of finding new, fast-growing companies, investors are more likely to retreat toward a large-cap safe-haven view.

A lack of investor interest can potentially create a vicious cycle in which the unwillingness of market participants to invest leads to a scarcity of capital for smaller firms. Offering fewer new issues leads to less interest being generated in small-cap stocks, and less interest in new stocks means less capital is available for small-cap firms.

Without capital for secondary firms, growth becomes muted. For investors to take on additional risk—more specifically, small stock risk— newly minted securities must offer superior growth and therefore higher returns. A less liquid asset class cannot thrive without promising above-average growth to investors.

Witness, for example, the surge in the small-cap market upon the introduction of Nasdaq in the early 1970s. Nasdaq allowed smaller companies easier access to the capital markets. As a result, investors basked in a long-run small-cap bull market for more than a decade after the opening of Nasdaq. It was not by simple chance, therefore, that small-cap firms significantly outpaced large caps during this period. Similar developments appear to be occurring in Europe—in Germany's "Neuer Market," for example. The new German exchange, opened in March 1997, allows younger firms to issue stock with fewer restrictions compared to the large bourse.

The availability of capital and the cost of capital play significant roles in the size effect. As discussed in later chapters, the abundance or scarcity of capital is critical in the rotations between small and large firms.

3. *Because small caps are less liquid and riskier than large caps, small-cap stocks should generate returns in excess of large-cap stocks.* If investors are to take on the incremental risk of investing in secondary stocks, they should have a reasonable belief that the returns will be above average. As a result, the historical returns for smaller-cap stocks should offer investors some supporting evidence that they will be compensated for the increased uncertainty of secondary stocks.

4. *Small-stock investing should benefit one's portfolio in terms of diversification.* If the price swings of secondary stocks are not perfectly correlated with those of large stocks, then the small-cap segment can be said to benefit one's portfolio. Investors need to have some tangible benefit from investing in any risky asset. If the correlation levels of secondary firms and the large-cap segment are low, then combining both groups should yield a more diversified basket. As a result, even if the delivered returns for smaller stocks are short of expectations, one's investment portfolio is nonetheless enhanced simply if variability in returns is muted.

Put another way, if the ebb and flow of small-cap stocks were completely dependent on large companies, there would be little incentive to invest in the secondaries. After all, one could simply create a leveraged position in large caps, through futures or options, and synthetically accentuate the returns of a large-cap portfolio. As a result, one would not need to take on small-cap risks, yet would benefit if the market returns increased.

A More Delineated Investing Landscape

The existence of the consultant and of a more savvy consumer of investment products has forced a more delineated market landscape. The current investment targets established for managers are so well defined that they could almost feel "pigeon-holed." Investment managers in the past may have had the luxury of loosely defining their target market. For the most part, a manager could claim that he or she invested in the stock market and simply get measured against the Dow Jones Industrial Average or, more recently, the S&P 500. It is quite possible that investment managers have always nibbled away at the secondary markets, whether intentionally or unintentionally, but were simply graded under the banner of a stock fund.

Identifying the small-cap effect and secondary stock performance vis-à-vis benchmarks has allowed investors to better understand and manage their equity market risks. The differences among small and large stocks are significant. Characteristics such as the variability in stock returns, the stability in earnings, the liquidity of the asset, and the information flow of the underlying securities reflect the differences. The uniqueness of the small-stock market requires a somewhat different skill set from traditional investment managers. An opportunistic eye is a valued trait among all investment managers. Yet skills such as the ability to trade and to develop independent and multiple-research sources become especially relevant when investing in smaller companies. As a result, the manager's process and priorities can be different from those of a large-cap investor. More importantly, such differences are endemic to the small-cap market and are likely to remain traits that segment small from large stocks.

THREE

Major Small-Cap and Large-Cap Cycles

A CLOSE LOOK at previous small-cap cycles provides insight into the nature of investor preferences for smaller or large firms. The complex nature of risk taking is a dynamic element that underlies market rotations. These cycles exist because of the ebb and flow of investors' risk

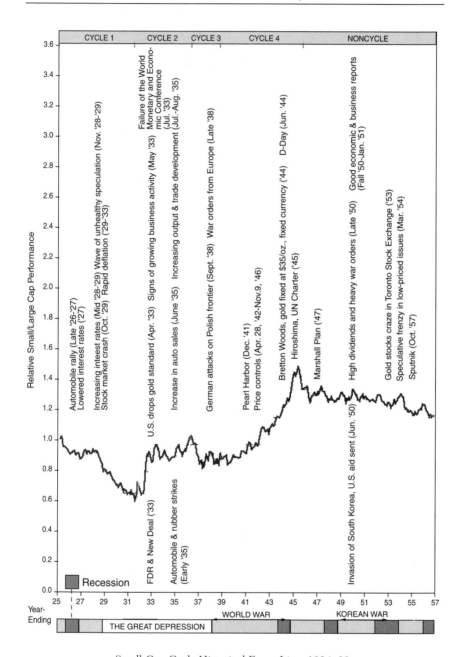

Small-Cap Cycle Historical Event Line: 1926–99

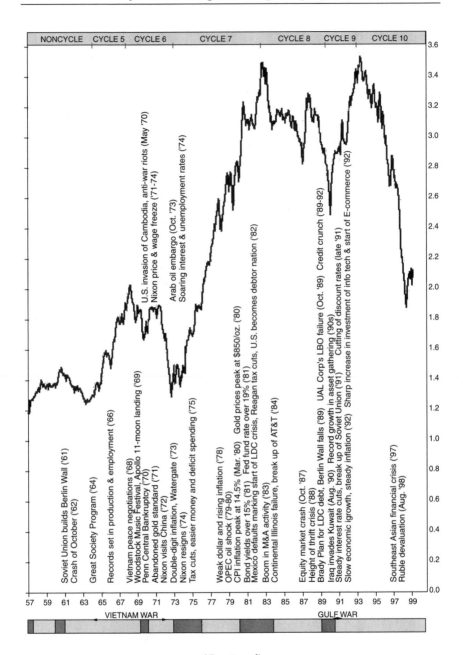

(Continued)

appetites for safe-haven prospects versus those requiring aggressive risk taking.

During periods when investors have flocked to the small stocks universe, they have overlooked the associated business risk and illiquidity as they pursued growth and higher returns. Because risk taking is dynamic in the marketplace, size preferences are unlikely to remain constant. The result is cycles in which small caps are more in favor than large caps and vice versa. But the historical premium that small stocks have returned offers little solace to investors who have unknowingly placed their chips on the secondary market in a down cycle. Second-tier hopefuls or smaller companies can sometimes lag the safer, more established franchises of large stocks for extended periods.

Since 1926, the market has seen ten major cycles of small-cap rotations and one notable noncycle in which large caps and small caps traded periods of superior performance. The average cycle lasts approximately five and one-half years. The shortest small cycle occurred in 1991, when small caps significantly outpaced large caps for approximately three and one-quarter years. The longest of the cycles began in 1973 and lasted for nine and three-quarter years. On the preceding pages is a chart representing the long-term relative peformance of small- versus large-cap returns, accompanied by a timeline of significant historical and economic events occuring during these cycles.

CYCLE 1—A PERIOD OF EXTREMES (DECEMBER 1925–MAY 1932)

The sudden and dramatic swings of the early small-cap cycles reflected the turbulent economic and political setting of the times. One of the earliest measured cycles was a seven-year bear market that began at the very end of 1925 and ended in 1932 (Figure 3.1). This especially difficult era encompassed a roaring bull market, the great crash of 1929, and the start of the Great Depression. Not surprisingly, most invested assets fared poorly during this era. Shares aggressively ran up through 1928 and, just as dramatically, subsequently collapsed. This seven-year period should not be considered a period in which large stocks outperformed small, but rather a period in which large stocks simply lost less ground.

This period contained both the most dramatic increases in share prices and the worst market correction recorded in the 20th century. The Dow Jones Industrial Average jumped 37.5 percent in 1927 and increased even more dramatically in 1928 with a whopping gain of 43.6 percent. The smaller, riskier firms also thrived in these go-go years.

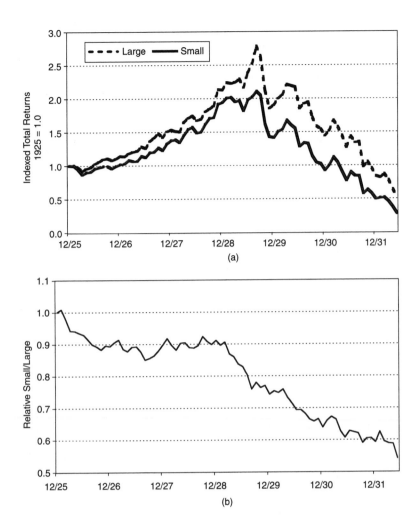

Figure 3.1 Cycle 1: (a) Small- vs. Large-Cap Performance and (b) Relative
Performance (December 1925 to May 1932)

Economic Statistics

Real GNP	−2.8%
GNP Deflator	−3.6%
Industrial Production	−7.5%
CPI	−4.1%

Business Cycle

Trough	Nov. 1927
Peak	Aug. 1929

S&P 500 Earnings Growth

Earnings Period	Average
1926–32	−13.2%

Annualized Statistics

	Companies				Long-Term Gov't Bonds	Treasury Bills
	Large	Mid	Small	Micro		
Total Return	−10.0%	−15.9%	−18.2%	−23.3%	3.7%	3.0%
Volatility	27.0%	29.9%	30.3%	32.2%	5.3%	0.4%

Smaller stocks jumped 34.7 percent in 1927 and 41.0 percent in 1928. In 1929, however, the Dow lost 17.2 percent and small stocks lost 27.1 percent of their value. Even more devastating than the 1929 crash was the slow and painful grind of the bear market. Large stocks lost 24.2 percent in 1930 and another 42.2 percent in 1931. Small stocks lost 34.8 percent and 46.4 percent in those same years—a reflection of the riskiness of this aggressive and illiquid market segment.

Speculation peaked in the early part of this cycle as investors aggressively used margins to increase their equity exposure. The U.S. equity market appeared immune from the economic difficulties in Europe, although Canada, like England, was mired in its own depression. Even though some of the economic turmoil overseas affected the domestic economy, the domestic market appeared unaffected in the early part of this cycle. Investors were fascinated by Charles Lindbergh's transatlantic flight and Henry Ford's mass-produced automobiles. This fascination supported the markets' fervor for airline- and auto-related shares during the later stages of the bull market and prior to the 1929 crash. This apparent rush to risk taking fueled a run-up in smaller stocks early in this first cycle.

S&P 500 earnings (the S&P 500 was known then as the Stock Composite Index and comprised 233 companies) lost an average of 13.2 percent annually during this period. Much of the profit contraction occurred after the crash; companies were simply going bankrupt. Concerns over profitability forced investors to higher market capitalization stocks.

The lack of capital played a significant role in the size preference. The Fed raised rates several times, to curb banks in their use of Federal Reserve loans for market activity in 1928 and early 1929. Market volatility began to increase by mid-1929 and eventually led to the great crash in October 1929. The Federal Reserve was slow to take action to offset the effects of the crash. Confidence in the markets and banks had begun to wane. Weakening share prices followed further breaks. Economic growth had begun to collapse. Commodity prices tumbled as overall demand dried up. Unemployment peaked at around 24 percent in the latter stages of this cycle. Public confidence shriveled. The darkness at the close of this era removed from the marketplace any speculative fervor that had been created only a few years past.

United States Government bond yields trended down for most of this period, before ending near the level where they had begun. Bond yields, which were 3.86 percent in 1925, fell to levels as low as 3.29 percent in 1930 and bounced back up to 3.68 percent by 1932. During this period,

Aaa–Baa spreads went from 139 basis points (bp) in 1925 to 135 bp in 1930 and then surged to 429 bp in 1932. Only blue chips could get access to capital in this dark era.

The credit markets also reflected the difficulty for riskier firms to raise capital. Credit spreads narrowed during the go-go 1920s, but started to widen before the October 1929 crash. Spreads widened to as much as 627 bp by the end of this cycle in May 1932—over six-times greater than the low for the cycle: 86 bp in December 1927. Prior to the crash, both the PPI (producer price index) and the CPI (consumer price index) went from inflationary to deflationary readings. After the crash, little pricing power existed, as evidenced by lack of increases to the PPI or the CPI.

Cycle 2—A Time to Rebuild (June 1932–February 1937)

The 1932–37 cycle began with an aggressive attempt by President Franklin D. Roosevelt to jump-start a downward spiraling economy through fiscal and monetary measures. Public confidence also began to reemerge. The government's stimulative measures caused investment spending to balloon in a short time. Recovering economic activity soon followed a dramatic rebound in share prices.

This period contained two of the most dramatic rebounds in the history of the U.S. equity market (Figure 3.2). The Dow jumped 54 percent in 1933—the most dramatic single-year increase in the history of U.S. equity prices. Two years later, the Dow again bounded another 48 percent. Although these figures appear overly robust, remember that the U.S. equity market had collapsed from the crash of 1929 and entered a multiyear bear market. By the end of that collapse, investments had withered significantly. Large stocks lost 76 percent and small stocks lost 86 percent from 1929 to 1932.

The five-year period between 1932 and 1937 favored smaller stocks. In some ways, this was only a marginal recovery of the wealth that had been lost in previous years. Large stocks recovered by 46.5 percent in 1933, but smaller stocks more than doubled. The index rose 104.2 percent that year. Smaller stocks jumped by 41.5 percent in 1935 and gained another hefty 36.4 percent the year after. Economic growth surged as the economy came out of the first leg of the Great Depression, and that surge supported the recovery of smaller stocks. Real GDP growth was 7.8 percent per annum from 1932 to 1936. Comparisons,

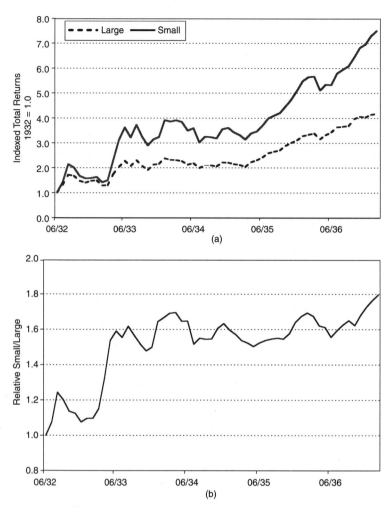

Figure 3.2 Cycle 2: (a) Small- vs. Large-Cap Performance and (b) Relative Performance (June 1932 to February 1937)

Economic Statistics		Business Cycle	
Real GDP	7.8%	Trough	Mar. 1933
GDP Deflator	1.3%	Peak	May 1937
Industrial Production	17.9%		
CPI	0.8%		

S&P 500 Earnings Growth

Earnings Period	Average
1933–36	27.0%

Annualized Statistics

	Companies				Long-Term	Treasury
	Large	Mid	Small	Micro	Gov't Bonds	Bills
Total Return	34.5%	49.0%	54.6%	66.9%	6.3%	0.2%
Volatility	31.9%	41.2%	47.9%	60.3%	4.3%	0.1%

however, were "easy," given that the economy was declining by more than 10 percent annually in the prior years. Corporate earnings, as measured by the S&P 500, rebounded fiercely in this reflationary period. Corporate profits grew at a staggering 27.0 percent each year during this cycle.

Nonetheless, this was still a difficult time for most Americans. The unemployment rate was still in the teens (17.2 percent in 1939, down from 24.9 percent in 1933). The economic conditions took many years to improve. Volatile and weak commodity prices were signs that fears of deflation and stagnation still lingered in 1935.

Government bond yields fell sharply from 3.68 percent in 1932 to 2.68 percent in 1937. Corporate spreads such as Aaa versus Baa narrowed from 429 basis points (bp) in 1932 to 177 bp by 1937. The pricing environment during the Great Depression was very volatile. There was both deflation and inflation. In short, this small-cap cycle could be considered Fed-induced or capital-induced.

CYCLE 3—THE WINDS OF WAR (MARCH 1937–DECEMBER 1939)

The cycle from 1937 to 1939 was a most volatile period that favored large caps (Figure 3.3). Small stocks lost 42.1 percent in 1937 and regained 37.7 percent the following year. Large stocks lost 31.8 percent in 1937 but reclaimed 25.1 percent the year after. Although equities in general lost ground, small stocks lost more than twice as much as large stocks over the nearly three-year cycle, with a 10.3 percent loss for small stocks versus 5.1 percent for large stocks. The concerns overseas and mixed economic results placed smaller stocks at a disadvantage.

The economic backdrop from 1937 to 1939 was tentative. Business activity underwent a noticeable slowdown as spending on public works slowed. The government placed more emphasis on balancing the federal budget, which also accounted for the slowing growth conditions. With unemployment in the high teens, these were still difficult times for most Americans.

The conflict in Europe initially caused share prices to rally in 1938 as war orders for Europe bolstered the U.S. economy. However, investors became more nervous as U.S. involvement with the war overseas became more prominent. Real GDP growth averaged 3.1 percent per year between 1936 and 1939. Both consumption and investment were losing steam after rapid growth in the preceding period. Corporate

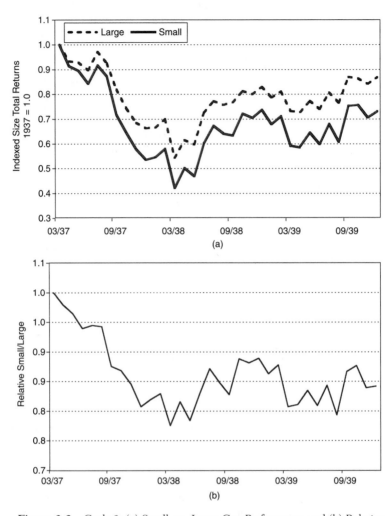

Figure 3.3 Cycle 3: (a) Small- vs. Large-Cap Performance and (b) Relative Performance (March 1937 to December 1939)

Economic Statistics		Business Cycle	
Real GDP	3.1%	Trough	June 1938
GDP Deflator	0.1%	Peak	Feb. 1945
Industrial Production	1.1%	**S&P 500 Earnings Growth**	
CPI	−0.5%		

Earnings Period	Average
1937–39	2.7%

Annualized Statistics

	Companies				Long-Term	Treasury
	Large	**Mid**	**Small**	**Micro**	**Gov't Bonds**	**Bills**
Total Return	−5.1%	−7.8%	−10.3%	−13.1%	5.4%	0.1%
Volatility	28.2%	37.1%	40.9%	49.8%	5.7%	0.1%

profits severely slowed as economic growth peaked. S&P 500 earnings grew an average of 2.7 percent during this cycle.

Inflation remained benign. Government bond yields continued their decline from 2.68 percent in 1937 to 2.36 percent in 1939. Credit spreads were volatile. They doubled to over 300 basis points (bp) during the first half of the cycle and then fell to 198 bp to close the period. Again, uncertain access to capital played a significant role. Investors kept a large-cap bias.

CYCLE 4—THE WAR YEARS (JANUARY 1940–MAY 1946)

In the early part of the 1940–46 cycle, investors were clearly more concerned with the dramatic events overseas than with investment opportunities. Share prices were broadly weak during the first several years of World War II (Figure 3.4). Small stocks lost 5.7 percent in 1940 and another 8.4 percent the year after. Later in the war years, however, the market began to rebound. Small stocks posted a staggering 20.2 percent increase in 1942, 38.7 percent in 1943, 29.8 percent in 1944, and a whopping 56.8 percent in 1945. Although large stocks also gained ground, their gains were not nearly as impressive as those of the small-cap market. Smaller firms outperformed large-cap stocks by approximately 10 percent annually over this six-year period. The unusually sharp increase in government spending may have been the most significant factor during this cycle.

Unsurprisingly, federal defense spending dominated economic growth while private investment contracted by 7.7 percent annually. After the United States entered the war, employment and production rose steadily, and by 1943, the United States had entered an economic boom. Real GDP growth jumped, averaging 9.5 percent between 1940 to 1945. Inflation was also high; the GDP price deflator averaged 4.2 percent, and the consumer price index (CPI) averaged 4.3 percent.

Contrary to the economic growth statistics, corporate profits remained fairly flat over this period. S&P 500 earnings marginally grew at 1.6 percent during these years. Note that earnings growth was slower than during the previous large-cap bull market.

The interest rate environment remained stable. Government bond yields were hump-shaped. They went from 2.3 percent in January 1940 to the mid-2s in 1943–44, and fell back toward 2 percent by the end of the cycle. The Fed was quiet during this period. The discount rate stayed

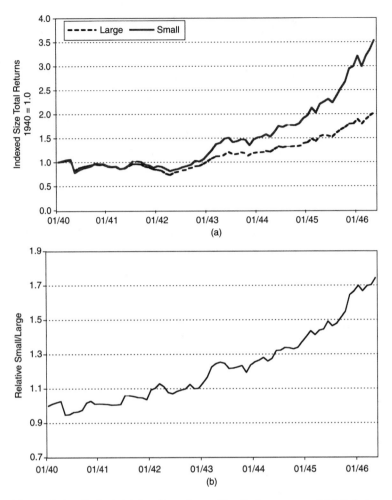

Figure 3.4 Cycle 4: (a) Small- vs. Large-Cap Performance and (b) Relative Performance (January 1940 to May 1946)

Economic Statistics		Business Cycle	
Real GDP	11.1%	Trough	June 1938
GDP Deflator	4.4%	Peak	Feb. 1945
Industrial Production	4.5%		
CPI	4.6%		

S&P 500 Earnings Growth

Earnings Period	Average
1940–45	1.6%

Annualized Statistics

	Companies				Long-Term	Treasury
	Large	**Mid**	**Small**	**Micro**	**Gov't Bonds**	**Bills**
Total Return	11.2%	19.5%	21.3%	27.7%	3.9%	0.2%
Volatility	14.4%	17.8%	19.3%	21.8%	2.9%	0.0%

at 1.0 percent and the prime rate held steady at 1.5 percent. Aaa and Baa bond yields drifted lower. Credit spreads narrowed sharply during World War II as interest rates generally fell. Lower credit issues saw the greatest decline in yields. This relative lowering of capital costs again seemed to support the rebound of smaller companies.

Prices were greatly affected as resources were shifted to the war effort. Both the producer price index (PPI) and the consumer price index (CPI) swung from being deflationary to inflationary during this period.

Noncycle—The Post-War Era (June 1946–November 1964)

The period from 1946 to 1964 represents one of the most unusual periods in the historical relationship between small- and large-cap stocks (Figure 3.5). Smaller and large stocks traded periods in which they outperformed each other, with little consistency in the performance results. Over this lengthy period, large stocks edged out smaller stocks by approximately 1 percent each year. For 18 years, however, there was little sign that smaller stocks bested large stocks, or vice versa, in a consistent fashion. Except for this 18-year period, all other performance cycles have been noticeable and severe. Most cycles typically exhibit a multiyear period of outperformance by smaller or larger stocks. It is possible that the unusual circumstance of a war-driven economy returning back to a market-driven economy, combined with an economic boom, caused all assets to balloon.

In three separate sequences, both small and large companies in the market posted strong results. Small and large stocks gained a whopping 20.7 percent annually between 1949 and 1952, in the first of these sequences. These performance statistics are curious because smaller companies marginally outperformed the larger stocks even in the presence of a strong market in 1949 and 1950. The results were similar in 1954 and 1955 when the market shot up in response to President Dwight D. Eisenhower's tax reform promises and a looser monetary policy by the Fed in 1954. Small stocks gained 56 percent in 1954 and 18.8 percent in 1955, and large stocks jumped 48.4 percent and 28.4 percent, respectively, in those years.

In 1958 and 1959, the markets again bounded to new highs. Small stocks jumped 56.1 percent in 1958 and 14.8 percent in 1959, versus a strong 40.8 percent and 13.2 percent, respectively, for the large caps. The lengthy period from 1946 to 1964 contained four separate business

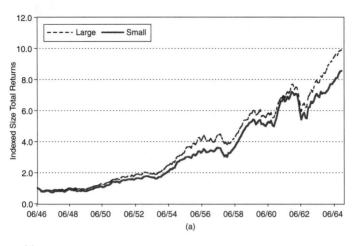

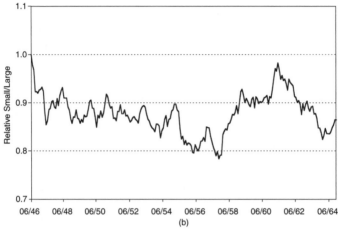

Figure 3.5 Noncycle: (a) Small- vs. Large-Cap Performance and (b) Relative
Performance (June 1946 to November 1964)

Economic Statistics

Real GDP	4.0%
GDP Deflator	2.3%
Industrial Production	5.0%
CPI	2.8%

Business Cycle

Trough 1	Oct. 1945
Peak 1	Nov. 1948
Trough 2	
Peak 2	July 1953
Trough 3	May 1954
Peak 3	Aug. 1957
Trough 4	Apr. 1958
Peak 4	Apr. 1960

S&P 500 Earnings Growth

Earnings Period	Average
1946–64	9.8%

Annualized Statistics

	Companies				Long-Term	Treasury
	Large	**Mid**	**Small**	**Micro**	**Gov't Bonds**	**Bills**
Total Return	13.0%	12.7%	12.0%	10.5%	1.7%	1.9%
Volatility	12.2%	12.6%	13.4%	14.4%	4.0%	0.3%

cycles and encompassed the Korean War and the emerging Cold War. The cycle troughs subsequently generated dramatic market results and covered the following periods: October 1945–November 1948; October 1949–July 1953; May 1954–August 1957; and April 1958–April 1960.

As World War II came to an end in 1945 and the Marshall Plan to rebuild Europe started in 1947, the economy underwent a period of new economic expansion. Real economic growth early in this period was negative as the military-based economy shifted back to a private enterprise system. Federal government spending was negative, which contributed to negative GDP growth from 1945 to 1947. Private investment exhibited wide swings during this transition period. Meanwhile, real personal consumption surged above 10 percent in 1946. At the same time, the GDP price deflator accelerated rapidly; growth was in excess of 10 percent in 1946 and 1947.

This curious and lengthy postwar era also reflected a robust profits cycle. The average S&P 500 earnings growth over this 18-year period grew annually at a strong 9.8 percent. Much of the growth, however, was centered at the start and end of the cycle. Corporate profits were especially strong during the first four years and the last three years. Earnings growth was fairly anemic during the interim decade. This stop-and-start type of profits picture may have caused a less than clear size distinction.

Inflationary pressures started to develop in late 1945. Inflation in the CPI and PPI jumped from approximately 2.5 percent for both rates in mid-1945 to 16.5 percent and 28.5 percent, respectively, in mid-1946. Inflation continued to be volatile through the early 1950s; periods of inflation and deflation occurred for both the CPI and the PPI. But inflation was dampened and stabilized by 1952, and this restrained inflationary environment lasted through the first half of the 1960s. The Fed increased the discount rate from 1.0 percent at the beginning of this cycle to 3.55 percent by the end of the cycle. Consequently, the prime rate increased from 1.5 percent to 4.5 percent. Corporate bond yields also increased; Aaa went from 2.62 percent to 4.4 percent, and Baa yields went from 3.29 percent to 4.83 percent.

Credit spreads peaked in mid-1949 and trended down through 1951 as the level of interest rates also fell. After 1951, the level of interest rates began their steady march upward. Spreads remained steady, and fluctuations generally followed the business cycle.

Fed policy in this noncycle, however, did bounce around. The Fed adopted an active monetary policy, after having negotiated with the Treasury Department its right to determine its own independent monetary policy decisions. From 1 percent in 1955, the funds rate went to about 3 percent in 1957. The Fed eased in 1958; the funds rate went below 0.75 percent in May 1958. The rate was raised again by August 1958 and through 1959, and got to about 4 percent in early 1960. The Fed started to ease and took rates down to about 1.5 percent in early 1961. At that point, the Fed started to tighten; rates went up toward 3.5 percent by 1964. Again, capital costs appeared to increase and similarly subside within the same period.

CYCLE 5—THE VIETNAM ERA (DECEMBER 1964–DECEMBER 1968)

During the four-year period beginning in 1964, smaller stocks significantly outperformed large stocks at a rate second only to that of the second small-cap cycle that began in 1932 after the Great Crash. The secondary market outperformed large stocks by roughly 12 percent annually over this four-year period (Figure 3.6). Generating robust results, the small-cap index gained over 20 percent annually, except for 1966, when it lost 5.8 percent. This era brought prosperity but also sowed the seeds for political and social unrest in the years that followed.

Symbolic of this small-cap cycle was robust economic growth partly caused by the Vietnam War. The Fed struggled to control inflation during much of this period. By 1967, interest rates had risen to their highest level in 46 years. Meanwhile, the budget deficit had ballooned due to defense spending. Investors also expressed concerns about financing the war through taxation. Disintermediation, or the entry of capital markets offering corporate clients alternatives to financing, entered the banking industry. One such example involved the introduction of commercial paper, or short-term corporate notes, which began to displace traditional corporate-related lending.

The small-cap cycle started while the economy was halfway into an extended economic expansion. During this cycle, real GDP growth averaged 5.0 percent, and inflation started to take an upward trend. Inflation held steady during the first half of the decade. Corporate profits, as based on S&P 500 earnings, slowed from the prior cycle but continued to grow at a healthy 6.3 percent.

The economy appeared to be operating on all cylinders during this small-cap expansion. Consumption, private investment, and government spending were strong. Inflation started to trend higher as the economy continued to grow at a healthy clip (in excess of 5 percent) and the Johnson

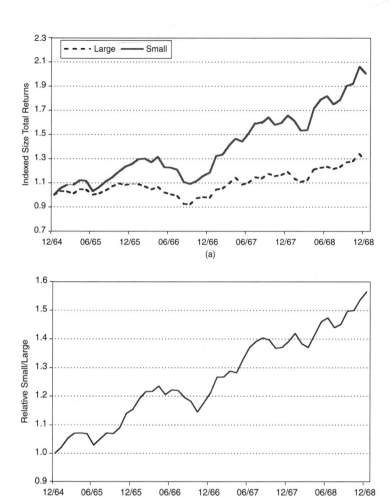

Figure 3.6 Cycle 5: (a) Small- vs. Large-Cap Performance and (b) Relative Performance (December 1964 to December 1968)

Economic Statistics

Real GDP	5.0%
GDP Deflator	3.4%
Industrial Production	6.1%
CPI	3.3%

Business Cycle

Trough	Feb. 1961
Peak	Dec. 1969

S&P 500 Earnings Growth

Earnings Period	Average
1965–68	6.3%

Annualized Statistics

	Companies				Long-Term	Treasury
	Large	Mid	Small	Micro	Gov't Bonds	Bills
Total Return	6.4%	12.1%	18.4%	27.2%	1.4%	−8.2%
Volatility	10.7%	12.3%	14.4%	17.8%	6.5%	0.2%

Administration initiated its Great Society program. Consumer price index (CPI) inflation and producer price index (PPI) inflation were largely in sync; their spread was within ± 2 percent of each other through 1966. Nonetheless, PPI inflation was about 2 to 3 percent greater than CPI inflation for most of 1967–68.

The segment is curious because small stock returns were incredibly robust as the Fed was tightening, and interest rates were generally rising. However, the figures suggest that credit spreads, such as Aaa or Baa versus 10-year Treasuries, were narrowing through 1966 before widening over the balance of the period. In this fifth cycle, the narrowing of cost of capital appears as a potential driver of the small-cap market.

CYCLE 6—THE COMPLEX YEARS (JANUARY 1969–NOVEMBER 1973)

Large-cap shares squarely outpaced smaller companies from 1969 to 1973 (Figure 3.7). Although economic growth was reasonably strong, capital flows into smaller companies were muted. Except for 1971, small-cap stocks underperformed large stocks each year in this cycle. This was a politically difficult period for the nation; the concerns of investors were raised enough for them to overlook the fairly strong economic backdrop. The latter part of this cycle was especially dramatic. Small stocks lost 26.5 percent in 1973 and another 24.9 percent the year after. Although large stocks fared better, they too lost ground. The large-stock index fell 12.9 percent and 28.0 percent, respectively, in 1973 and 1974.

Yet economic growth accelerated throughout the cycle. An economic expansion began in November 1970 and lasted until November 1973, but smaller firms lagged behind.

Socially and politically, America faced a great amount of unrest as civil disobedience demonstrators took to the streets. This complex period also brought the end of the Vietnam War (1971), the installation and removal of wage and price controls (1971–74), and U.S. abandonment of the gold standard (August 1971). As the nation braced for the possibility of impeachment hearings on President Richard Nixon, the outbreak of the Arab–Israeli war led to the first oil embargo in October 1973. It is possible that the ensuing oil embargo spurred the rebound of smaller stocks in the next cycle. Oil stocks rallied on skyrocketing oil prices. Because the majority of the oil and gas companies were based in the small-cap market, a rally among those stocks fueled a small-cap rebound.

Figure 3.7 Cycle 6: (a) Small- vs. Large-Cap Performance and (b) Relative
Performance (January 1969 to November 1973)

Economic Statistics		Business Cycle	
Real GDP	3.5%	Trough	Nov. 1970
GDP Deflator	5.2%	Peak	Nov. 1973
Industrial Production	3.9%		
CPI	5.4%		

S&P 500 Earnings Growth

Earnings Period	Average
1969–73	8.0%

Annualized Statistics

	Companies				Long-Term Gov't Bonds	Treasury Bills
	Large	Mid	Small	Micro		
Total Return	3.0%	−2.6%	−4.6%	−10.0%	5.4%	5.5%
Volatility	13.5%	17.5%	20.5%	23.3%	9.7%	0.4%

Real GDP growth was strong but slower than in the prior cycle. It averaged 3.5 percent during this period, with private investments increasing. Government spending declined, largely because federal defense spending slowed as the Vietnam War ended. Manufacturing generally slowed but inflation accelerated.

Corporate profits grew much faster (roughly 8.0 percent) than in the prior cycle. Profits growth languished during the first half of this cycle, then bounced back sharply to the end of the cycle. CPI and PPI inflation rates (about 2.5 percent and flat, respectively, in 1967) were trending higher. They peaked at about 6.2 percent and 5.0 percent, respectively, in late 1969. The realities of inflation were also masked because of the government's efforts to reinvigorate the economy and to institute wage/price controls.

The Fed continued tightening monetary policy well into this cycle. The discount rate rose from an average of 5.16 percent to 6.44 percent during this large-cap cycle. The cost of borrowing for businesses also increased. The bankruptcy of Penn Central, in June 1970, also shocked the markets. This cycle cooled inflationary concerns, but likely contributed to the widening in credit spreads.

The Fed funds rate continued to climb higher in 1969 and exceeded 9 percent by August 1969. After peaking at around 9 percent, the Fed went on an easing cycle through March 1971, when funds reached 3.75 percent. From that low, the Fed hiked rates aggressively through September 1973, when funds reached 10.75 percent.

CYCLE 7—THE RAVAGES OF INFLATION (DECEMBER 1973–JULY 1983)

In the longest small-cap cycle to date, small stocks outperformed large stocks by 10.9 percent annually from 1973 to 1983, except for 1980, when the small-cap index (+31.6 percent) marginally lagged the large-cap benchmark (+32.5 percent). This cycle included a number of phenomenal small-cap years (Figure 3.8). For instance, small caps appreciated 56.6 percent in 1975 and 40.1 percent in 1976. The large-cap market also generated strong results but paled in comparison to the secondary markets. Large stocks gained 31.6 percent and 20.8 percent, respectively, in 1975 and 1976. Even in a difficult year such as 1981, when large stocks lost approximately 8.4 percent of their value, the small-cap sector managed to eke out a gain of 3.8 percent. The Arab oil embargo and strong capital spending levels during this cycle may have spurred

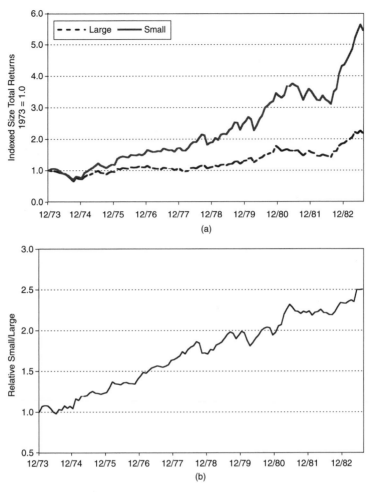

Figure 3.8 Cycle 7: (a) Small- vs. Large-Cap Performance and (b) Relative Performance (December 1973 to July 1983)

Economic Statistics			
Real GDP	1.9%		
GDP Deflator	7.2%		
Industrial Production	1.3%		
CPI	8.4%		

Trough 2	July 1980
Peak 2	July 1981

Business Cycle

Trough 1	Mar. 1975
Peak 1	Jan. 1980

S&P 500 Earnings Growth

Earnings Period	Average
1974–82	5.8%

Annualized Statistics

	Companies				Long-Term	Treasury
	Large	**Mid**	**Small**	**Micro**	**Gov't Bonds**	**Bills**
Total Return	8.5%	13.6%	19.4%	24.3%	5.6%	8.5%
Volatility	16.6%	18.2%	19.5%	22.5%	12.3%	0.9%

significant gains in oil and gas and technology stocks, which propelled the small-cap benchmarks well ahead of the large. A majority of the exposures to energy and technology stocks were primarily small-cap-based during the 1970s.

The 1973–83 cycle is especially interesting because it included two oil shocks, or sharp rises in oil prices, which greatly distorted the financial markets, the economy, and the levels of inflation. This cycle also included two economic expansions, from March 1975 to January 1980, and from July 1980 to July 1981. The oil shocks contributed to a slowdown in real GDP growth. The average of 3.5 percent in the preceding large-cap cycle fell to an average of 2.1 percent. At the same time, prices rose sharply. The GDP price deflator averaged 7.6 percent, and the CPI averaged 8.4 percent per year during this period. As a result, interest rates soared to new highs.

Earnings growth slowed from the previous cycle to approximately 5.8 percent annually. A great deal of the increase in corporate profits occurred between 1975 and 1980. Companies tried to contain costs through vertical integration, which entailed acquiring all or most of the inputs required for their production processes. The hope was that vertical integration might stem inflationary risks. As a result, the conglomerate was born.

These years were not only difficult economically but were politically complex. The nation witnessed the second set of trials to impeach President Richard Nixon, who eventually resigned. In addition, warfare and the outbreak of violence in the Middle East, Southeast Asia, Africa, and Central America made for unsettled times at the international level. These global concerns may have muted stock returns, but they did not materially affect the outperformance of small stocks.

Oil shocks and inflation scares dominated this period. The first few years brought a sharp rise in oil prices, which pushed the producer price index (PPI) to exceed the consumer price index (CPI). Both exceeded 10 percent; the PPI went above 20 percent. CPI inflation finally caught up with and then exceeded PPI inflation in mid-1975, by which time CPI and PPI inflation had already started to decelerate. The two began to move in tandem, but a new bout of inflation pressures began in 1975 and lasted through the end of this cycle. The Fed was extremely aggressive in fighting inflation. The Fed also shifted its policy from money growth to the Fed funds rate. Between the Fed policy and the inflationary environment of the period, interest rates were very volatile. The Fed's rate hikes continued through July 1974, when funds approached 13.0 percent. The

Fed then started to ease aggressively. By February 1976, the Fed funds rate was down to 4.75 percent, and it stayed between 4.0 percent and 6.0 percent through mid-1977. The Fed started to hike aggressively in 1977. At the start of that year, funds were around 4.60 percent. They raced above 10 percent by year-end 1978, and continued to head much higher.

The market viewed the appointment of Paul Volcker as Federal Reserve Board chairman in July 1979 as a constructive measure. The effective Fed funds rate went from a low of around 5.0 percent in 1976 to over 19.0 percent in 1981, before the Fed began to ease. The prime rate also approached 19 percent during this period, and the borrowing rates for Aaa- and Baa-rated debt doubled to over 14.0 percent, the peak for the cycle. Spreads peaked to 269 bp in late 1982; they were in the low 70s in mid-1979. Spreads relative to the base interest rate scenario appeared benign in this period. A combination of the muted capital spreads and the unique exposure to energy and technology contributed to a significant amount of the gains enjoyed by small-cap investors over this period.

The recession that began in 1973 was supply-, not demand-induced. Interest rates, in general, peaked in the middle of the recession, when the economy also faced record rates of inflation. Rising budget deficits became the new and dominant force in the bond market by 1975. Deficits kept increasing and did not follow the stylized cycles caused by economic expansions and contractions.

As a result of the difficult backdrop, stock valuation levels, especially for large stocks, fell to single digits. In fact, the relative valuations of smaller to large stocks began the cycle at a 30 percent discount to the large-cap market in price-to-cash flow terms, and ended the cycle at an astounding 60 percent premium by 1983. This dramatic valuation disparity set the stage for the significant number of mergers and acquisitions that followed, and bolstered large stocks' share prices in the next cycle.

CYCLE 8—THE GO-GO EIGHTIES (AUGUST 1983–OCTOBER 1990)

In the period from 1983 to 1990, large-cap stocks outperformed small-cap stocks by almost 5 percent annually. This was one of the longest periods of outperformance by large stocks (Figure 3.9). A dramatically weak dollar favored U.S.-based firms with high foreign exposure and may have significantly accounted for the preference for larger stocks in this period.

Figure 3.9 Cycle 8: (a) Small- vs. Large-Cap Performance and (b) Relative Performance (August 1983 to October 1990)

Economic Statistics		**Business Cycle**	
Real GDP	3.8%	Trough	Nov. 1982
GDP Deflator	3.9%	Peak	July 1990
Industrial Production	2.8%		
CPI	4.1%		

S&P 500 Earnings Growth

Earnings Period	Average
1983–89	9.9%

Annualized Statistics

	Companies				**Long-Term Gov't Bonds**	**Treasury Bills**
	Large	**Mid**	**Small**	**Micro**		
Total Return	13.8%	11.5%	8.6%	4.4%	13.4%	7.4%
Volatility	16.3%	17.9%	18.4%	19.9%	11.4%	0.5%

In addition, larger firms reaped the benefits of falling debt costs as interest plunged throughout the decade.

Although the returns of both large and small stocks were healthy, large stocks outperformed small-cap stocks for five of the seven years in this cycle. The aggressive antiinflationary stance that the Fed took during the 1970s began to curtail inflation and inflationary expectations. As a result, this curtailment ignited a bull market that continued through the 1990s, nearly 20 years later. This period also marked a sharp increase in defense spending due to the support of President Ronald Reagan for a strong military. Other key events during the period were the breakup of AT&T, significant problems in the American rust belt, and the equity market crash of 1987. The international financial system also witnessed a scare when a drop in oil prices caused great problems in Mexico and Latin America. A real estate crisis in the United States weakened the U.S. banking system and almost wiped out the savings and loan (S&L) industry. The bailout of the thrifts extended into the early 1990s and severely drained the resources of the federal government. News at the tail end of this cycle also centered on the end of the Cold War, as marked by the fall of the Berlin Wall and the reunification of East Germany and West Germany in 1989.

The 1980s marked a most innovative period for the financial markets. Derivative structures such as the use of options, futures, and protection schemes (e.g., portfolio insurance) became recognized as methods by which institutions could offset risk. The 1987 market crash forced institutions to rethink the pricing of derivative instruments. During this period, the Fed allowed banks to compete with investment banks in the debt underwriting business.

A dramatically weaker dollar during this period encouraged international investors to aggressively acquire U.S. financial assets, as well as hard assets such as real estate. The weaker dollar also created a constructive backdrop for U.S. companies competing overseas.

Economic growth was healthy, averaging 3.6 percent between 1983 and 1990. It was led in large part by personal consumption, which averaged 3.5 percent. Government spending was healthy because of the surge in defense spending. One of the key factors behind the growth in consumption and the idea of economic well-being was the drop in the unemployment rate. After peaking at around 11 percent in 1982, it fell to 6 percent by the late 1980s. In addition, corporate profits began reaccelerating over these years; S&P 500 earnings grew annually at 9.9 percent.

Debt growth boomed during this period. All sectors were increasing their debt. Households were borrowing to fund their consumption, the federal government was borrowing to fund its defense spending and other programs, and corporations were increasing their leverage, which reflected, in part, the mergers and acquisitions boom during the 1980s. Foreign investors played an increasingly important role in funding activities in the United States through their purchases of U.S. dollar assets.

The Fed's resolve in fighting inflation eventually forced the inflation rate lower. After averaging 8.4 percent in the preceding small-cap cycle, the CPI averaged only 4.0 percent between 1983 to 1990. Credit spreads were also declining during this period, despite the lingering concerns regarding the health of the financial system. The LDC debt crisis, the real estate crisis, and the thrift crisis were great blows to the financial system. All three can be linked to the drop in oil prices.

The compelling valuation levels of equities and the fact that large-cap stocks were especially cheap at the start of this cycle, coupled with falling inflation, spurred a tremendous amount of corporate action in the form of buyouts and mergers and acquisitions. The disinflationary decade of the 1980s generated a wealth of business for bankers as corporations retraced their steps and attempted to pare down their size. Without the uncertain pricing environment of the 1970s, the costs associated with vertical integration became unwarranted. Aggressive use of high-yield financing to accomplish the new corporate structure became the order of the day.

As valuation levels began to run up, speculation in the financial markets became apparent and led to creative new forms of valuing firms, such as private market value, in order to justify the higher multiples. In October 1987, investors faced the second great crash of the U.S. equity market in this century. The S&P 500 posted a single-day loss of 20.5 percent on October 19, 1987. The Russell 2000, a measure of small-cap returns, lost 12.5 percent. Even though small caps lost less ground than the overall market on that dark day, they continued to lose more ground well into that fateful month and ended up losing an additional 11.4 percent for the remainder of October. Conversely, the S&P 500 reclaimed 12 percent over the days following the crash in October. Unlike the response to the crash of 1929, the Fed aggressively eased its monetary policy to add liquidity to the financial system. The bull market for large stocks pushed valuations of smaller stocks from a 60 percent premium over large companies down to a paltry 10 percent premium by the end of the cycle.

CYCLE 9—THE TRANSITION PERIOD
(NOVEMBER 1990–DECEMBER 1993)

One of the shortest small-cap cycles, the period from 1990 to 1993 was nonetheless one of the strongest periods for small-cap stocks (Figure 3.10). Over this three-year period, small-cap benchmarks outperformed the large-cap benchmark by almost 13 percent annually. This truly represented a renaissance period for smaller stocks, especially considering that the market had long been dominated by large caps. This cycle may have been primarily driven by the falling cost of capital faced by smaller firms. The Fed had cut interest rates several times, allowing favorable terms for marginal companies.

This period marked the beginning of the current economic recovery that began in March 1991. Although real economic growth, as measured by GDP, as of 2000 has continued to be much stronger than anyone would have expected, especially this late in the cycle, the beginning of the economic expansion got off to an anemic start. After averaging 3.6 percent from 1983 to 1990, the economy was mired in a "growth recession," with growth averaging only 1.4 percent between 1990 and 1993. A mini-oil crisis coincided with the Persian Gulf War in January 1991. In addition, earnings growth was paltry over this period. The weak economic backdrop squeezed corporate profits to a slight gain of 0.6 percent over these recovering years.

Competition and privatization continued to blossom, however. Even some of the Latin American countries started to privatize, in hopes of resolving some of their economic problems. One of the largest examples was Mexico's privatization of Telmex, a Mexican telephone company. Smaller firms and bankers were wise to the robust small-cap cycle. As a result, a record amount of small-cap initial public offerings (IPOs) were brought to market. Indeed, more shares chasing the same dollars may have cut short the small-cap cycle.

Both consumption and investment were anemic early in this current expansion. It was a period in which arguments surfaced about excess capacity and the idea of firms not having much pricing power. One of the developments that emerged during this period was the image of the frugal consumer of the 1990s as compared to the extravagant consumer of the 1980s. Consumers started to hunt for bargains, and firms had to find ways to generate profits without raising prices. Although talks about deflation or disinflation or the new-era economy had not yet materialized, the early 1990s may have planted the seeds of the fast

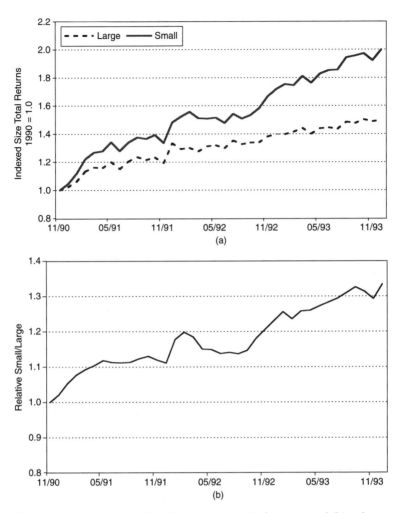

Figure 3.10 Cycle 9: (a) Small- vs. Large-Cap Performance and (b) Relative
Performance (November 1990 to December 1993)

Economic Statistics

Real GDP	1.6%
GDP Deflator	2.9%
Industrial Production	2.6%
CPI	2.8%

Business Cycle

Trough	Mar. 1991
Peak	N/A

S&P 500 Earnings Growth

Earnings Period	Average
1990–93	0.6%

Annualized Statistics

	Companies				Long-Term Gov't Bonds	Treasury Bills
	Large	**Mid**	**Small**	**Micro**		
Total Return	15.5%	24.8%	28.2%	30.8%	14.9%	4.0%
Volatility	10.6%	12.2%	12.7%	14.5%	6.8%	0.4%

growth and low inflation that materialized near the second half of the decade of the 1990s.

Interest rates continued to fall in this cycle. Having successfully handled the equity market crash in 1987, Fed Chairman Alan Greenspan continued to enhance his reputation. The Fed embarked on a long easing program to jump-start the economy. Between mid-1989 and 1993, the funds rate fell from about 9.8 percent to 3.0 percent. Not until late 1993 and early 1994 did the economy start to exhibit signs of robust growth. The cut in rates allowed the spreads between prime and Treasury to narrow dramatically. This favorable cost-of-capital environment may have been the key contributor to the small-cap bull market.

The economy continued to become increasingly more service-based, and concerns about service inflation started to grow. (Service inflation is not reflected in the PPI, which is based primarily on goods prices.) Concerns about the strength of the U.S. dollar, which weakened in 1991 and 1992, and rising medical care costs represented key factors that played into inflation fears. Such concerns may have been the seeds that caused the unwinding of the small-cap rally by 1994.

Interest rates were generally declining, and credit spreads were narrowing during this period. Despite this seemingly supportive environment, credit growth was decelerating. Debt growth went from over 9 percent in 1989 to almost 2 percent in 1992. The 1989–92 credit crunch coincided with the weakness of the banking system, risk aversion, and the deleveraging of corporate America. Easy monetary policy seemed ineffective in pulling the economy out of the 1990–91 recession at that time.

The spreads between prime rate and Treasury were as wide as 192 basis points (bp) early in the cycle and narrowed to a negative 104 bp by early 1992. The relative valuations of small-cap stocks went from a 1.1 times, or a 10 percent, premium over the large-cap price-to-cash-flow levels to a 1.4 times, or a 40 percent, premium. By 1994, a great deal had been priced into the outlook for smaller-cap stocks.

CYCLE 10—GLOBAL FRANCHISES AND THE GOLDILOCKS ECONOMY (JANUARY 1994–JANUARY 2000)

The period from January 1994 to 2000 has perhaps been the golden age for equity investing (Figure 3.11). Large stocks outpaced smaller stocks at one of the highest levels in the past 70 years, and the largest, safest companies generated astounding returns. Over a four-year period, from

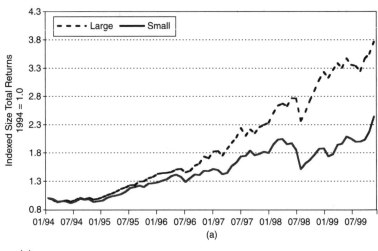

Figure 3.11 Cycle 10: (a) Small- vs. Large-Cap Performance and (b) Relative Performance (January 1994 to December 1999)

Economic Statistics		Business Cycle	
Real GDP	3.4%	Trough	Mar. 1991
GDP Deflator	1.8%	Peak	N/A
Industrial Production	4.5%		
CPI	2.4%		

S&P 500 Earnings Growth

Earnings Period	Average
1994–99	12.5%

Annualized Statistics

	Companies				Long-Term Gov't Bonds	Treasury Bills
	Large	Mid	Small	Micro		
Total Return	24.5%	18.4%	14.6%	15.2%	6.2%	5.0%
Volatility	13.9%	14.4%	15.4%	17.9%	8.6%	0.2%

1995 to 1999, large stocks generated returns of over 20 percent each year.

The most significant divergence between small- and large-cap performance occurred as the U.S. markets struggled with the collapse of many emerging markets in Southeast Asia. The subsequent recoil caused a dramatic flight to quality. In August 1998, the small-cap market experienced one of the worst months in its history: It fell 18.3 percent. There had been only six other months, scattered over the previous 70 or so years, with more severe losses.

The continuing disinflationary environment of this cycle helped to lower global interest rates. Although investors were concerned about insufficient savings and the lack of available capital (given the demand from emerging markets), hindsight suggests that capital and liquidity were abundant. Investors richly rewarded global franchises in this era. Companies such as Coca-Cola, Merck, and General Electric enjoyed a lengthy period of dramatic multiple expansion. The size premium narrowed significantly in this period, and outperforming large stocks detracted from the historical outperformance of small-cap firms.

After an anemic start, economic expansion started to take off. Between 1993 and 1998, real economic growth accelerated and averaged 3.4 percent; meanwhile, inflation fell. This performance is counterintuitive to most economic models. Later in this cycle, the period was dubbed "the Goldilocks economy"—an economy that was not too strong to cause inflation fears but quite robust for a healthy economic backdrop. Not too hot and not too cold, but just right.

Robust growth, using GDP, was exhibited at both the domestic and international levels early (1994–95) in this large-cap cycle. In particular, the U.S. market and the emerging markets, such as Asia and even eastern Europe, were the primary beneficiaries. Europe still lagged, however, and Japan continued to weaken.

Earnings growth rebounded sharply as corporate America went through a belt-tightening exercise to improve profits and reward shareholders. S&P 500 earnings grew at a dramatic 12.5 percent annually over the entire cycle. The period also marked a consumption boom and a big surge in investment spending, especially in technology. Improving efficiency and productivity was key in helping corporations to increase and preserve profitability. Furthermore, the interest rate environment, in general, was benign despite rapid growth. A key factor in bringing down the interest rate was a decline in inflation and in inflationary expectations.

Several factors contributed to the decline in inflation: a strong U.S. dollar; productivity gains; a drop in oil and other commodity prices; and a decline in medical care costs, as the result of HMOs, competition, and the threat of legislative changes from President Bill Clinton's health care initiative. Although CPI inflation generally outpaced PPI inflation during this period, the degree to which it did so is questionable. Remember that inflation measures are simply the price samples of a basket of goods. The sample basket is a best estimate of the makeup of relevant goods consumed in the economy. The basket is fixed, but we know that consumers' tastes and needs are dynamic. With respect to government spending, the switch from chronic federal budget deficits to what appears to be chronic budget surpluses flushed the market with liquidity, which may have benefited the financial markets and investment spending.

The Fed actively promoted the notion of adjusting monetary policy preemptively to stem inflation and promote economic growth. For example, it tightened monetary policy aggressively in 1994–95 by raising the federal funds rate from 3 percent to over 6 percent. Fed Chairman Greenspan's efforts appeared to succeed in extending the expansion while also preventing inflationary pressures from developing. The spread between prime and Treasury remained quite wide (over 2 percent) during this cycle. Except for a few minor adjustments, the Fed stayed largely out of the picture from 1995 until 1998, when it eased interest rates by 75 basis points to increase liquidity and prevent a global financial crisis.

The crisis was provoked by the woes of Long Term Capital Management (LTCM), a hedge fund that was on the verge of defaulting on huge currency and interest rate contracts. Many investors believe that the Fed took sudden actions in the fall of 1998 in response to the peril LTCM represented to the financial markets. By swiftly cutting interest rates, the Fed attempted to prevent market fears from erupting into a financial panic. Over the duration of this crisis, the small-cap market collapsed significantly to diverge from the blue-chip averages. The bond markets were rocked over this short time period as well. Quality bond yield spreads jumped significantly—a fast and furious knee-jerk reaction that well captured the increased market aversion to risk. Relative small-cap valuations fell from a 40 percent premium in 1994 to a discount of 30 percent by the end of 1999.

Smaller stocks began rebounding in 1999 as Asian economies began settling and even rebounding. In addition, the cost of capital spreads reverted to 2 percent from the extreme 4 percent level witnessed in 1998.

FOUR

A Changing Landscape— Significant Recent Trends Affecting the Small-Cap Market

MARKETS, LIKE all systems, are dynamic and evolve over time. Although past events and results are important sources for insights into the behavior of the markets, investors must also take into account the evolving nature of the financial markets. The New York Stock Exchange (NYSE) had 1,057 companies listed in 1950. As of 2000, the latest rally recorded some 3,748 companies trading. The average daily trading volume on the NYSE reached 1.98 million shares traded in 1950. By the end of 1999 that number had grown to 809.20 million. In

93

addition, Nasdaq was trading 1.08 billion shares by the end of the millennium. The trading systems available to investors are much more sophisticated than they were just ten or fifteen years earlier.

As the U.S. equity market has evolved, the pricing efficiencies for all stocks, large and small, have similarly evolved. More important, the evolutionary nature of the equity markets has caused the size equation, or the relative performance between smaller and large-cap firms, to similarly change and diverge even further than before.

Studies of the financial markets' history, past performance cycles, and other traditional relationships serve to bridge the past with the changing landscape as equity markets mature and evolve. The correlation between small- and large-cap firms has diminished significantly since the 1950s (Figure 4.1). The decline in correlation, as discussed in Chapter 5, suggests that smaller firms, when added to a large-cap portfolio, are likely to offer a more diversified portfolio. Such trends in correlation imply that the domino principle may become more pronounced with time.

Even though factors that affect the relationship between small and large caps can appear unending, a handful of changes have been truly significant and are most likely to have a continuing effect. Among the innovations that have introduced new wrinkles to the small-cap investment process are: the evolution of the Internet, the increased access of smaller

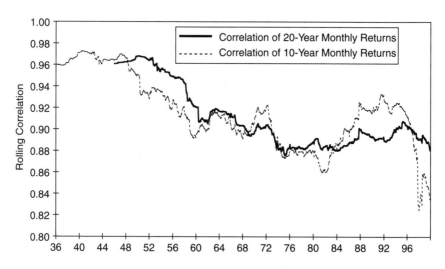

Figure 4.1 Correlation of Small-Cap vs. Large-Cap Stocks

firms to capital, the increase of professionally managed assets, a tighter linkage between corporate managers and shareholders, and the use of futures and derivatives. Although many of these changes are generally beneficial for the small-cap market, not all changes necessarily increase the premium that small caps have traditionally received in the market.

INFLUENCE OF TECHNOLOGY AND THE INTERNET

Although the commercial implications of cyberspace may remain an unsolved mystery for some time, the Internet is clearly changing the rate and method by which communication occurs and information is disseminated. Of all the current changes influencing the market, the evolution of the Internet may have the most significant impact on the relationship between large and small caps. Two critical factors have an impact on the relationship of small stocks versus large stocks:

1. The Internet enables all firms, large and small, to operate on a broader scale. For example, the increased connectivity between smaller firms and their customers may give the average start-up opportunities that were not previously available to such companies.
2. The Internet gives the investor ready access to information on the most undiscovered but obscure investments.

These two factors combined are likely to have a favorable impact on smaller caps and may possibly increase the returns from this market in the future.

Greater Scope of Operations for Small Caps

One of the most compelling arguments for company mergers and expansion is that such actions enable companies to operate on a larger base and benefit from economies of scale. With a sizable operation, a company can tap into a broad customer base that offers large market share and more pricing power. A broader distribution channel creates powerful economics. Not only does each additional customer widen the scope of a company's customer base, it also drives the marginal cost of production down. This is the case for all business lines. Money-center banks have aptly posed this corporate strategy to investors as they continue to consolidate.

Retailers such as Wal-Mart and category killers such as Home Depot have similarly garnered investor approval and funds.

Because of the "Size is good" argument, investors have bid up large stocks, especially since the latter half of the 1990s. More important, mega-size firms have answered investors' hopes in spades as share prices have rocketed to record-high levels. With the advent of the Internet, the argument favoring big companies has been instantly placed on its head. Companies no longer need to be everywhere or even to be large to connect with their intended markets. A tiny start-up with the right product can tap into markets anywhere, anytime. Although this begins to sound like a pitch for selling an Internet initial public offering, the basic benefits that the Internet offers are indeed vast.

Because its benefits are available to all corporations, the Internet, in this sense, does not have an impact on the size equation. On the other hand, developed franchises that had always benefited from their sizable geographic and business penetration no longer carry such a unique market advantage. Prior to the Internet, smaller companies had little choice but to settle for limited distribution of their goods and services. The Internet now offers smaller companies the ability to tap directly into markets and therefore compete head-to-head for business and eliminate previously existing boundaries.

There are some limitations to this argument. For instance, capital-intensive industries, such as aerospace and defense, still represent significant capital and investment spending hurdles for start-ups. Most industries, however, are subject to a reshuffling of the deck because of the Internet. As the Internet becomes more developed for business-to-business transactions, smaller and smaller firms with solid business models may also find it less challenging to get products and services to their customers. Several industries have already begun to feel the competitive pinch of this newfound technological intermediary. Traditional businesses such as retailers now face competition from Amazon.com and other online retailers ("e-tailers") that have been able to create franchises overnight. The brokerage business has similarly been challenged by newly initiated competitors, such as E*Trade. Even though these new start-ups are unlikely to replace the solid existing franchises, the Internet's new medium of communication is likely to lower the hurdle for smaller, less developed, franchises. Any business development that helps good companies with solid business models to reach their intended customer more ably is likely to increase the valuations of these companies.

Increased Information Access for Investors

As a giant data warehouse, the Internet allows investors to research investment opportunities more efficiently. Larger firms enjoy a richer valuation, partly because of their ability to attract investors. A wider universe of interested buyers can, in turn, have a positive influence on share prices. Because the Internet provides easy access to information, it gives interested investors a significant opportunity to identify and become familiar with smaller firms. Even though the Internet is growing at a geometric rate and creating a deluge of information that is only likely to increase, it nonetheless allows the most distant observer to easily tap into undiscovered investment ideas. The dramatic flow of information may, at times, be overwhelming, but interested observers who are skilled at using this new technology will benefit greatly.

Online technology offers very cheap ways for the management of smaller firms to communicate with investors. Thanks to the Web, virtual visits or audiovisual interactive presentations are quite simple and affordable for companies to arrange. More important, the scale of this communication medium is boundless. Microcap firms in distant places can instantly broadcast their business goals and strategies to investors worldwide.

The Internet might also be credited with creating a new breed of investor: the online trader whose interest goes well beyond the scope of large-cap blue-chip investments. With the rise of this new investment consumer, the demand for undiscovered investment opportunities can be expected to grow and may lead to greater potential interest in smaller stocks. This trend is likely to increase smaller stock valuations.

The incredible bull market of the 1990s captured the interest of the most distant observers. The new day trader may symbolize the peak of this speculative fervor; at the same time, other independent investors and thinkers are also likely to be attracted to this new investment forum. Although the profile of the Internet investor is likely to gyrate with the swings of the market, the electronic investment bug has tapped into a sizable segment of the investment population. This contingent is likely to remain.

Although the Internet might account for higher valuations of smaller firms, the increase of information flow about these firms might eventually lower the excess returns traditionally produced by smaller stocks. Nonetheless, the benefits from the Internet are more than likely to outweigh any slippage in the long-run expected return of smaller stocks.

GREATER ACCESS TO CAPITAL FOR SMALL CAPS

The current universe of smaller companies in the U.S. stock market is vastly broader than it was before the mid-1970s. The richer set of growth companies in the current small-cap market did not exist in the small-cap market of the 1940s. Simply put, aggressive young companies of that era were limited in their ability to tap into the capital markets. The NYSE, which was appropriately dubbed the Big Board, primarily housed large, mature firms. The NYSE's stringent issuance standards prevented smaller firms from raising capital in the public markets.

In 1971, the creation of The National Association of Securities Dealers Automated Quotation System (Nasdaq) allowed younger and more aggressive small companies to enter the equity markets. This financing revolution significantly broadened the U.S. equity market and, in turn, enlarged the small-cap market. The nature of the smaller capitalized market changed forever as hundreds of small, young firms promised a world of growth and competed for investment dollars.

This fundamental change in access to capital significantly altered the contours of the small-cap market and created a polarized setting. When the new set of young, emerging growth firms issued securities into the small-cap market, the majority of the firms in the market were no longer cyclically inclined or fallen angels. (As discussed in Chapter 1, fallen angels are stocks that were once stellar performers but have since fallen out of investors' favor.) The small-cap market became a market of polar extremes. On the one hand, it remained concentrated with numerous deep-value situations; on the other, a sizable chunk of young, high-octane growth companies began to filter into its roster. This was especially notable in the mid-1970s, when spending on technology goods drove the demand for faster growing technology companies. By contrast, technology stocks were virtually nonexistent in the large-cap market. As a result, the underwriting of young and emerging technology companies aggressively broadened the small-cap market and permanently altered its profile.

The small-cap sector is no longer made up solely of slower or cyclical stocks that carry below-average valuations. It has now been joined by hundreds of fast-growing companies, many of which promise growth in excess of 30 percent over the subsequent three to five years. This significant change in the small-cap market can only suggest that its returns are unlikely to behave as they have historically.

This market change, which involves greater access to capital for small caps, has two major effects:

1. The ongoing small-cap market is likely to behave less like the value-driven market of the past because of the increased underwriting of fast-growing smaller firms. Many such firms can now rise out of the less cyclically driven sectors, such as health care, medical devices, education, and so on. As the small-cap market continues to evolve, the economic sensitivity that has historically accounted for size rotations from small to large caps, and vice versa, may no longer play quite the same role.

2. The profiles of the small-cap and large-cap markets are likely to diverge further as underwriting of aggressive growth companies increases. This can only cause the small-cap market to behave less and less like its large-cap counterpart. As the correlation between small and large caps declines, the benefits of diversification should continue to increase.

Beyond the United States, other major markets are beginning to enter the stage in which smaller companies can more readily come to market. For example, Germany's Neuer market, Japan's liberalization policies, and the Canadian Venture Exchange, which was reorganized in November 1999 to be specifically aimed at smaller firms and start-up ventures, represent currently created opportunities for capital to be siphoned to young upstarts. Freer flow of capital creates true small-cap investment opportunities. Thus, such markets, if successful, might experience a significant boom in secondary stocks. As a case in point, one of the most significant and lengthy small-stock bull markets of the 20th century began a scant two years after the inception of the Nasdaq markets.

INSTITUTIONAL INVESTING

The economics of the professional money management business changed considerably in the 1990s. More banks and brokerages have recognized the benefits of increasing assets under management to bolster their fee-generating abilities. Fees are terrific because they are more stable. Investors prefer stable earnings streams to those that are variable. More stable earnings lead to higher valuations for underlying firms. As a result, asset management firms such as Putnam or Pimco have become adept at consolidating assets, based on the argument that economies of scale are produced when millions—or, more appropriately, billions—of dollars are consolidated and entrusted to a handful of managers. These economies of scale ultimately strip away the inefficiencies operating in the investment management process. Why should a firm pay ten managers and their support staff to manage a billion dollars each, when one asset manager can control the whole pot and they need to pay only one fund manager? This cuts the cost of doing business by one-tenth. The example oversimplifies the value-added that each professional manager represents, but it offers insight into the powerful difference in economics.

As assets balloon to unimaginable size, however, their sheer volume forces investment managers to focus on more liquid investments. This focus on liquidity can only limit the ability of managers to invest in thinly traded securities, such as those found in the small-cap market. The need to optimize and manage sizable funds efficiently raises a fundamental question: Does the need of institutional investors for liquidity pare down the small-cap premium?

Although the impact of megafund managers is unlikely to change the long-term merits of investing in small stocks and the small-cap premium, it might exacerbate ongoing trends. In the past, a preference for large stocks would have caused large companies to outperform smaller stocks. At the current time, when a handful of astute investors can swing billions of dollars instantaneously into or out of some asset class, the notion of marginally gaining exposure to the megacaps can result in a stampede out of smaller capitalization firms. This change in preferences can transform the benchmark returns and create sizable disparities between large and smaller stocks. Similarly, if smaller stocks are in favor, then only a marginal rotation out of large and into smaller capitalization stocks by a handful of megasize funds can cause smaller-cap stocks to balloon overnight.

Even though the size relationship is affected by these ongoing fundamental changes, investors ultimately seek valued franchises whether they are highly liquid or illiquid. If a company has a sizable market capitalization, this simply represents that it has, in the past, distinguished itself among its peers. Market capitalization does not define whether a company can subsequently remain an industry leader. Subsequent returns are dependent on the company's being able to produce subsequent incremental gains.

Although the high volume of assets for investment can change the focus of the marketplace over shorter periods, fundamental investment opportunities or economics should win out over longer spells. An investor, whether an individual or an institution, will not remain fixated on a set of investment opportunities if there is no compelling reason for doing so. Because large-cap stocks make up a majority of the market in terms of aggregate value, the majority of assets, by definition, will remain in the large-cap segment. However, if investment managers see opportunities elsewhere (for example, in small stocks), they are likely to shift their focus to other market sectors. As the marginal dollar is siphoned to lower capitalization assets, a new small-cap cycle begins.

All investors chase returns. Even though the investment community is comprised of a host of players with varying objectives, they all compete to generate the best returns. Because of this very basic goal, investment managers are unlikely to choose to retain highly liquid positions that are deemed inferior in value. Some investors enter the market and participate in a minimal and conservative manner; others search for more extravagant returns. The existence of these differing investment styles ultimately makes up a market. The interested parties, both owners and bidders, have preestablished notions of an asset's worth. When both parties reach mutual agreement and a suitable price point for the asset is reached, a transaction occurs.

Stretched or extreme valuations, discounted or dear, may tempt some participants to tender or extend an offer for an asset. When asset valuations make a compelling argument for investing, the value hunter with few constraints takes notice. The interest of this investor places a floor in the "undervalued" asset. If enough value buyers begin to act, the market benchmarks begin to reflect a change. More investors are drawn in when word begins to filter out to other market participants, such as momentum buyers. If the reasoning underlying such market interest is valid, investment managers with seemingly well-defined investment philosophies may be led to consider opportunities that might not otherwise be within their purview. Traders call this phenomenon "not fighting the tape."

The chase to own the best assets can supplant consideration of issues of liquidity. Hence, a well-mapped investment philosophy of managing the most liquid assets might become quickly unhinged as the market begins to act adversely or perversely. As market interest swells to a quiet roar, this buildup can fuel an extended period of outperformance of a terribly illiquid asset class in the face of business strategies demanding more liquid assets under management.

The preference for more liquid assets could fundamentally change if clients begin rewarding their investment managers for being invested in timely fashion. Clients would no longer chase after the best performing fund managers but would instead reward managers who most quickly put their assets to work. As much as the industry is changing, however, it is unlikely that clients would neglect the primary criterion in selecting an investment advisor: the best possible performance within the given investment objective. Of course, anything is possible. If the evaluation of fund managers begins to focus on those who have most efficiently invested some sizable chunk of assets, then it may be time to rethink the preference for large, liquid stocks versus small, less liquid stocks.

The new trends in the investment management business should not change the fundamental premise that small- or large-cap choices are a function of investors' preferences for risk taking. The investment business is nonetheless undergoing a significant evolution from a cottage industry of "independent" managers 30 years ago to a handful of behemoths that dominate the industry globally. This change has resulted in two significant effects:

1. Stock prices are likely to experience increased volatility as fewer players make shifts in their sizable holdings.
2. With only a handful of sizable decision makers, the duration of small- and large-cap cycles may possibly shorten as investors fiercely compete to arbitrage potential market returns between small and large caps.

INCREASED AGGRESSIVENESS OF LARGE CORPORATIONS

Large-cap blue-chip corporations are no longer the stodgy, slow-moving organizations they once were. General Electric (GE) is a prime example of a megasize player with all, or almost all, the get-up-and-go of a hungry microcap start-up. Its corporate strategy of being among the top three in a business line smacks of discipline that will likely continue to propel its market capitalization above the levels previously thought possible. The newfound aggressiveness of mature large-cap firms represents a change in the financial market landscape. In short, these behemoth organizations have aggressively embraced their business and consequently provided rewards to their shareholders. As a result, the premium that small caps have received in the past may not predict their long-term status.

Large organizations are no longer satisfied with the traditional confines of their competitive landscape. They are aggressively seeking to grow market share and increase profit margins at both the local and global levels. (GE, for instance, generates 35 percent of its total revenues from sources outside the United States. Only two decades ago, its foreign exposure was much lower.) As a consequence, the risk profile of the large, "safer" blue-chip firms may be unlike that of the past 50 years. The traditional business challenges for corporate management required the ability to navigate successfully in an uncertain business environment, launch new products, and compete for market share and pricing power. The new corporate culture requires management to face the added burdens of forecasting economic growth and demands across different countries and cultures. Management teams of multinational firms must grapple with a host of complexities unfamiliar to the Fortune 500 companies of the past. For these firms, growth and associated risk may be more pronounced than might be expected from historical measures.

The motivation behind this sweeping change may be tied to two basic factors: (1) shareholder activism and (2) change in corporate reward structure. Shareholders have taken more aggressive steps to ensure that corporate managers are making decisions that best maximize shareholder value. The California Public Employees' Retirement System (CalPERS) may be the best example of this newfound shareholder activism. CalPERS leveraged its asset holdings—over $168 billion, as of January 2000—to influence corporate boards and proactively force decisions that are shareholder-friendly. In a January 6, 2000, press release, CalPERS vowed to end dual-class shares of Tyson Foods, Inc. Dual-class shares offer two-tier stocks that have different voting rights. CalPERS argued that the dual-class stock structure severely limits the ability of shareholders of the company to exercise their ownership rights. As of January 2000, CalPERS owns roughly 1.8 million shares valued at $29 million. This level of activism among shareholders forces management structures, even in the largest companies, to make decisions that are equity-friendly.

The payout structure for corporate officers has significantly changed over the past few years. The use of options and of compensation tied to the performance of the company's stock has further aligned the interests of management with those of equity holders. This suggests that corporate managers may act in a more entrepreneurial manner to boost shareholder value.

Before the widespread use of incentive-based compensation plans, the nature of smaller companies meant that their managers, compared to their large-company brethren, were more closely tied to the value of their stock. The realignment of shareholder and management interests in larger firms suggests, however, that the entrepreneurial edge that resonated in smaller firms may be increasingly present in larger blue-chip organizations. This rejuvenation of the large-cap corporate culture may lead to shrinkage of the small-cap premium.

USE OF OPTIONS, FUTURES, AND OTHER FINANCIAL ENGINEERING TECHNIQUES

The increased use of derivative instruments such as options and futures has created a significant amount of debate in the financial markets. These complex structures have been represented as new wonder tools that allow market participants to address more easily their existing concerns in the financial markets. Others believe, however, that these new financial engineering techniques may be at the heart of an increasingly volatile market.

Although both views are still debated, many of the developments in the options and futures markets have effectively revolved around the most liquid assets in the financial markets. A majority of contracts written on the exchanges still involve the largest companies—IBM, Microsoft, and so on. In addition to all the benefits associated with the new derivatives, a subtle but relevant side effect has been that an already efficiently priced market has been transformed into a market in which new information can be arbitraged in nanoseconds.

Investors can readily create, in moments, a leveraged position for any given megacap security, such as GE or IBM, with marginal slippage. Take the Fidelity Magellan Fund as an example. With slightly under $100 billion in total assets as of September 1999, it holds a 4.7 percent stake in GE—its most sizable holding. That amounts to a stake of almost $4.3 billion worth of GE in the fund! Upon learning new information, an investor can easily hedge a long position by selling short the stock or buying a put to temporarily suspend a long position. This allows the investor to create a sizable position and simultaneously minimize the trading costs and tax consequences that might be associated with exiting from this position. An investment that affords an investor many exit strategies is extremely important. Being unable to readily exit an investment is the ultimate investor nightmare. Attempting to utilize derivative structures among smaller stocks can become quite difficult if the stock is not terribly liquid.

In similar fashion, investors can increase or decrease an exposure to an entire asset class. By using options and futures on an index, an investor can shed or double his or her exposure to an entire segment of the market as easily as hedging a stock position. The size of a typical contract for a large-cap exposure, of course, dwarfs the positions placed for a corresponding small-cap position. A look at the volume in dollars indicates that small-cap instruments, such as the futures contracts for the Russell 2000, have less than half of 1 percent of the size of the Standard & Poor's 500 contracts. These figures do not include the contracts for the Dow Jones Industrial Average, the Russell 1000, or the Nasdaq 100, which are primarily large-cap structures. The instruments for these indices allow investors to make lightning-fast changes in exposure for sizable assets.

Table 4.1 summarizes the annual trading volume and open interest of several commonly used contracts. For 1999, the period ended on August 12.

Options and futures instruments permit investors to place active "bets" in a seamless fashion. Because the large-cap contracts can offer what might appear to be boundless leverage or gearing, participants are more able to eradicate, at will, randomly floating arbitrage opportunities.

Ultimately, market inefficiencies offer opportunities to investors. The bias toward liquid assets in financial engineering tools dictates that the large megacap shares are likely to be scrutinized by investors far more than they have been in the past. Because derivative contracts are increasingly being used as liquid strategies in the investment arena, the less liquid small-cap segment of the equity market may be less exploited, thus giving rise to greater opportunities. It is ironic that such new instruments, which offer investors more opportunity to capture existing market

Table 4.1 Average Daily Futures Volume in US$ by Year, 1997–1999

Index	All ($)	1997 ($)	1998 ($)	1999 ($)
S&P 500	43,892,367,819	60,210,348,849	33,571,672,222	34,896,439,669
Russell 2000	213,496,297	146,797,055	223,413,030	298,670,060
S&P Midcap	194,900,371	153,694,584	208,023,198	237,024,814
DJIA	1,379,129,969		1,215,441,344	1,624,662,906
Nasdaq 100	759,871,921	310,977,586	549,914,773	1,748,149,145
Russell 1000	248,508,826			248,508,826

inefficiencies, also make it more difficult for active investors to find opportunities in the large-cap landscape.

The pricing inefficiency that currently exists between the large-cap and small-cap worlds might continue to diverge because of the large-cap bias that is common in many financial engineering tools. Because the ability to price information changes at lightning-fast speed, large-cap active managers may find it more difficult to add value in the future.

PART II

NAVIGATING IN THE SMALL-CAP UNIVERSE

FIVE

Asset Allocation and Small Caps

THE PERFORMANCE cycles of small- and large-cap stocks can be extreme. Not unlike that of the overall U.S. equity market in the past decade, the outperformance of large megacap shares has been dramatic. A bull market for secondary stocks can be equally compelling. Should one attempt to opportunistically trade in and out of the secondary market? Although evidence suggests the existence of factors or relationships that might cause one to lean toward smaller or larger firms, efforts at market-timing the size or small-cap turns can nonetheless be humbling.

The secondary market and the blue-chip sector are complementary segments of the equity market, but factors such as volatility, marketability, and information flow cause small caps to behave quite differently from large caps. The differences between small and large caps support an asset allocation approach to investing in smaller companies. A basic premise of asset allocation—the process of adding a particular asset to the portfolio mix—is to exploit returns that are unique to that particular asset and concurrently lower the portfolio's volatility. Even though it is challenging to strike the proper balance among dissimilar assets, this effort may provide ample rewards. This is especially true in the context of riskier assets such as small-cap stocks.

The small-cap universe benefits from its unique exposures to a variety of industries. For example, many secondary market industries simply do not exist in the large-cap blue-chip universe. Start-up biotechnology efforts of the late 1980s tended to exist only in the small-cap market. Similarly, health care companies were primarily a small-cap exposure in the early 1990s. As health care costs skyrocketed during that period, a market solution became increasingly necessary. A number of managed care companies went public. The outlook for this new industry was bright and was primarily characterized by smaller capitalization. Except for the three largest stocks competing in this field (Aetna at $5.1 billion, US Healthcare at $4.8 billion, and United Healthcare at $3.9 billion), all the players were below $1.6 billion in market capitalization in 1992. In fact, the majority were under $1 billion around that time.

As with the managed care industry, business outsourcing firms which provide services that allow large corporations to run more efficiently primarily inhabit the secondary market. The changing educational and training needs of a new digital-age economy create a wealth of investment opportunities, and many of the public companies that compete in this space are essentially small-cap firms. A number of factors underscore the benefits of diversifying one's portfolio by investing in small-cap stocks. Not only is value added from the higher rate of return of the combined portfolio, but diversification also creates the potential for a less volatile portfolio. A more varied collection of assets leads to a less correlated portfolio. Assets with unique return streams are considered less correlated and therefore beneficial because as one asset weakens, the remaining assets are less likely to follow suit. The nightmare condition for any investors is to helplessly watch their bond holdings collapse as their stocks lose ground. If their assets are less correlated, the potential benefits that arise from combining the assets in a portfolio are heightened.

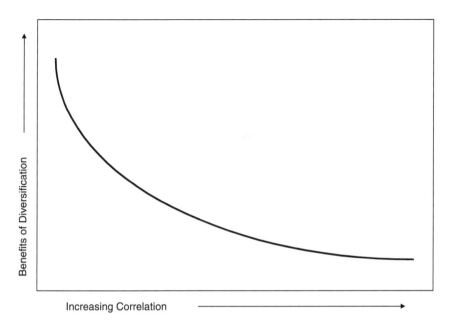

Figure 5.1   Correlation and Diversification

Figure 5.1 represents the theoretical relationship between the diversification of assets and the related benefits. The basic relationship suggests that as correlation levels increase, or as assets become more similar, potential benefits of diversification fall.

USING THE ASSET ALLOCATION MODEL TO YIELD AN EFFICIENT PORTFOLIO

A close examination of the traditional asset allocation model, based on seminal work by Nobel Laureate Harry Markowitz on modern portfolio theory, suggests that when bonds and stocks are combined, they yield a more efficient portfolio. The portfolio of combined assets generates a higher rate of return, with lower variability, as the result of lower-risk asset or bond returns. An efficient frontier between stocks and bonds represents the allocation of unique assets in order to produce higher returns with muted variability. Table 5.1 presents the long-run total return for the asset classes.

According to a simple stock/bond analysis, a portfolio with minimum risk should hold at least 15 percent in stocks for the long run. In fact, a

40 percent holding of stocks with a 60 percent bond mixture increases the rate of return 1.3 percent annually with more than a 4 percent decrease in annualized volatility. This is surprising. How can any exposure to a riskier asset—stocks, in this instance—yield a better behaved or less volatile portfolio? Ultimately, combining these assets benefits a portfolio because stocks and bonds do not move in perfect tandem. In some instances, a portfolio pulled down by a faltering stock market can be supported by a resilient bond market. In similar fashion, a skyrocketing stock market can dramatically inflate one's portfolio. This important trait can be reduced to a single statistical figure called the correlation between two asset classes.

Correlation is a measure, ranging from −1 to +1, of the tendency of two series of numbers to move together. If two assets are perfectly correlated, this is represented by a straight line connecting the two assets. The correlation figure would thus be 1.0. In other words, if the return of one asset goes up 2 percent for some period, the other asset also registers a 2 percent gain. An inverse relationship between the assets would be represented by a −1.0 correlation. For example, if one asset experiences a 2 percent gain, the other exhibits a 2 percent loss.

Figure 5.2 represents an efficient frontier curve between stocks and bonds. The equity proxy is based on the returns of the Standard & Poor's (S&P) 500, and the bond proxy is represented by long-term Treasury bonds. The lower end of the curve represents complete exposure to bonds. Since 1926, such exposure has yielded a 5.19 percent rate of return with 7.7 percent variability. The upper end of the curve represents a full exposure to the equity market or the S&P 500. From the mid-1920s to 1999, stocks have significantly outperformed bonds; their total rate of

Table 5.1 Return and Risk of Small and Large Stocks, the S&P 500, Bonds, and Cash

	Long Term Annualized	
	Return	**Standard Deviation**
Stocks		
Small	11.7%	23.0%
Large	10.6	17.9
S&P 500	11.3	19.6
Bonds	5.2	7.7
Cash	3.8	0.9

* Figures are estimated from 1926 to Dec. 1999.

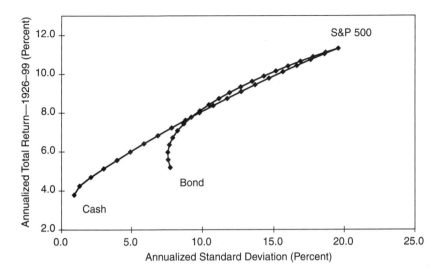

Figure 5.2   Risk/Return Relationships: S&P 500 Stocks vs.
Fixed-Income Instruments

return has been 11.3 percent with 19.6 percent variability. Large stocks
have yielded a 10.6 percent rate of return with a 17.9 percent variability.
Plot points between the two endpoints represent varying combinations of
a stock/bond mix. For instance, a 50 percent stock/50 percent bond exposure yields an 8.7 percent rate of return with an 11.2 percent variability.

When there is a perfect correlation between bonds and stocks, the
allocation decision becomes a matter of the investor's preference for risk.
A more risk-averse investor could opt for a heavier bond exposure. A
more aggressive investor might lean toward being overweight in stocks,
which would produce a higher, but less certain, return.

If the two assets in question are less than perfectly correlated, there
is a scalloped curved line between the two assets. Statistically, bonds are
thought to have a 0.20 degree of correlation to stocks.

Although volatility sounds like a theoretical concept, the importance
of a less volatile portfolio cannot be overestimated. Lower variability represents a "sleep at night" factor—the ability to feel that one's investments
are secure. The less certain the investments, however, the less comfort
an investor will have in planning for the future. Losing ground is expensive. If a portfolio declines 30 percent, it requires roughly a 43 percent
gain to reinstate its level prior to the loss. For example, if a $100 portfolio
experiences a 30 percent loss, at the end of the day the portfolio is worth

$70. A 30 percent gain on $70 yields only $91. A 43 percent appreciation would be needed to recover from $70 to $100.

APPLYING AN ASSET ALLOCATION
FRAMEWORK TO SMALL STOCKS

A similar allocation model can be applied to the small stock market. Figure 5.3 represents a combination of small-cap stocks and bonds. The correlation between small-cap stocks and bonds is 0.18, which is lower than the bond–large stock correlation figure. (Microcap stocks have roughly a 0.14 correlation with bonds.) Figure 5.3 depicts an even more "scalloped" relationship. A 100 percent small stocks exposure can yield a higher rate of return: 11.7 percent with 23.0 percent volatility. Although small stocks outperform the market rate of return, they are accompanied by a much higher degree of uncertainty.

This uncertainty in asset returns—primarily, equity returns—is a powerful reason to consider an exposure to the small-cap asset class in the context of a more diversified portfolio. A 40 percent exposure to small stocks offers an annualized return of 8.4 percent. The return is 7.7 percent with a 40 percent exposure to large stocks. The higher return with

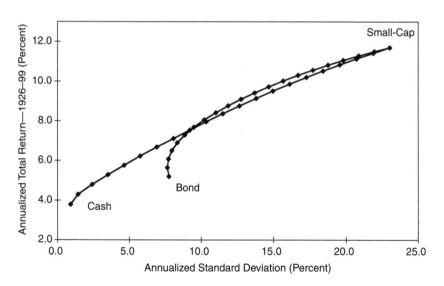

Figure 5.3   Risk/Return Relationships: Small-Cap Stocks vs.
Fixed-Income Instruments

the small-cap allocation is not a free lunch; the small-cap exposure increases the overall portfolio volatility by 1.75 percent. Interestingly, if an investor required an 8.4 percent rate of return using large caps as the primary equity vehicle, roughly 55 percent of the asset base would have to be allocated to equities.

Although the preceding interesting exercise might excite proponents of small-stock investing, it yields a fairly impractical conclusion: having a whopping 40 percent invested primarily in small stocks. A 40 percent exposure does not even include the normal 20 percent of the market that midcap shares typically represent. This portfolio may be especially impractical when the investor has a conservative pension plan with billions of dollars to invest. Nonetheless, one cannot ignore the simple conclusion from such an analysis: Compared to the bond market, small stocks are very different—even more so than the large-cap equity market. Although a 40 percent small-stocks exposure is perhaps impractical, the lower equity exposure gained by using small stocks to generate a risk/return profile that is comparable to the use of large stocks makes it difficult for a long-term investor to entirely avoid the small-cap asset class.

SMALL STOCKS AND THE EQUITY EQUATION: WHAT PROPORTION MAKES SENSE?

The stock investment decision relates to how much stock and what proportion of fixed-income securities make sense, not to timing when stocks should outperform. Similarly, the question of capitalization size may be more than simply a market timing issue of investing in big caps one day and small caps the next. As one of the more humbling parts of the size puzzle, the investor must negotiate the twists and turns of whether secondary firms outshine their large-cap counterparts. Reframing the size issue in asset allocation terms may help an investor to avoid the pitfalls of applying market timing to the small-cap market.

The more relevant, and perhaps more manageable, question for a long-term investor is whether to completely "bet" on a single asset. Being fully invested in a safer asset class such as bonds may not make sense over the longer term. Similarly, allocating an entire equity position or exposure to large blue-chip stocks over the long run may also fall short of sound investing. Beyond looking at the proportion of stocks to bonds, the investor must determine the proportion of small stocks that belong with large stocks in the total equity puzzle. By determining some minimum risk level between small and large stocks, an investor can arrive at a healthier long-term portfolio position.

Figure 5.4 shows the risk/return trade-off between small and large stocks from 1974 to 1999. The correlation between small and large stocks cannot be as dramatic as the stock/bond relationship. Even though small stocks are very different from the blue-chip sector in terms of such factors

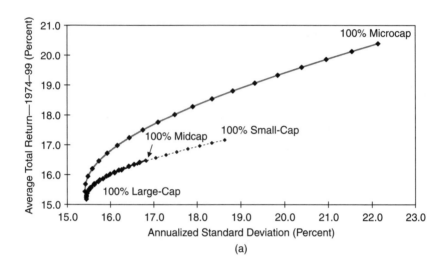

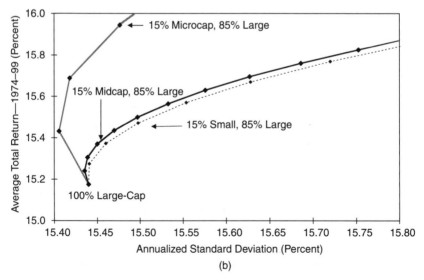

Figure 5.4   Risk/Return Relationship: Small vs. Large Stocks

as variability, sector exposures, and liquidity traits, secondary stocks and blue chips are complements in the total equity market. Conversely, bonds are a completely different instrument with a very different set of obligations to the holder. Debt holders have direct claims to specific assets of the borrower/company. The returns are typically based on a fixed agreement for a predetermined time frame. Stockholders have a residual claim on assets of a company. Unlike bonds that are accompanied with coupons, stocks promise minimal payouts over the life of the shares. The shares of a corporation never mature; traditional bonds do. As a result, the correlation level between bonds and stocks, 0.2, is much lower than, say, the correlation level between small and large stocks—roughly, 0.9. Put another way, the benefits of combining large and small caps are not, or cannot be, as great as the benefits from incremental changes in bond/stock allocations.

However, certain levels of exposure to small-cap stocks make good sense. A 25 percent exposure to small stocks increases the annualized rate of return by 50 basis points, or half of a percent, with a marginal increase in variability, or roughly 20 basis points. The mix of data does not point to a 40 percent exposure to small stocks, as with the bonds/small stocks mix, yet a marginal exposure appears to make the total portfolio more efficient. Upon close inspection, a minimum variance, or lowest risk, portfolio should accord a 10 to 15 percent weight to this fledgling sector.

Where do midcap stocks fit into the picture? The minimum variance approach yields a 15 percent midcap exposure in the total equity puzzle. The optimal midcap and large-cap mix yields a 15.4 percent rate of return with a 15.5 percent volatility. Again, another snapshot of a smaller stock bias yields a figure different from zero. Exposures beyond the 15 percent level become an issue of an investor's preference or tolerance for risk.

THE INCREASING RELEVANCE OF ASSET ALLOCATION BY SIZE

Asset allocation analysis using historical data, as in Figures 3.2–3.4, implies that the risk/return relationship between large and smaller companies is constant. This simplistic assumption is needed to simulate the trade-off between large and small company exposures. The historical data provide very useful correlation levels between the two assets. A critical question must be addressed in this asset allocation exercise concerning small- versus large-cap exposure: Are correlation levels constant through time? In other words, can one assume that the level of interrelatedness between smaller and large firms is constant or not significantly different from the long-run assumptions?

If the relationship is fixed, are the long-term implications of the analysis likely to remain meaningful? A close look at the correlation levels over time strongly suggests that smaller stocks and large stocks, as asset classes, are less similar today than in prior decades. More important, the level of correlation between smaller and large-cap firms has been declining. Going forward, a lower correlation between two assets implies that the benefit of diversification is likely to increase.

Figure 5.5 represents the correlation of returns between the small-cap index and large-cap index. Notice that the correlation levels between smaller and large-cap firms in the early 1940s was approximately 0.96. The long-run correlation figure, approximately 0.93, is in contrast to the 0.85 correlation level over the decade from 1988 to 1998. These changes in correlation levels are significant because they imply that the benefits of diversification between smaller and large-cap firms are likely to be more significant than the historical data imply. Simply put, if the trade-off of returns between large and smaller companies is less related than in the past, the variability of a combined portfolio of small and large stocks is likely to be more muted.

The fall in correlation between smaller and large stocks is compelling because one can reasonably argue that such a pattern is more likely to

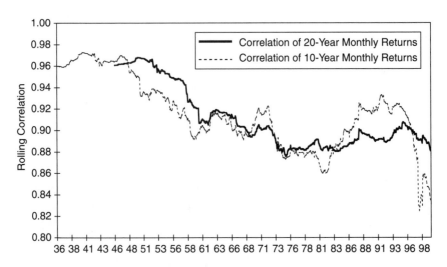

Figure 5.5   Correlation of Small-Cap vs. Large-Cap Stocks

continue. Smaller companies today are less related to large companies of the past for a good reason: Large companies are going global. As a result, the revenue stream and therefore the earnings stream of megacap global franchises are less likely to be related to the more domestically based small-cap universe of companies. Most important, the trend toward globalization is likely to intensify, not reverse. Hence, the interrelationship between smaller and large firms will continue to fall, thereby increasing the asset allocation benefits of a combined small- and large-cap portfolio.

GLOBAL DIVERSIFICATION

Diversifying assets has been a popular yet sound investment mantra in the 1990s. Thanks to this concept, investors have cast aside the comfortable confines of their domestic markets to pursue international exposure more aggressively. The logic is: If economies operate on varying economic cycles, investments among a diversified set of countries are more likely to offset the vagaries of any single market.

As investors are generally aware, large-cap stocks, and even select smaller companies' stocks, are far more exposed overseas than they were only a few short years ago. Coca-Cola, for example, sold $12.1 billion of products overseas in 1999, or roughly 62 percent of its total revenues. This figure was about 51 percent in 1986. As of 1999, large companies derived approximately 26 percent of their revenues from overseas business (see Figure 5.6). Anecdotal evidence suggests that this figure is increasing. Because corporations are more aggressively pursuing growth across markets, the profit cycle of multinational firms has become increasingly linked to global concerns.

The issue of size, or small stocks and diversification, has special significance in the context of global investing. As has been noted, large-cap stocks have a more international revenue stream than small stocks. As a result, the realized diversification benefits of holding large, blue-chip stocks is likely to fall short of estimates based on past data. Small, more domestically based companies are more likely to diversify a basket of global equities.

Furthermore, although shareholders can benefit from corporate ventures into faster growing markets, the holder of a global portfolio may actually face some disadvantages. As a case in point, consider the significant rally among U.S. large-cap stocks in the late 1990s. This rally took place as the market began to reward blue-chip firms for taking on more overseas investments. However, as overseas economies soured in late

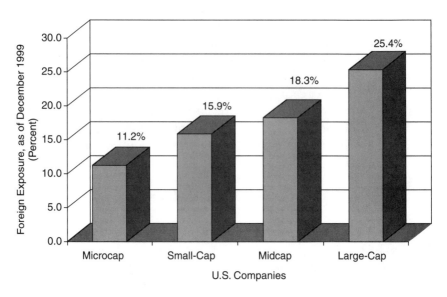

Figure 5.6   Foreign Exposure by Size

1997 and early 1998—for example, in Southeast Asia—concerns rippled across continents to seemingly unrelated markets. Returns across very developed markets tumbled. The United States markets fell 12.2 percent; those in the United Kingdom tumbled 10.6 percent. Germany lost 13.2 percent, Japan lost 10.0 percent, and Canada was weakened by 27.1 percent during the summer of 1998 (June through August).

Although globalization has opened the door to newfound opportunities, it has also introduced added risks to traditionally safer blue-chip firms. Witness the "Asian contagion," in which a meltdown of Asian economies and financial markets spread around the globe. This may be symptomatic of the new global landscape, in which shocks to one segment of the world are more likely to have a sharper ripple effect than in the past. In theory, diversification of one's portfolio represents the market's immune response system to single-market shocks.

THE DOLLAR AND THE SMALL-CAP CYCLE

Shifts in the U.S. dollar and the resulting impact on the U.S. small-cap cycle support the contention that large companies are increasingly global. In a rising dollar environment, smaller and more domestically based firms tend to outperform their larger and more internationally exposed counterparts. Because large firms tend to play a more significant international role than their small-cap counterparts, the dollar movements should offer some discriminating information.

As the U.S. dollar weakens, products of domestic firms become cheaper abroad, and competing products from nations with rising currencies become more expensive. Conversely, a strengthening dollar places firms with significant international exposure at a disadvantage. As the dollar strengthens, U.S. products become more expensive, lowering the profitability of such firms.

Figure 5.7 reflects the relative performance of small to large shares (right scale) versus the trade-weighted dollar (left scale). The trade-weighted dollar represents the U.S. currency versus the currencies of the other G10 nations.

One can argue that the secular, or long-term, fall in the dollar during the 1980s significantly contributed to the outperformance of large shares during most of those years. Figure 5.7 depicts the secular fall in the dollar and the corresponding weakness among secondary stocks during the 1990s. This long-term decline in the dollar suggests that companies that invested internationally additionally benefited because of currency effects.

One can argue that companies with an eye on global opportunities can fuel faster growth than if they were to remain solely domestic players. Multinational companies are likely to exhibit similar profit cycles. Because the average investor tends to be more focused on company-specific issues that drive profitability, he or she may be less aware of the

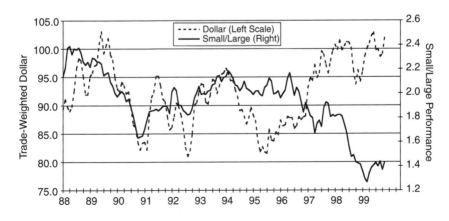

Figure 5.7 The Small-Cap Cycle and the Dollar

portfolio side effects for companies that are invested globally. As a result of the shift in geographic business mix, however, major financial markets are likely to be tied more, not less, closely.

Moreover, the push toward globalization forces profit cycles to converge. This suggests that expected correlation figures among international large-capitalization companies are likely to be higher than the historical data might suggest. If the secondary markets in some countries are indeed more domestically based, then smaller-cap firms may truly represent a unique venue that allows investors to remain regionally diversified.

To retain the traditional benefits of diversification vis-à-vis global markets, one can lower exposure to multinational firms and/or consider small caps as an additional asset class. By adding the smaller-capitalization segment, the overall portfolio becomes more diversified from a geographic perspective.

The success of a global megacap portfolio is predicated on solid global growth trends. It is possible that such stocks earned a significant valuation premium during the 1990s because these global brands have been able to take advantage of faster-growing international markets. Yet, one needs to reconcile whether the markets have properly priced-in the risks associated with a less diversified basket of blue-chip stocks.

Recognizing the impact of a more closely knit financial market structure may be a more subtle exercise. Measurable factors such as changes in currencies and interest rates may not necessarily indicate such secular shifts in correlation. Some of the change in market interrelationships may not become evident until dramatic shifts occur in interest rates and currencies. In most instances, currencies and interest rates are relatively stable. Therefore, it can be difficult to pinpoint linkages among companies by calculating the correlation of daily price returns.

One approach to this more complex global investment landscape might include structuring two tranches of equity to represent a global basket. The first might include a "true" global franchise segment, and the second could contain those companies that are more locally based. By segmenting the locally based companies from the global franchises, one can better control regional exposures for a diversified portfolio.

The global franchise segment allows for one's exposure for a broad play on global themes and sectors. A more domestic or local group would allow one to properly control for cross-border correlation levels. Even though implementing the global tranche is a complex task, this structure begins to address some of the more difficult issues surrounding a more tightly linked global marketplace.

EXCEPTIONS TO THE RULE

The evidence in the United States suggests that adding smaller companies to one's asset allocation may yield a more globally diversified portfolio, but this may not be true for all countries. In fact, though not common, the secondary markets in some countries can reflect a more sizable foreign exposure than their large-cap counterparts. For example, the level of foreign exposure appears to be lower for small companies in the United States and the United Kingdom, but the level appears to be higher in Japan.

Within the U.S. market, there appear to be certain sector exceptions. Even though the average level of foreign exposure of smaller companies appears to be fairly low, some specific sectors hold unusually high levels of such exposure. For example, small technology shares are significantly exposed overseas.

Figure 5.8 represents the foreign exposure of the large- and small-cap groups on a sector basis. To no one's surprise, the large-cap sectors [Figure 5.8 (a)] are much more exposed abroad than their smaller counterparts. Interestingly, the distribution of foreign exposure is less broad-based as one gets to the small-cap segment [Figure 5.8 (b)]. The large-cap segment contains five sectors (Basic Industrials, Energy, Capital Goods—Technology, Capital Goods, and Consumer Staples) with a foreign exposure level of 25

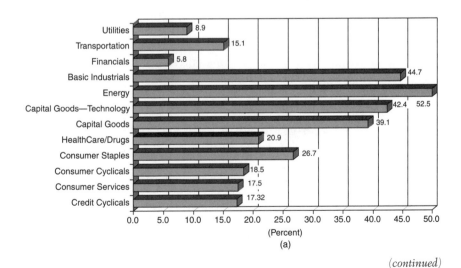

(continued)

Figure 5.8 Foreign Exposure by Sectors: (a) Large-Cap; (b) Small-Cap

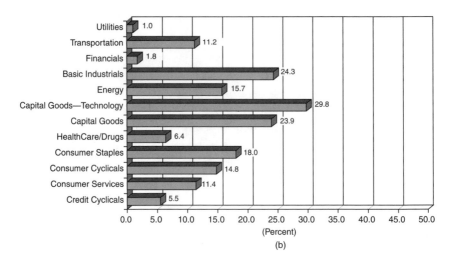

Figure 5.8   (Continued)

percent or greater. The small-cap segment contains only one sector over the 25 percent level: Capital Goods—Technology has nearly 30 percent exposure overseas.

Certain segments within the smaller technology sector can be terribly dependent on overseas economies. For instance, companies in the telecommunications equipment sector can have a majority of their revenues from overseas. In 1999, Brightpoint, Inc., a $577 million capitalization company in the wireless equipment business, gained more than 60 percent of its total revenues from overseas sources. As much as the small-cap market appears to have minimal international exposure, certain exceptions, such as the telecommunications sector, can be profound.

SMALL STOCK EXPOSURE AS A PROPORTION
OF THE TOTAL EQUITY MARKET

Another approach to the size puzzle might be defined by the total assets currently invested in the market. In other words, a market-neutral exposure to an asset class would simply be the exposure of that asset in the total market. The total market value of small stocks makes up 7 percent of the total U.S. equity market, or $1.06 billion in total assets. Interestingly, even though the $1.06 trillion small-cap market (1999 estimate) is only a secondary market in the United States, it is nonetheless more sizable than any of the more than 30 emerging markets and most of the mature equity markets except France ($1.1 trillion), Germany ($1.2 trillion), the United Kingdom ($2.6 trillion), and Japan ($3.9 trillion).[1] The total capitalization of the U.S. small-cap market does not include the roughly $1.7 trillion in midsize publicly traded companies in the United States.

This point estimate or latest snapshot of 7 percent is somewhat dependent on market trends. If the market has taken a megacap trend over past periods, it is quite possible that most recent weights exaggerate the large-cap exposure. As large stocks outperform small, they make up a greater proportion of the market with each tick-up in share prices. Hence, an outperformance in some asset class, such as large caps in the late 1990s, yields exaggerated large-cap exposures.

Figure 5.9 illustrates the market exposure of small stocks in the United States during the past few decades. Note that the weights of smaller stocks reached a high of approximately 18 percent at the peak of the small-stock rally in the early 1980s. A more reasonable approach might be to smooth out this effect by taking a simple average of the ratio over a long period of time. The data go back only to the mid-1970s. This approach suggests that a market-neutral holding of small stocks is roughly 12 percent. Even though this proportional approach tackles the asset exposure level in a different manner, it appears to arrive at a figure not terribly different from that of the more theoretical risk/return approach discussed previously.

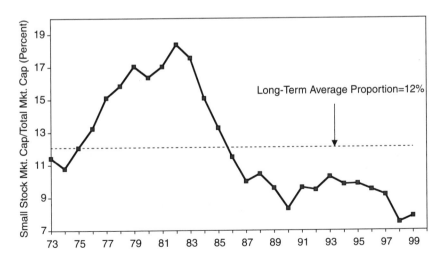

Figure 5.9 Small-Cap Stocks as a Percentage of U.S. Market Capitalization

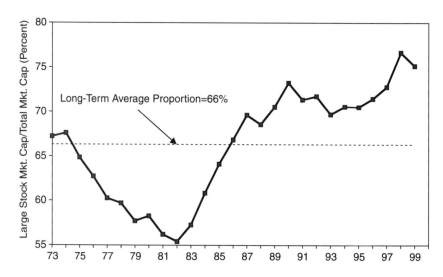

Figure 5.10 Large-Cap Stocks as a Percentage of U.S. Market Capitalization

One can tackle the large-cap market via the same process that is used to determine an optimal large-cap holding. Figure 5.10 reflects the large-cap proportion of the U.S. equity market over time. Like the small-cap market at its peak in the early 1980s, the 78 percent of exposure of large caps in 1999 perhaps reflected a raging bull market for megacap stocks. The longer-term average of 66 percent suggests a more conservative exposure to large-cap stocks.

The small-cap estimate of 12 percent and the large-cap exposure of 66 percent indicate that midcaps are likely to hold roughly a 20 percent exposure. These figures should sum close to 100 percent. The remaining 2 to 5 percent should account for a microcap exposure.

EXPOSURE TO SMALL CAPS OVER THE LONG TERM

What is the proper exposure to small stocks for the long term? The preceding analysis suggests that a minimal exposure of 15 percent for small stocks is appropriate. If an investor were to combine a small-cap and a mid-cap exposure, this might lead to a significant 25 to 30 percent of equity holdings in smaller firms. Besides statistical analysis, the investor's outlook for investment returns in the upcoming years, and his or her tolerance for risk, must also enter the investment decision.

For instance, examine the traditional exposure of stocks and bonds. Many Wall Street strategists tend to have an average stock holding of 54 percent of the total portfolio. Yet the historical data might suggest that a minimum risk level of 25 percent allocated to equities would be more appropriate. What accounts for this (54−25) 29 percent difference between the data and the experts? If, according to the data, only a minimum proportion should be invested in stocks, any excess over 25 percent must derive from the strategist's outlook for stocks over the near term. The more bullish the outlook for a particular asset, the greater the exposure to that asset. In this instance, the excess exposure to stocks is a moving target.

A historical perspective of the proportion of small to large stocks can also offer investors some guidance toward a minimum holding for smaller firms. A small stock holding above the 15 percent level recommended for small stocks depends not only on the investor's bullishness on equity but also on the outlook for small versus large stocks. Chapter 6 sheds light on this important and complex topic of size rotations.

Finally, as noted above, another variable in determining exposure to an asset class is the investor's appetite for risk taking. Ultimately, the basic guide for exposure to an asset class is an investor's own comfort with the risk associated with that asset.

TIME HORIZON OF INVESTMENTS

In determining the ability to assume a risky investment position, one critical component relates to the time frame of the investment. Even though an investor can be extremely risk-averse, a longer-term time horizon enables the investor to tap into riskier assets.

Suppose an investor can invest a sizable amount of assets in either Treasury bills or emerging market securities. These assets have completely different expected returns and risk contours. One asset is effectively a short-term guaranteed-income contract; the other is a promise of great returns with very little certainty. If the investor needs to turn over that cash for a down payment on a house or for paying off an outstanding debt in one year, the choice of investments becomes very limited. A quick glance at the yearly payout patterns on various emerging country markets, for example, could quickly make even the most daring gambler stick with Treasury bills. A short-term time horizon simplifies the decision process, rendering moot any comparisons between the returns on T-bills versus those from emerging markets. The rational investor simply realizes that the upcoming term payment is near. Although the expected return of Treasury bills is far below the dramatic returns produced by emerging markets, the investor has little choice but to invest in T-bills, given a one-year investment window.

Longer holding periods, however, can act to dampen the volatility associated with assets. Although the expected return for a risky asset might be uncertain in the short term, as the holding period extends, the predictability of the assets increases. For example, consider the science of weather forecasting. The technology for predicting weather has become much more advanced and precise. Nonetheless, even nonprofessional forecasters have a better chance of correctly estimating that the temperature is likely to fall between the months of August and December in the northeastern United States, than a meteorologist would have in estimating the change in temperature between the first and the third weeks in August for the same locale.

Likewise, it is extremely difficult to predict how one stock will fare versus some other stock from one day to the next. Yet, if an investor has a basic understanding of the fundamentals of the companies involved and the general economic backdrop, he or she can more easily identify the company that is less likely to lose market value, say, one or two years hence.

On simple examination, there is indeed support for the popular conception that small stocks are riskier than large stocks. More important, the secondary market is much more volatile than the blue-chip market. The long-term volatility of small stocks is roughly 23.0 percent annually, compared to 17.8 percent for the large-cap benchmarks. But volatility goes both ways. A stock that registers a dramatic change in price, whether up or down, is labeled as being highly volatile. To many investors, a stock that is bounding to new highs offers welcome risk. They only become concerned when asset prices fall.

Probability-of-Loss Approach to Assessing Risk

To assess the risk of the small-cap market, investors can examine performance in terms of the probability of loss over varying investment horizons. What is the chance of losing money in the small-cap market over a one-year period? More important, what is the probability of losing money in the small-cap market versus the large-cap market?

Figure 5.11 represents the chance that various instruments, such as equities, stocks, bonds, and cash, will lose ground over several investment time frames. The figures presented are simply the number of rolling holding periods, such as three-months, one-year, two years, and so on, over the available history of the asset returns. These figures are summed over the total number of observed periods. Note that the small-cap percentage is placed in the context of other financial instruments, such as cash or Treasury bills, long-term government bonds, and large stocks.

It is perhaps not surprising that, over the past 75 years, the probability of loss for cash in a three-month holding period is almost nil at 1.7 percent. Under this probability-of-loss approach, the next riskiest assets are long-term government bonds, with a 31.6 percent probability of loss, and large stocks, with a 31.3 percent chance of losing money over a three-month holding period. By comparison, the small-cap shares have a 33.6 percent chance of losing ground within the same time frame.

As discussed previously, given a three-month time frame, the asset allocation decision might be uncomplicated. Investors would simply select cash as a safe-haven asset and shy away from other risky ventures such as stocks. When the holding period is extended from three months

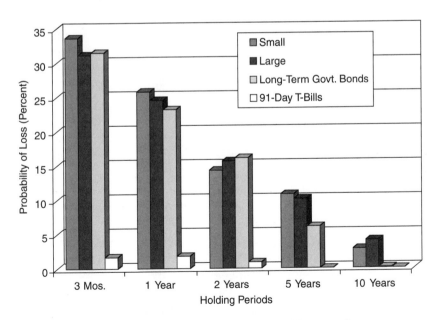

Figure 5.11 Probability of Loss per Holding Period

to one year, the probability of loss for the safe assets marginally declines from the probability for a three-month holding. The riskier assets display positive changes, however. The probability of loss for large stocks declines from 31.3 percent to 24.6 percent, and the chance of losing money is cut by 21 percent. Similarly, small stocks appear more resilient if the holding period is extended beyond three months. The probability of loss for small stocks declines 23 percent. The one-year holding period of 25.9 percent drops from 33.6 percent over the one-year time frame.

In fact, the riskiness of smaller companies continues to drop as the time frame extends over an even longer holding period. The two-year holding period figures suggest that the probability of loss for small caps is not terribly different from that of large stocks. Although large stocks have a 15.7 percent chance of capital losses over a two-year holding period, the probability for small stocks is also a compelling 14.3 percent. Notice that holding periods beyond two years suggest that small-stock results are no riskier than large company returns.

Why do risky assets appear safer over a longer time frame? Part of the answer relates to business cycles over the past 75 years. If one can make the simple assumption that stock prices are based on the success of corporate ventures, then it is easy to accept the historical results presented above. Remember that most business cycles over the past 75 years have lasted less than a decade. Even if a business cycle deteriorates, as long as it bounces back before a decade lapses, there is a good chance that risky assets, tied to the general health of corporations, will rebound to reflect a more robust or, at least, a recovering business environment. The length of business cycles might explain why asset returns are less volatile over longer holding periods; these periods allow assets that have collapsed to rebound under improving circumstances. Hence, the positive trends found in lengthy holding periods are likely simply because business cycles, though many, have reflected a resilient and prosperous economy over the past 75 years.

The probabilities of loss discussed above reflect an incredibly supportive backdrop for equity investing. The absolute returns for equity investing during the past century were quite strong. Naturally, if the rewards outstrip the traditional risks associated with equity investing, an analysis of long-term holdings is more than likely to continue pointing toward risky assets as being desirable investments.

This evidence makes a compelling case that investors should not avoid risky assets if they are taking a longer-term approach. Nonetheless, they must exercise caution, given the historically prosperous backdrop of the U.S. equity market. It is indeed quite likely that this type of analysis has driven Wall Street strategists to recommend equity positions above a level that would be supported by traditional risk/reward analysis.

In the same light, recommendations on exposure to secondary stocks may be warranted at levels above the recommended long-term proportions that the historical data might suggest. Bear in mind, of course, that an increased exposure to secondary stocks is predicated on the investor's having a more flexible and longer-term investment horizon.

SIX

Drivers of
Secondary Stocks

ALTHOUGH THEIR record has been tarnished since the late 1990s, secondary stocks have fared better than large caps over the long term. Yet their superior long-term performance has also been accompanied by cycles in which small companies have swung in and out of favor.

As discussed in Chapter 1, these shifts in size preference, whereby small caps outperform large caps, and vice versa, tend to ripple across the entire equity market. Furthermore, these size rotations appear to operate on the margin. That is, midcap stocks outperform large stocks, small stocks outperform midcap stocks, and microcap stocks outperform small-cap stocks in a bull market for smaller stocks. As the tide turns to favor small-cap firms, the smaller companies within a large-cap universe like-wise tend to outperform their megacap counterparts. Because of this domino effect, attempts to solve the size puzzle are relevant for the small-cap investor, the asset allocator, and even the perennial large-cap blue-chip bettor. To be successful, active investors need to understand the factors that drive this shifting cycle of preferences for small- or large-cap firms.

What is the price of not paying attention to the size factor? If an investor could perfectly target when a cycle will swing in favor of small versus large stocks—and when it will swing back again—the rate of return would exceed the small-cap benchmark by 3.3 percent and the large-cap benchmark by 4.4 percent. By 1999, instead of earning $3,969 from one dollar invested in small stocks in 1926, one would have earned $32,374. From a practical standpoint, this might not be an attainable goal, but the comparison graphically illustrates the cost of not taking a view on size. Figure 6.1 represents the absolute performance of small- and large-cap firms since 1926. Table 6.1 presents the annualized rates of return and

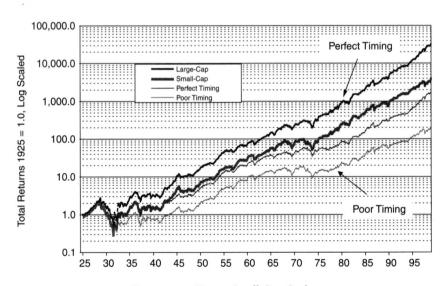

Figure 6.1   Timing Small-Cap Cycles

the annualized volatility for the performance comparisons of small- and large-cap stocks.

The performance series shown in Figure 6.1 are placed in the context of a hybrid line that comprises the best performing results for each of the past ten small-cap cycles. The fourth line at the lower end of the chart represents an investor who is getting the cycle turns completely wrong. This run of poor timing represents the lower end of the investment spectrum. Simply put, the size factor can significantly enhance or detract from an active investor's efforts. Although it may be difficult for an investor to take a position on size, serious investors cannot afford to ignore this factor.

Savvy investors who recognize that the environment is favorable for small-cap investing can confine their focus to a narrower subset of investments. Conversely, if the market appears enamored of "safer" blue-chip firms, a manager can be more cautious about proceeding with the small-cap market and migrate to a larger sector.

Ultimately, size preferences represent the waxing and waning of investors' risk-taking appetite. The motivating factors, or drivers, that account for changes in risk preferences have two main components:

1. Long-standing, or static, effectively constant traits and relationships, which may account for the small-cap return premium over the long term. The inherently riskier nature of smaller firms, for example, can be considered a static trait.
2. Dynamic drivers that account for the cycle shifts or rotations in size between small- and large-cap stocks. These performance cycles exist because investor risk tolerances are not constant or stationary. As risk preferences change, so also do preferences for small- or large-cap stocks. The dynamic drivers that influence the propensity of investors to take on additional risk fall into three broad categories: (a) cyclical growth, (b) credit and cost-of-capital relationships, and (3) profitability.

Table 6.1

| | Small-Cap | Timing Small-Cap Cycles | | |
		Large-Cap	Perfect	Poor
Annualized Return	11.8%	10.6%	15.1%	7.5%
Annualized Volatility	23.0%	17.8%	21.0%	20.1%

Valuations also offer some strategic guidance as to the size-rotation decision. Investors can look at valuations to determine whether risk has been fairly priced in the small-cap market. Measures of value allow investors to determine whether it is too early or too late to enter into a small-cap proposition.

SMALL CAPS OUTPERFORM LARGE: FACT OR FICTION?

Historically, small stocks have generated an excess return, or size premium, over large stocks, which is in keeping with the excess risk that typically accompanies smaller firms. The size premium represents a market risk premium. Assets are priced according to their underlying risks. Small caps are expected to provide a higher rate of return than large caps, to compensate for their higher risk. As discussed later in this chapter, other static factors such as the law of large numbers and the effect of analyst neglect also argue for the existence of a size premium. Nonetheless, a number of arguments can be made against the validity of a size premium as well.

Some of the more compelling factors that have been cited as arguments against the existence of a size premium include: measurement error, inferior profitability comparisons, and the erratic nature of spikes in small-cap returns. Another popular but qualitative argument holds that small companies are inferior to large companies in terms of product and services, management depth, balance sheet, and similar factors. Other relevant issues investors must reconcile, before taking on a small-cap position, relate to the illiquidity of small stocks, which interferes with the ability to invest quickly.

Flaws in Performance Data

Historical data are always subject to frailties of human error. By extension, a measured effect is only as good as the database from which it is drawn. One way in which critics debunk the size premium is to claim that the data are flawed. They argue that databases tracking security prices as far back as the 1920s must contain some degree of error. Yet the services that provide such pricing data claim that they accurately capture all events that have been transacted in the equity markets. Factors such as survival bias, or databases that do not account for companies that have gone bankrupt or not "survived," or other data hitches such as flawed data entry, certainly leave open the possibility that compelling small-cap returns have been measured less than perfectly.

Because of the robust sample size, however, it becomes difficult to argue that errors in the data, which are clearly drawn at random, consistently bias the smaller stock returns. The sizable universe of companies makes it more likely that the measured returns over the long term are closer to the realized returns.

Another issue that has surfaced relates to the definition of small stocks. According to this argument, as laid out by Bill Fouse,[1] small stocks have generated excess returns in the past because large companies were accidentally included in the sample of small companies. In the initial studies on size, size groups were reconstituted over five-year periods, which meant the sample size of the small-cap index remained unchanged for five years. As a result, some of the more successful small-cap ideas could have migrated to the large-cap universe but were mistakenly credited to the small-cap universe. Although this argument has some merit, the lengthy five-year holding period would also be likely to cover collapsing secondary stocks that small-cap investors would be unlikely to hold. These stocks, which would be incorrectly credited to the small-cap index, would detract from small-cap performance measures. Accordingly, it might be more appropriate to assign weakening issues to a group outside the small-cap universe. For instance, faltering secondary stocks that are losing market value might be more appropriately assigned to a segment of microcap stocks. Even though the upward migration of shares can produce an upward bias in small-cap benchmarks, downward migrations can likewise create a downward bias in returns. Although investors need to examine all benchmark results with a critical eye, a migration bias may be less relevant than other issues. Because the markets are fluid, there are always likely to be migration effects, whether upward or downward. Over the long term, these effects are likely to cancel each other out and have little impact on any potential return bias.

To determine the significance of the migration effect, the holding periods of a small-cap benchmark could be shortened—for example, from five years to four years. The benchmark results could then be analyzed to determine whether they are significantly different when the rebalancing frequency is cut down to three years, two years, or one year. In one simulation, several identical small-cap portfolios were created to vary only by the length of the holding periods. The portfolio results were nearly identical. Based on this study, there seems to be little evidence that the performance of a small-stock index calculated over a five-year holding period varies greatly from that of an index with a four-year holding period. In fact, the results appear to be fairly uniform across holding periods.

The significant number of companies that comprise the small-cap market accounts for the stark similarities among small-cap benchmarks reconstituted across holding periods. In other words, once a benchmark is constructed with several hundred companies, as most small-cap benchmarks are, the averages are more likely to converge, reflecting quite similar results. Although index turnover can appear significant, the net performance results do not necessarily vary because of the tendency for a broad core of small-cap names to remain in an index over lengthy periods.

Suspect Small-Cap Cycles

The size premium has also been questioned in relation to performance cycles. In an argument posed by Jeremy Siegel,[2] a Wharton School professor and noted author, the degree to which small stocks outperformed large stocks in the 1970s was unusually strong and possibly suspect. According to this thinking, if the 1974–83 period were removed from the long-run performance analysis, the remaining data would yield a large-cap premium.

That ten-year-period appears to have represented a bonanza for small-stock investing. Figure 6.2 presents the performance of the Ibbotson Small Stocks Index versus that of the Standard & Poor's 500. Note that the long-run data from 1926 to 1999 indicate that a dollar invested in small-cap stocks would be worth approximately $6,545, compared to approximately $2,842 for large stocks over the same time frame. If the years 1975 through 1984 were removed, however, large caps would have generated $2,004 and outpaced small stocks, which would have gained only $1,202 over this period.[3] The period in question represents an unusual time, one of oil shocks and devastating inflation. Although it might seem reasonable to remove an anomalous subset of returns, this analysis neglects the possibility that unusual events have occurred in practically every decade. If the 1975–84 period were removed from the analysis, this elimination would also erase a bear market for large caps that occurred during the first half of this time frame. This approach inadvertently

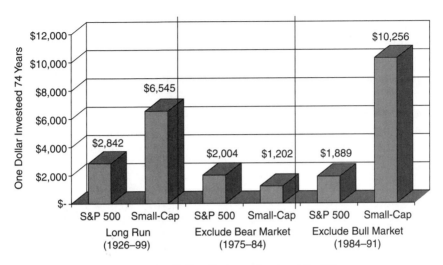

Figure 6.2 Small-Cap Cycles in Good and Bad Times

assumes that investors can adeptly time a large-cap bear market. It turns out that besides being a period in which small-cap returns were stellar, the 1970s also marked a bear market for large-cap returns.

Likewise, most of the subsequent period from 1984 to 1991 should be removed from analysis because large stocks exhibited unusually high returns during those years. In this time of severe disinflation long-term government bond yields fell from the mid-teens to roughly 5 percent over a 10-year period. Investors are unlikely to face such a significant period of disinflation within the foreseeable future. If the 1984–91 period were removed from the analysis, the long-run performance results, not surprisingly, would show that small stocks outperformed large. In fact, as presented in Figure 6.2, the margin of small-cap outperformance would be even greater than that of the long-run time series data. As this discussion demonstrates, selective measurements can cloud any analysis, including an analysis of the small-cap premium.

Large-Cap Dominance

One of the more popular arguments against the existence of a small-cap size premium regards the dominance of the large-cap franchise. It is argued that small companies are inferior to large companies and therefore make poor investments. Among the factors cited for large companies' being sound investments are: recent technological advances such as just-in-time inventory and e-commerce; a financial landscape that ties together global markets more closely; and fewer layers of corporate management, resulting in more efficient operations than in past decades. Bear in mind, however, that these changes should benefit all firms, both large and small. For example, improved technology increases productivity for *all* companies, not just for large companies. Similarly, if global markets are indeed more closely linked, this implies that smaller companies, as well as large companies, should find it easier to market their products or services overseas.

One pivotal component of the "large is good" argument relates to the economies of scope and scale from which large firms can benefit. They can leverage these economies to take a dominant market-share position, squeeze out inefficiencies, and streamline costs to yield greater profitability. The larger a firm becomes, however, the greater the challenge to operate it efficiently. The question then becomes whether senior management can corral middle management to push through its corporate goals effectively. In an Op-Ed piece in *The New York Times,* David C. McCourt, Chairman of RCN Corporation, made a forceful argument that big is not necessarily better:

> The most profound emotion running through the executive offices of the nation's former telecommunications monopolies these days must be terror. The clearest example of this terror is the steady stream of megamerger announcements, which somehow feel incomplete without mentioning the word billions. . . . If 100 years of business history has taught us anything, it is that Godzilla can't marry King Kong and live happily ever after. For all the headlines these deals generate, the megamergers are unlikely to create great companies. . . . Federal Express was not born of a megamerger. Neither was Microsoft, Wal-Mart or Sony. Companies that become industry leaders are marked by strong values, clear goals and better ideas. . . . Moving from a destroyer to a battleship doesn't just give you a bigger boat, it gives you a bigger boat to turn around. . . . Railroads didn't become airlines. Western Union didn't become AT&T. Horse-drawn buggy makers didn't go on to lead the automotive revolution. These kinds of shifts don't happen, because companies that dominate a certain technology find it close to impossible to cannibalize their own business to embrace the changes being imposed on them. . . . Unfortunately, the eyes of the terrified often see bigger as better, even when the reality dictates the opposite.[4]

Although McCourt clearly disagrees with the "bigger is better" argument, the "large company, good investment" mantra has been partly based on the superb stock performance of large companies in the latter half of the 1990s and much of the 1980s. In *The Synergy Trap,*[5] Professor Mark Sirower of New York University assails the large-is-good argument by identifying the significant number of hurdles that firms face as they attempt to become megaplayers. Ultimately, many companies overpay to grow. As a result, even if a combination makes good business sense, management still faces tremendous difficulties in generating profitable results. The hurdles for these newly formed entities are significantly higher because of the premium they typically pay to achieve so-called synergies.

Further, as noted in *The Synergy Trap,* the value combinations tend to be overestimated. As a result, the odds are typically against a firm's being successful by simply acquiring size or buying other companies to become a larger force. If a deal is properly structured and priced, it is possible for even a poor business combination to yield successful results. The "large company, good investment" argument is especially appealing because one can easily follow the commentary of corporate change and can point anecdotally to the success of blue-chip stocks as evidence. But can the largest companies dominate the equity performance race over time, simply because they are "good" companies? Small-cap cycles in the past have not depended on large-cap stocks' being inferior companies. The outperformance of small companies from 1991 to 1993 did not imply that large blue-chip firms such as Merck, Coca-Cola, and Microsoft were inferior businesses. Yet the secondary market handily outpaced its blue-chip brethren.

A critical but faulty assumption behind this argument is that great companies are synonymous with great stocks. This logic is flawed because the value of a firm is based on expectations of growth. If the market has already priced-in a rosy outlook for a company, what incremental or ongoing evidence drives existing valuations higher? If all good news has already been taken into account in the price of a company, the equity component of this company quite possibly is a questionable investment.

If large companies were to dominate the equity markets because they are fundamentally "better" than small companies, size rotations would cease to exist. As discussed in Chapter 1, however, size rotations from small to large caps, and vice versa, have been a strong force in the market and are likely to continue. Simply put, a small-cap bull market is as likely to occur as a rally among blue chips.

If the logic underlying the "large companies are good companies" philosophy were sound, it is reasonable that the largest companies would likely dominate the market. However, if the largest of the large companies continued to grow in market capitalization, the corresponding valuations of these firms would likely become excessive. At some point, expectations would reach unsustainable levels and cause such favorite stocks to subsequently correct.

Whether or not market participants agree with the "large is good" hypothesis, the dedicated large-cap investor is likely to migrate to attractively valued large companies under extreme valuation conditions, such as when one segment of large companies is severely overvalued in comparison to the remainder of the market. As long as investors are opportunistic in their trading and buy companies for reasonable value, they are likely to trade out of overvalued companies, causing a rotation within their large-cap universe. This "value" rotation within the large-cap market implies a marginal shift toward smaller firms as well as cheaper stocks. The evidence clearly indicates that if a size swing occurs in the large-cap market, a concurrent rotation also occurs across the entire market. Stock prices in major markets such as the United States, the United Kingdom, Japan, and Australia, for example, consistently suggest that swings in size occurring in the large-cap market also ripple through to the secondary market. This rotation refers to the Domino Principle which is discussed in Chapter 1.

Figure 6.3 illustrates how rotations within the large-cap market appear to trace rotations in smaller capitalized firms. If large firms were simply better companies and therefore merited the exclusive attention of the equity market, the startling correlation between intra-small-cap and intra-large-cap cycles would not exist.

Liquidity of Large Stocks

The illiquidity of smaller stocks is the most credible argument against the existence of a small-cap premium and perhaps the one most difficult to dismiss. As discussed in Chapter 2, small companies can be extremely illiquid. Active small-cap investments are therefore unlikely to replicate simple benchmark or historical results. Because the large-cap benchmarks are several times more liquid, however, active large-cap investment results are more likely to be representative of the historical data.

This argument suggests that the historical paper-based benchmark performance results, as seen in popular indices such as the Russell 2000 or the Merrill Lynch Small Cap Composite, are perhaps several hundred basis points above actual investment returns. Remember that benchmarks such as the Russell 2000 and S&P 500 are simply paper-based calculations of stock prices as they are quoted on the exchange. The price of

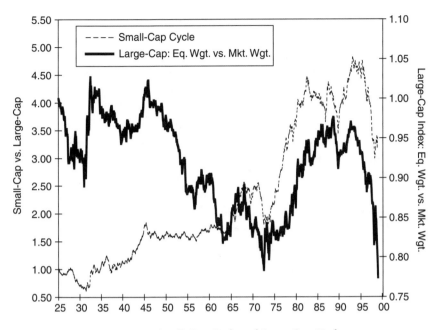

Figure 6.3   Small-Cap Cycle and Large-Cap Market

a stock can differ significantly, depending on how liquid the stock is, as investors attempt to make a purchase. The mathematics is sound; if the average bid–ask spread of a small firm is 2 percent, then one needs to subtract at least 2 percent from the annualized rate of return for small stocks.

The effect of liquidity on the small-cap premium is more complex, however. For instance, index funds based on the small-cap market can achieve performance results, adjusted for costs, not unlike those of their popular paper-based benchmarks. If trading costs were as prohibitive as is suggested by the simple trading-cost argument above, an index tracking effort would be unlikely to match its intended target. Nonetheless, as research has shown, passively managed small-cap funds can nicely match their paper-based benchmarks. In a study of the U.S. small-stock market, Rex A. Sinquefield noted that the success of passive funds was primarily dependent on the managers' attention to trading costs.[6] With respect to the United Kingdom small-cap market, Elroy Dimson and Paul March, professors of finance at London Business School, found that the Hoare Govett Small Cap Index Investment Trust, an index fund that tracks that market, exhibited a tracking error of 1.46 percent and underperformed its benchmark by only an annualized 0.37 percent per annum in 1993–98.[7]

Based on the illiquidity of small stocks, active small-cap managers might be expected to lag their benchmark results relative to their large-cap counterparts. Yet a look at active performance data suggests otherwise. Compared to large-cap investors, a greater proportion of active small-cap managers tend to outperform their benchmarks. Table 6.2 compares the proportion of small-cap funds that outperformed their benchmark to the proportion of large-cap active funds over most of the 1990s.

It is notable that the higher transaction costs associated with small stocks do not appear to significantly hinder the abilities of small-cap active investors. Ultimately, this edge exhibited by small-cap managers is compelling evidence that smaller stocks are less efficiently priced, and, as a result, allow investors to generate above-average results.

Even though trading costs can represent significant barriers to entry, it is possible that simple bid–ask spreads appear wider than the actual realized trading results of small-cap funds. One explanation is that when a fund is fully invested, the fund manager can keep turnover to a manageable level. Investors need not completely overhaul their portfolios on a regular basis. Because trades would occur only on an opportunistic basis, the portfolio would never be completely sold to make room for new candidates.

Table 6.2 Active Small-Cap vs. Large-Cap Fund Manager Results

	Large-Cap		Small-Cap		Percent of Total	
	S&P 500 Rank*	Total Number of Funds	Russell 2000 Rank*	Total Number of Funds	Large-Cap	Small-Cap
1990	154	385	123	140	40%	88%
1991	229	422	77	151	54	51
1992	254	468	45	177	54	25
1993	328	561	89	212	58	42
1994	153	649	150	267	24	56
1995	107	727	181	328	15	55
1996	211	804	256	392	26	65
1997	106	804	179	392	13	46
1998	198	804	227	392	25	58
1999	371	900	214	389	41	55

* Ranked within all funds for that year.
Example: 153 funds outperformed the S&P 500 in 1990.

Another factor may be that liquidity is a primary issue in the trading function. Trading is always a competitive factor in the investment business, but it is especially relevant in small-cap management. A small-cap investor can benefit significantly from trading a stock that is racing to new highs. The relative illiquidity of the stock can cause its price to jump more dramatically than the price of a more liquid stock, which allows its holders to benefit from the positioning of the trade. As a result, a small-cap stock that is trading higher is likely to benefit its holders more than a large-cap idea that has similarly appreciated. A skillful small-cap trader might thus have more of a competitive advantage than a similarly talented large-cap trader.

Finally, it is also possible that the simple bid–ask spreads might represent an overly difficult trading environment faced by investment advisers. After all, the small-cap market contains many dormant investments that have collapsed. In those situations, trading may be nonexistent, and the spreads measured may be unusually wide. Simple aggregate small-cap statistics reflect not only the hundreds of stocks that normally trade but also the shares that have fallen off the beaten path.

Greater Scale of Large Stocks

The incredible bull market that began in the late 1990s has forced the money management industry to rethink its core business strategy. When millions of dollars are entering the equity market on a daily basis, managers need to be concerned about efficiently getting those funds invested. The profitability of an asset management firm lies in the fees generated from the assets it manages. If a firm can more easily grow assets through large-cap products, which can rapidly increase the assets being managed, the firm is likely to hold a more favorable disposition toward large-cap investing.

This creates a difficult setting for investment managers who need to grow assets but are investing in more thinly traded securities. Creating a position in blue chips can be accomplished in a seamless manner, but attempting to place, into smaller stocks, one-tenth of the assets one might place in a large-cap fund can be a challenging task. Proponents of the big-cap bias are quick to claim that the need to invest sizable dollars continues to force the average money management firm to migrate toward large-cap products. This argument creates, in some respects, a new motivation to invest in large stocks.

The liquidity benefits of large stocks are compelling; they suggest that swings in favor of large caps can become accentuated. However, investors ultimately care more about performance than efficiency. Investment managers are rewarded or penalized according to the degree to which their performance varies from the rest of the pack or from the benchmark. This variation typically is measured in mere basis points. Unless investors change the basis of distinguishing a good manager from a marginal performer, the liquidity and scale factors of large stocks are unlikely to create a new paradigm of investing.

STATIC DRIVERS AND THE SMALL-CAP PREMIUM

The topic of whether small caps generate a return premium is hotly debated. Many efficient market proponents consider the size premium to be an anomaly. In an efficient market, they say, excess returns should be arbitraged and would thereby dissipate; that is, investors would bid-up the value of smaller firms, expecting higher returns. At some point, the overvalued small-cap market would only generate returns similar to those of blue-chip firms.

By viewing the small-cap excess return as an anomaly, one is forced to accept as predominant a low-risk, high-return scenario in which large stocks dominate the market. Yet the basic rules for pricing risk suggest otherwise. Examples of risk pricing are legion. For instance, the insurance industry has priced risk for very lengthy periods—a healthier, younger person pays a radically lower premium than an unhealthy, older counterpart. The fixed-income market appears to price risk similarly, with the result that riskier assets tend to offer significantly higher yields. Junk bonds have been so priced as far back as the 1800s.

As noted at the beginning of this chapter, a simple and elegant argument in favor of a small-cap premium is that small caps, by nature, exhibit a premium because they entail greater risk. A size premium exists because smaller stocks typically are neglected assets. The information-rich world of large-cap stocks is less likely to generate excess returns from neglected assets.

In many ways, it is somewhat intuitive that secondary stocks should outperform large stocks. Small caps need to compensate investors for taking on the burdens of added risk. If smaller firms are indeed riskier ventures, their long-term rates of return need to be superior to those of safer blue-chip businesses or they will not attract investors and capital. If the returns of smaller companies were truly inferior, a capital market for small companies might not exist.

A similar argument can be applied to private equity or securities sold to a limited number of investors. By definition, the returns of a private stake cannot be easily measured. Yet private investment vehicles have always existed. If the realized returns were not commensurate with the level of risk taking, these forms of financing would also dissipate or vanish.

This risk-based argument is posed by Jonathan Berk, of the University of British Columbia, who argues that small-cap returns must be superior to those of large caps because of the higher discount rates embedded in smaller companies.

> The present value of a stream of cashflows depends on the cashflows' riskiness. All else being equal, riskier cashflows require higher discount rates, and so have lower present values than less risky cashflows. Since the market value of a company is the discounted expected value of its future cashflows, if the market value of two companies with the same expected cashflows is compared, the riskier company will have a lower market value than the less risky company. Thus market value is a measure of the firm's discount rate or riskiness. [8]

If the market value of an asset is the sum of the future discounted cash flow, then the higher discount rate or expected return of a small firm forces its current market value to fall well below that of a large-cap firm. Remember that the discount rate of a stock is made up of a risk-free rate—or the cost of money for a riskless asset (Treasury bills are often seen as a riskless asset)—and a risk premium. One can easily argue that the risk premium of a smaller firm is higher than that of a blue-chip franchise. See Chapter 2 for a discussion of risk characteristics of small caps.

The Law of Large Numbers

Just as trees do not grow to the sky, companies cannot grow infinitely. The law of large numbers also comes into play—namely, incremental growth is more difficult to sustain as a firm gets larger. In other words, for companies that have a large base of revenues/earnings, growth is a more difficult task. Because the market rewards growth rates and not simply large numbers, large-cap firms can be at a disadvantage. For instance, a company with $100 in revenues needs to make an incremental $10 in revenues to grow 10 percent. A smaller firm with only $10 in revenues needs only $1 of incremental revenues to grow 10 percent.

The same dilemma exists in the financial markets. What are the chances that a $200 billion company will continue to appreciate at or above market returns? Conversely, a small company valued at 1/100 the size of a large-cap firm can more easily appreciate at or above market returns. Put another way, how much money is needed to drive up General Electric or Microsoft an incremental 10 percent? That figure, without a doubt, is substantially higher than the amount needed for a $100 million company to jump 10 percent. The growth of a company, in terms of revenues or earnings, is also a function of size. How fast can a firm with $100 in revenue grow, versus a company with $1,000 in revenue? The reality is: The larger the base, the more difficult it is to sustain growth without creative financial engineering. This becomes more challenging when a company is generating a few hundred million dollars in earnings. Ultimately, the rate of change matters most in measuring the success of a business or of investment results. Share prices move on incremental changes in information. No matter how large a firm, if management warns that it is likely to fall short of earnings expectations, share prices are likely to tumble. As a company gets bigger and bigger, it becomes more and more tied to the overall growth of the economy. Unless the underlying economy is expected to offer significantly faster growth than in past periods, a gargantuan firm ultimately struggles to continue its growth.

Oxford Health Plans, a health care provider, represents a good example of a successful small-cap firm that faced greater difficulties as it became larger. The company fared quite well as a rapidly growing small provider of health care services. However, the stellar results began to dissipate as Oxford broadened, and later struggled to retain, its fast growing profile. The stock quickly fell from grace and became a small cap again.

Investing in smaller companies offers great investment leverage. A $100,000 stake in a $50 million firm is far greater than a $100,000 stake in General Electric or any other $200 billion company. As a small firm expands its cash flow and its franchise, shareholders are likely to realize benefits commensurate with their ownership stake. In short, having a greater stake in a firm with fewer limitations on growth implies a higher long-term rate of return.

Small Caps as Neglected Asset Class

Another argument for why the small-cap premium exists is: Small caps are a neglected asset class. The average small-cap firm causes much less fanfare than its large-cap counterparts. Figure 6.4 shows Wall Street's coverage of microcap, small-cap, midcap, and large-cap firms. The smaller companies within an equity market tend to be neglected. Although 19 analysts, on average, cover the large-cap segment, only six cover small stocks.

By nature, neglected assets tend to outperform well-followed companies. Companies for which there is a wealth of information tend to carry valuations that are commensurate with their potential. On the other hand, underfollowed firms may have tremendous potential but trade at a significant discount. As investors become more aware of the opportunities that lie in such undiscovered gems, the movement toward these ideas can create dramatic jumps in valuation and share prices.

The underfollowed nature of small caps may lead to inefficient pricing. If an asset is priced less than efficiently, investors may find it easier to capture excess returns from such an investment. Comparable opportunities are far fewer among companies that are under the severe scrutiny of the investment public. The large-cap market has become an efficiently

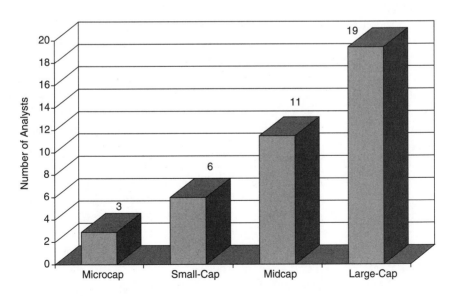

Figure 6.4 Analyst Coverage by Size

priced asset class. As a result, excess returns are tougher to find in the megacap investment space.

DYNAMIC DRIVERS

If the deck is as stacked in favor of the secondary market as the evidence in this chapter suggests, why do small caps experience cycles in which they severely underperform? Underlying the small-cap results are dramatic swings in stellar asset returns between the megacaps and the underlings of the secondary market. For small caps, the periods of underperformance can be as long lasting as a bull-market run. This can cause the staunchest long-term investors to question a buy-and-hold small-cap strategy.

For investors, the dilemma in recognizing and capitalizing on the size premium, or the outperformance of smaller stocks relative to large stocks, concerns the tendency of small caps to experience sharp cycles or swings in which they fall in and out of favor with the market. Not surprisingly, the mere existence of a size premium comes under attack in periods when small stocks severely underperform. For instance, Bill Fouse's article, "The 'Small Stock' Hoax," referred to earlier in this chapter, was written in 1989, approximately six years into a significant large-cap cycle. The argument that the 1970s, an era of superior small-cap performance, should be removed from performance analyses surfaced during the large-cap rally in the latter half of the 1990s.

The size premium debate exists largely because the periods in which small stocks underperform large stocks can be lengthy. The level of underperformance can be drastic; this was the case in May 1998, when small stocks collapsed 29.4 percent in four months. It is quite easy to question small-cap historical returns when the markets appear to dictate a preference toward large, safe companies. The natural temptation is to believe that "things are different this time."

Ultimately, the shift in preference to and from smaller firms relates to the basic fabric of risk taking. If investors are willing to assume more risk, lower market-cap stocks are likely to outperform large caps. Conversely, when market conditions arouse fear and concern in the minds of investors, the tendency to grab for safety overwhelms the outlook for the long term. The need to secure assets causes investors to rotate out of the riskier asset classes, such as small stocks.

Although the propensity of investors for risk taking is an open-ended and complex topic, it is still useful to examine the willingness of investors to assume more (or less) risk. This analysis can yield fruitful insights into the twists and turns of size preferences. A number of broad factors influence investor preferences for risk taking. As discussed in Chapter 1, these factors fall into three broad categories: (1) cyclical growth, (2) relative cost of capital, and (3) profitability. Combined, these factors appear to account for significant swings in the appetite for risk taking and in market rotations between large and small stocks.

Patterns of cyclical growth provide a useful gauge of investors' ability to assume greater risks. A healthier, more robust economic backdrop tends to drive the interest of investors toward riskier companies. Broad macroeconomic indicators—such as industrial production, the gross domestic product, the strength of the local currency, and inflation measures—tend to reflect major swings in cyclical growth and are used to measure the overall health of the economy.

The cost of capital also plays a significant role in investors' ability to assume greater risks. Large companies generally have easier access to capital, which leads to lower capital costs and many more choices in financing. As financing conditions improve overall, however, secondary firms tend to outperform large companies. In general, a lower *relative* cost-of-capital spread generally favors smaller firms.

Profitability also drives the demand for risky assets. Risk taking is less likely to occur if businesses are finding it difficult to turn a profit. As profitability increases, investors gain confidence and venture into firms that have risky business models. Earnings growth, forecasted earnings growth, and the pricing power of companies are among the measures that investors can use to assess profitability and decipher the size puzzle.

Economic and Cyclical Growth

If a worker is worried about keeping his or her job in tough times, he or she is unlikely to pursue risky investments. Likewise, an increased risk-taking posture for investors can only thrive when the economic backdrop is stable or robust. Thus, it is useful to assess the overall economic backdrop as a means of determining the market's appetite for risk. Most measures of economic change, such as industrial production and gross domestic product, generally support the argument that small caps outperform large caps when economic activity increases.

Smaller firms also appear to experience more leverage from the economy, partly because, to thrive, smaller marginal firms require a healthy economic backdrop. A look at the sector exposures of smaller firms indicates that small caps have greater economic sensitivity than large caps. (See Chapter 2 for a description of the sector bias in the smaller companies' universe.) Because, compared to large caps, a greater component of the small-cap market is more dependent on economic growth, the shares of small caps are more likely to react to the vagaries of the economic cycle.

Industrial Production

Small stocks generally tend to fare better when the economy undergoes a period of rapid growth. For example, during the most recent small-cap bull market, which began in 1991, small stocks significantly outperformed large stocks as the economy reaccelerated in the early 1990s. Economic growth is tied to industrial production. As industrial production expands, economic growth becomes more abundant. Industrial production is measured by an index that comprises 250 subcomponents from the manufacturing, mining, and utilities sectors of the economy. This measure is especially sensitive to consumer durables and business equipment. In the early 1990s, when small-cap stocks surged for an extended period, such a surge had not occurred since the early 1980s. It was no coincidence that industrial production had slowed through most of that decade.

The relationship between cyclical growth and small-cap cycles was sharply illustrated during the Great Depression. The calamitous breakdown of the economy caused the value of smaller stocks to collapse by one-third in the 1930s. Figure 6.5 relates the small-cap cycles to the change in industrial production over the long term.

A hard look at the industrial production data indicates that size rotations correspond with industrial production measures. Although the relationship has not been constant over the 70-plus years since 1926, the correlation appears to be significant and positive. There have been periods in which economic growth has appeared strong, yet a small-cap bull market has failed to materialize.

Figure 6.6 relates, in a more direct fashion, the performance of small-cap cycles to changes in industrial production. The annual change in industrial production is delineated with respect to small- and large-cap returns. The returns are grouped in periods of weak, moderating, and robust measures of industrial production between 1926 and Dec. 1999.

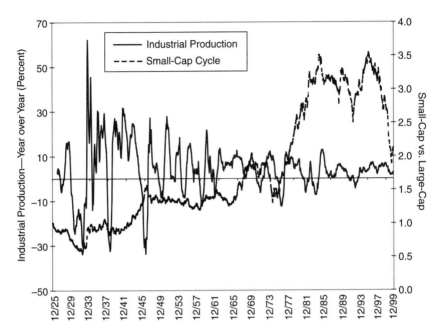

Figure 6.5 Small-Cap Cycle and Industrial Production

Both small- and large-cap returns are normalized for their respective average returns. This allows one to determine whether the change in a factor such as industrial production has an impact above and beyond the normal or average returns. As Figure 6.6 depicts, small-cap stocks have outperformed large stocks by approximately 6 percent during periods in which industrial production exhibited growth of more than 10 percent.

There appears to be only a marginal bias favoring smaller stocks when industrial production slows below 5 percent on a yearly comparison. In addition, small stocks begin to lag large caps (and the average small-cap returns) as industrial production turns negative. Statistical tests, such as a z-score, suggest that small-cap returns are especially compelling when extreme changes occur in industrial production data.[9]

Interestingly, subsequent one-year results between small and large stocks are especially robust; they favor smaller firms as industrial production bottoms out and small caps experience a rebound. This rebound or snapback effect exists partly because smaller stocks can be especially punished in times of sudden and weak economic growth. At such times,

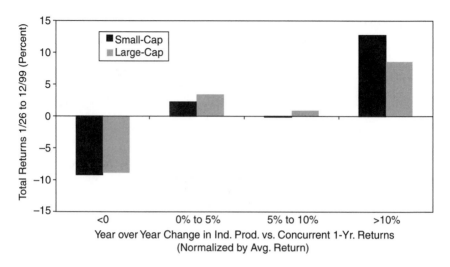

Figure 6.6   Small-Cap Cycle and Change in Industrial
Production—1926 to 1999

small-cap share prices are likely to tumble well below some fair and intrinsic value. As it becomes clear that production has bottomed, however,
the severely battered secondary markets are likely to rebound feverishly.
On average, small stocks outperform large stocks by roughly 3 percent
one year after industrial production declines.

A more current snapshot, showing comparisons from 1975 onward
between industrial production and small-cap performance, appears less
robust than might be expected from long-term data. This may be partly
due to the changing orientation of the economy, which has become considerably more service-based, compared to past decades. Service-based
companies are less economically sensitive than companies in the basic
industrial sector, for instance. Furthermore, recent economic cycles have
been much more muted than cycles of the 1930s, 1940s, and 1950s.
Nonetheless, the general connection between size and risk taking suggests that the positive relationship between cyclical rebounds generally
favors smaller firms.

Strength of Currency

The strength of the local currency also plays a role in size. If the local
currency is strong or appreciating, the economy is more likely to be

healthy, with low inflation. A strong currency, such as the dollar, suggests strong domestic growth relative to other economies. As the dollar appreciates, smaller firms tend to outpace large firms. Figure 6.7 relates the small-cap cycle to the trends in the U.S. dollar.

The existing disparity in foreign exposure between smaller and large stocks further contributes to this effect. Companies with significant international investments are more likely to struggle in the face of a strengthening local currency. A stronger dollar makes U.S.-based goods more expensive and less desirable in other countries. As a result, the demand for these goods slows. A stronger dollar creates additional difficulties as companies attempt to translate foreign revenues back to a stronger domestic currency. Because large firms in the United States are much more dependent on foreign sales and exports than their small-cap peers, a stronger dollar is more likely to adversely affect larger companies that have greater foreign exposure. (See Figure 5.6 for an illustration of the foreign exposure of firms of various sizes.)

Compared to large stocks, changes in the dollar have a less direct impact on the average small stock. The indirect effects on small stocks are

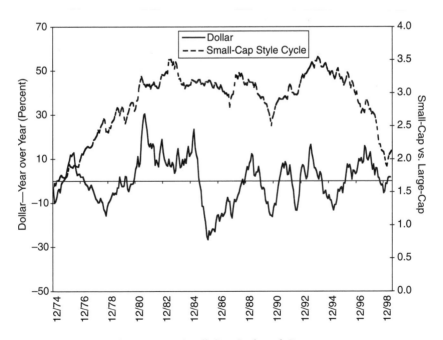

Figure 6.7 Small-Cap Cycle and Currency

significant, however. If the dollar falls, companies that have global operations should become more profitable because of their international exposure. These companies tend to fall into the large-cap category. As a result, in a falling-dollar scenario, large stocks should be rewarded in the marketplace relative to small stocks. Conversely, a rising dollar is more likely to place added pressures on firms with international operations. In this instance, the dollar leverage that previously favored large global companies now penalizes the same companies.

The secular, or long-term, fall in the dollar may have significantly contributed to the outperformance of large shares during most of the 1980s. As the U.S. dollar weakened, the products of domestic firms became cheaper abroad, and competing products from nations with rising currencies became more expensive. In addition, currency translation effects caused international business profits to appear even more robust as companies translated these revenues from a stronger currency into a weaker dollar.

A close look at the currency and size relationship suggests that a stronger dollar marginally favors smaller stocks. Figure 6.8 depicts the changes in the dollar with respect to small- and large-cap returns from January 1973 to December 1999. Smaller stocks outperformed in periods of a strong dollar. Again, these returns are normalized for the long-run average of small-cap returns. For instance, the small-cap index outperforms by one percent in a period when the dollar is strengthening between 0 and 5 percent. Curiously, the most significant statistics appear when the currency is especially weak. A terribly weak dollar appears to be detrimental to the smaller stock bias and is most statistically significant.

Inflation

Rising prices appear to support a bias toward smaller stocks. More significantly, collapsing prices, as measured by consumer prices or producer prices, spell disaster for small stocks. Typically, until the 1990s, a deflationary environment coincided with a very weak economy. In such instances, secondary stocks significantly lagged the big caps. The Great Depression of the 1930s represented an extreme example of this occurrence. As noted previously, in troubled times, blue chips are likely to lose less ground than their small-cap counterparts. Conversely, an environment with increasing prices generally reflects a more robust economic backdrop. An increase in business activity generally spurs more risk taking and therefore a preference for smaller stocks.

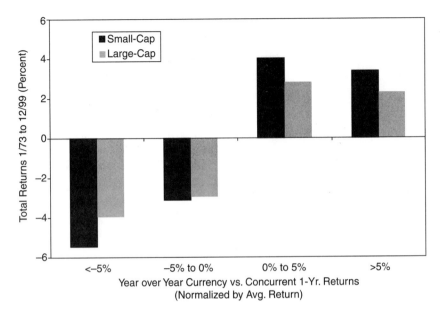

Figure 6.8 Small-Cap Cycle and Change in Dollar, 1973–99

The latter half of the 1990s might be considered a deflationary period. During this time, small stocks severely lagged large shares as the competition among firms intensified and, as a result, limited the ability of firms to raise prices on goods provided or services rendered.

A look at the consumer price index (CPI), which measures changes in the prices of goods and services to the typical consumer, supports the contention that there is a relationship between prices and small-cap cycles. (See Figure 6.9.) Similar support is provided by other measures of inflation, such as changes in the producer price index (PPI) of finished goods.

Inflation, an unwelcome by-product of faster economic growth, tends to hurt all parties. As prices begin to escalate, the benefits of excess growth may outweigh the costs associated with inflation for smaller companies. A comparison between small and large stocks over noninflationary and inflationary periods seems to support the general thesis that inflation, though generally harmful to equity returns, appears to be marginally more favorable for smaller stocks. Figure 6.10 suggests that smaller stocks, when adjusted for long-term results, have outperformed large stocks by roughly 3 percent during periods in which inflation ranged above 5 percent.

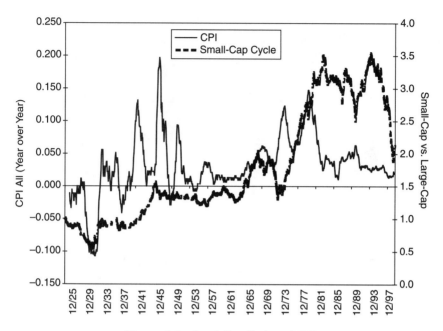

Figure 6.9   Small-Cap Cycle and CPI

The statistical tests suggest that inflation has a positive effect on the stock prices of small companies; nonetheless, it is doubtful that inflation truly helps smaller companies. If inflation is high, variables such as demand and the cost of inputs become difficult to forecast. In this environment, a marginal small-cap company is unlikely to have an edge against its megacap counterpart.

Although smaller stocks outperformed large caps in the 1970s, when prices were rapidly rising, this may have been a chance occurrence. The oil embargoes of the 1970s not only spurred inflation and inflationary expectations, they also increased investors' fondness for energy stocks. The small-cap market contained numerous oil and gas producers during that era. As a result, the share prices of these tiny energy companies were revitalized, which significantly boosted the small-company averages. In addition, the latter half of the 1970s exhibited a strong pickup in capital goods spending, which pushed technology stocks to the forefront of investor interest. Because many technology stocks in those years were primarily small caps, the bull market for technology investing in the late 1970s largely propelled the small-cap market.

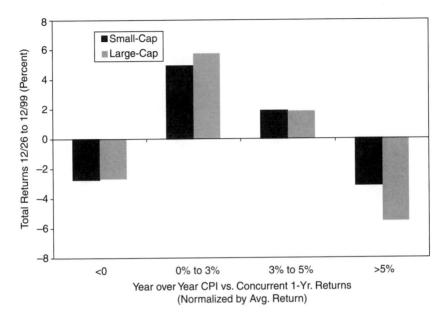

Figure 6.10 Small-Cap Cycle and Change in CPI: 1926–99

Cost of Capital and Access to Capital

The cost of capital and access to capital may be more relevant to the cyclical nature of small caps than most other economic measures. Although capital is essential to all firms, it is critical to younger emerging growth companies and also to struggling firms with a tainted track record.

Access to capital and, therefore, the cost of capital tend to be especially prohibitive for higher-risk firms. The average cost of Merck's liabilities, for example, is considerably lower than the amount a smaller-cap firm could raise in the debt markets. A sample of subprime lenders' rates, or the price of capital that smaller companies might face if they attempted to raise capital through borrowing, indicates that rates are at least 2 to 3 percentage points higher than those applicable to large caps. Although a difference of 2 to 3 percent does not sound dramatic, consider these levels in the context of a home mortgage. A difference of 3 percent in mortgage rates could put a significant portion of the housing market out of reach for the average home buyer.

The capital–size relationship is significant because smaller companies can generate growth only if they have access to cheap capital. If General Electric (GE) were offered as much capital as it needed, at no cost, for a 30-year period, could it grow faster than its current rate? Maybe; maybe not. By contrast, a smaller company with access to cheap capital can produce staggering growth. Take, for instance, a family-run restaurant. If this enterprise could raise cheap capital, it could create a set of franchises and post remarkable gains almost immediately. The quality of earnings and the sustainability of such a stream might be questionable; nonetheless, the access to capital would allow a small franchise to post extraordinary growth.

This may be the critical difference between small and large organizations. Small companies may find it easier for capital to generate bottom-line or earnings growth. A megacap, blue-chip franchise such as GE is most likely to be dominant in all the markets it deems relevant. Simply allowing it access to cheap capital is not necessarily enough to bolster growth. Smaller companies, on the other hand, are markedly handicapped by capital constraints and therefore rely on the ebb and flow of capital access.

A variety of capital measures, such as cost-of-capital spreads and fixed-income measures, offer insights into the twists and turns of smaller stocks. Although the cost of money should be higher for a small cap than, say, the borrowing cost for GE, the spreads can swing from being marginal to monumental in difficult periods. In short, an investor may find it very useful to focus on the changes in the relative cost of capital when identifying and grappling with market swings from small caps to large.

Fixed-income measures include relative debt costs, as measured by: the difference between bank lending rates and Treasury yields; the difference between higher-quality and lower-quality bond yields, known as quality spreads; and the slope of the yield curve, which refers to bond yields of a variety of maturities. Longer-maturity bonds generally (but not always) carry higher bond yields than short-term instruments. As a result, the yield curve tends to be upward sloping. These instruments/relationships provide useful signals on the trade-off between high- and low-risk opportunities.

Larger firms have a more dynamic and considerably lower cost of financing, because of their access to (1) a broader range of financial services, (2) instruments such as commercial paper and corporate bonds, and (3) more favorable terms of lending. These advantages make it more likely that large firms, rather than their smaller counterparts, will enjoy the benefits of a secular fall in bond yields. In fact, the precipitous drop of Treasuries in the late 1990s has had little or no impact on the debt-financing costs of smaller capitalization firms. In 1997, the prime rate, which is the lending rate for corporations, actually rose as Treasury prices rallied and bond yields fell.

A comparison between the 10-year Treasury bond and the prime rate reveals the financing dilemma that smaller firms must face. Even though the prime rate is no longer as relevant as it once was, it represents the cost of funding for preferred corporate customers and it reflects the less-than-dynamic change in capital costs for smaller, riskier firms. Given that smaller firms have lending terms that are even less favorable than the prime rate, the real spread relationship for smaller firms tends to be more adversely skewed. Figure 6.11(a) represents the yield to maturity for the prime rate and 10-year Treasury bonds. Besides suggesting that positive moves in bond yields are not necessarily reflected in the prime rate, this chart shows that a shift in the prime rate points to a more stepwise adjustment in financing costs for firms that borrow from banks. Because the prime rate is set by banks and not priced by the markets, the changes tend to move in strict 25-bp or 50-bp adjustments.

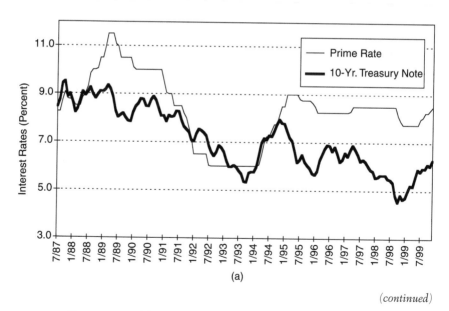

(a)

(continued)

Figure 6.11   (a) Cost of Capital: Treasury Notes vs. Prime Rate;
(b) United States: Cost of Capital Spread

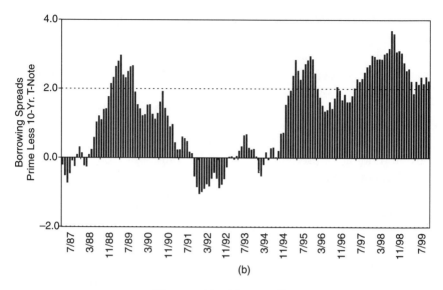

Figure 6.11   (Continued)

The last resurgence of the small-cap cycle began in 1990, after the Fed had eased interest rates several times and the spread had significantly narrowed. During the economic downturn of the late 1980s, spreads were almost 3 percent wide, or 300 basis points. As of July 1989, they subsided, and they reached roughly 100 basis points by September 1990. Only then did the small-cap market begin to recover. Concerns over the financial crisis in Southeast Asia and the Long Term Capital Management calamity in 1998 forced spreads to even wider levels than the peak level in July 1989. By October 1998, spreads reached an astounding width of 316 basis points.

Both the cost of capital and access to capital are linked to the economic backdrop in the size puzzle. If the economic backdrop becomes tenuous, banks may become even more conservative and primarily bid for higher-quality loans. This causes the real spread between the prime rate and the 10-year Treasury note to widen further.

The relative performance of small caps is inversely related to the spread between prime rates and Treasuries—in this instance, 10-year Treasury bonds. The wider the cost-of-capital spread, the more smaller stocks are likely to lag large companies. As support for this statement, consider bond yields and lending rates dating back to the early 1950s. A narrow spread between prime and Treasury suggests that smaller stocks are likely to outperform large stocks by roughly 2 to 3 percent. If the spread is significant (e.g., greater than 20 percent), smaller stocks are likely to lose roughly 3 percent against the large-cap sector, as depicted in Figure 6.12.

Cost of Capital and Federal Reserve Policy

Smaller stocks tend to exhibit more economic sensitivity than large-cap stocks. A slowing economic backdrop creates a difficult environment for marginal or small-cap firms. However, as the Fed eases its monetary policy, and investors once again regain their appetite for risk taking, some of those concerns may become more muted.

A stimulative, easy-money policy may cause the more economically sensitive components of the small-cap market to bottom out and subsequently to bounce. Another effect of easing policy is that the cost of capital begins to improve for marginal firms. Because access to capital is always prohibitive for smaller firms, the investment community is likely to warmly receive any action to tilt the scale toward more favorable borrowing costs.

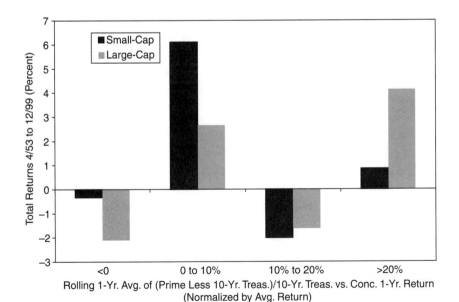

Figure 6.12 Small-Cap Cycle and Cost of Capital: 1953–99

Conversely, smaller firms are at a disadvantage when the Fed attempts to slow economic growth by taking a restrictive stance. Investors can easily forecast that economic growth is likely to slow as a result of the Fed's action. A rate hike tends to have an almost immediate impact on share prices. As another effect of a rate hike, the relative cost of capital immediately begins to rise. The prime rate typically increases in sync with Fed funds. Subprime lenders to small companies are likely to take a similar cue and act accordingly.

Relationship of Yield Curve to Size

The slope of the yield curve also can be used as a measure for pricing risk and, therefore, the market's appetite for riskier small-cap firms. For example, a steep yield curve indicates that (1) more competition for capital exists and therefore (2) greater risks are being taken by investors in the market. This occurs because inflationary expectations rise as economic growth picks up. As a result, the yields on longer-maturity bonds (e.g., the 10-year Treasury) begin to increase more so than shorter-term or

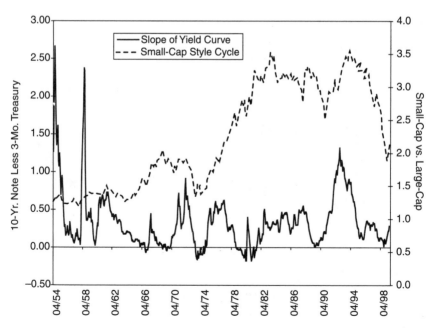

Figure 6.13   Small-Cap Cycle and 10-Year Note Less Three-Month Treasury Bills

3-month Treasury bills. In a steep yield curve, the yield on the longer end (or longer maturity) is at a 40 percent premium or higher, compared to the short end (or short maturity). At such times, small stocks have outperformed large caps by roughly 3 percent per annum. A flat or nearly flat yield curve (0 to 20 percent spread) implies that small stocks marginally lag large stocks. Figure 6.13 places the small-cap cycle in the context of the slope of the yield curve dating back to 1954. Figure 6.14 represents the relative performance of small- and large-cap stocks given ranges of yield curve data—namely, the difference between the 10-year note and the 3-month Treasury bills.

A flat or marginally inclined yield curve tends to favor larger stocks, although test results appear to offer only marginal insights into the market's size preferences in this situation. As noted by economists Arturo Estrella and Frederic Mishkin,[10] a flat yield curve generally implies fairly sluggish growth. According to their research results, a flat or nearly inverted yield curve, which occurs when short-term Treasury rates are higher than longer-term bond yields, suggests roughly a one-in-three chance that the U.S. economy will fall into a recession during the subsequent year. If the curve becomes completely inverted, a recession scenario is even more likely.

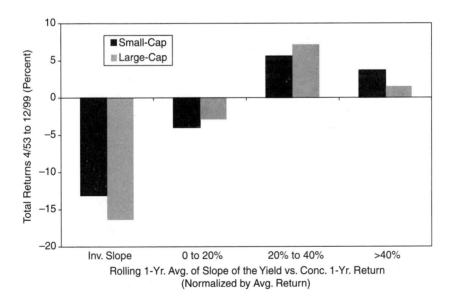

Figure 6.14 Small-Cap Cycle and Slope of the Yield Curve: 1953–99

When overall economic growth becomes sluggish, investors are more likely to focus on fairly conservative investments, which can be detrimental to the small-cap market. When the yield curve rises, as it did in 1990, the small-cap cycle rebounds. As the Fed began to ease its policy, the slope actually inverted before it turned positive. After almost a year of eased Fed policy, the yield curve steepened to roughly 130 basis points.

By contrast, the slope of the yield curve was effectively flat over the latter half of the 1990s, a period in which small stocks decidedly lagged large stocks.

Curiously, an inverted yield curve, although uncommon, seems to provide a favorable backdrop for secondary stocks. When the yield curve is inverted, small stocks are likely to outpace the market by a margin of 3 percent per annum. At first glance, this might appear counterintuitive. Bear in mind, however, that the market is a discounting mechanism. To some extent, an inverted yield curve suggests that growth is likely to subsequently rebound. The collapse in growth will slow by itself or the Fed will engineer a resurgence by aggressively cutting interest rates. In the latter case, the yield curve is likely to steepen in quick fashion and forecast a rebound in economic activity, which bodes well for small caps.

Quality Spreads

Unlike the cost-of-capital spreads discussed earlier, quality spreads are dynamic; they represent the difference between higher- and lower-quality bond yields. Bonds are priced regularly in the market and offer a pulse on the price of risk and, accordingly, on market preferences for small and large caps. In short, quality spreads and the small-cap cycle appear to have an inverse relationship; that is, as quality spreads in bond yields narrow, smaller stocks tend to outperform large stocks. Figure 6.15 represents the small-cap cycle, or the relative performance of small to large stocks, versus the spread of higher- and lower-quality corporate bonds dating back to 1926.

The yield spread between higher- and lower-quality bonds can be a fair measure of economic health and financial confidence. Generally, an increase in the spreads can mean one of the following: lower-quality bond yields are rising, the yield on higher-quality bonds is falling, or both extremes are diverging. Such an increase can represent a flight to quality, whereupon large and more liquid names are likely to outperform issues that are smaller and more thinly traded. Conversely, as adverse business

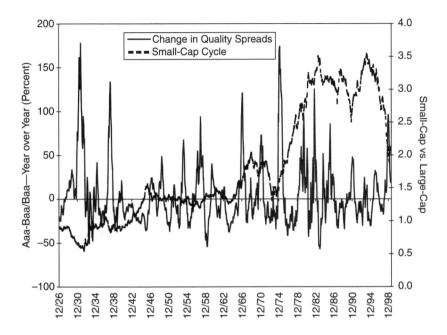

Figure 6.15 Small-Cap Cycle and Quality Spreads

conditions improve or bottom out, riskier ventures are viewed more favorably. This reduces the risk premium that riskier bonds can carry over those of higher quality. As a result, the quality spread narrows. With a more confident backdrop, investors are likely to tolerate more risk, and secondary stocks may therefore be regarded more favorably.

As noted previously, an inverse relationship generally exists between quality spreads and the small-cap cycle. The relationship is negative or inverse and statistically significant. The findings from 1926 to 1999, however, appear much more significant than those of the post-World War II era—perhaps partly due to the expanded scope of the small-cap market in the past 30 years. A greater percentage of aggressive growth stocks has entered the small-cap universe. These companies are unlikely or unable to participate in the bond market. As a result, variation in quality spreads may no longer provide the robust signals that were once supplied for small-cap investors.

In addition, the quality spreads of the 1990s may be less comparable to those of earlier years. Banks have been able to repackage lower-quality bonds in sizable tranches. This has created a more liquid junk-bond market. As a result, quality spreads (and therefore the relationship to small and large stocks) have remained quite muted through most the 1990s.

Profitability

If companies are struggling to turn a profit, marginal businesses are more likely to get squeezed in the process. Even though some small caps are considered to be exceptional franchises, they reflect a less stable business segment overall. As a result, given an economic backdrop that prevents companies from growing earnings in less-than-stable fashion, the investment community will postpone a foray into a riskier asset class such as small stocks.

Rising corporate profits are generally beneficial for small stocks. Figure 6.16 illustrates the relationship between the small-cap cycle and annual changes in corporate profits. Reported earnings growth, on an

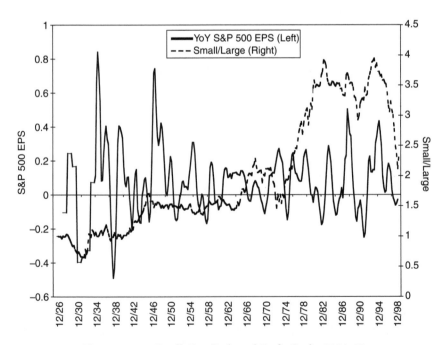

Figure 6.16   Small-Cap Cycle and Profit Cycle: 1926–99

annual basis, is positively related to the small-cap cycle. However, the long-term relationship does not appear to be robust. It is possible that the earnings relationship does not have a linear relationship to the small-cap cycle. As earnings accelerate, excessive growth might cause investors to become more concerned about measures to slow and contain growth. These concerns might cause the investors to exit the secondary market because they anticipate that robust profits growth is an unwelcome signal to inflation hawks.

Curiously, the positive relationship between growth in corporate profits and the small-cap cycle has been more robust over more recent periods, compared to the entire data sequence dating from the mid-1920s. In fact, a look at a market earnings forecast appears especially related to the small-cap cycle since the mid-1980s. Figure 6.17 represents the consensus forecast in market earnings for the S&P 500 profit cycle versus the small-cap cycle.

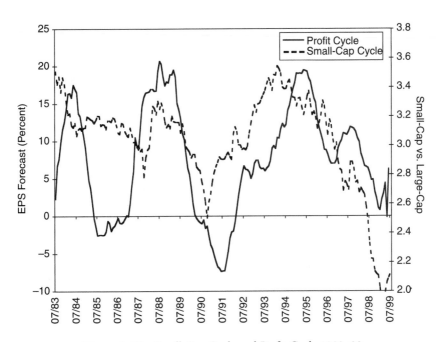

Figure 6.17   Small-Cap Cycle and Profit Cycle 1983–99

Pricing Power

One of the most important components of corporate profitability is pricing power. This pertains to whether companies have the flexibility to improve profitability by pushing costs to the end user. The pricing environment has become especially relevant since the 1990s; companies have been forced to pare away at expenses to bolster earnings. One could argue that the disinflationary process that began in the early 1980s has become more extreme, or even deflationary, since the latter half of the 1990s.

The difference between the prices of goods produced and goods consumed offers some insight into corporate profitability. A simple approach to measuring profits and evaluating their effect on the small-cap cycle is to consider the spread or ratio between producer prices and consumer prices. If producer prices are marginally rising in the face of stable consumer prices, it could reasonably be argued that companies are struggling on a relative basis. Similarly, if producer prices are falling faster than consumer prices, companies are more able to maintain or even increase profitability. A difficult pricing environment is likely to breed a more cautious

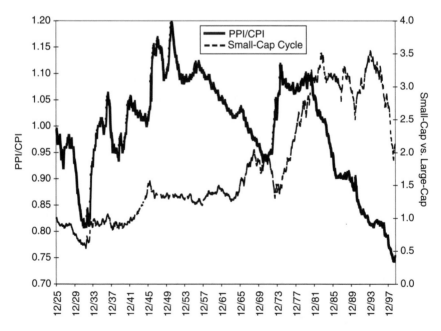

Figure 6.18   Small-Cap Cycle and PPI/CPI 1925–97

and cutthroat environment, which is hardly ideal for a fledgling investment. Figures 6.18 and 6.19 present the small-cap cycle in light of the pricing relationship of the Producer Price Index (PPI) to the Consumer Price Index (CPI).

A great deal of the motivation behind technology spending has come from corporations squeezed to enhance earnings in an environment that does not tolerate pricing flexibility. During the 1970s, for example, companies directed resources toward investment in technology, to gain better control over the bottom line. Inflation (not deflation, as was the case in the 1990s) motivated companies to invest in technology in the 1970s, when input costs were rapidly rising, and were wreaking havoc on corporate profitability. Similarly, a deflationary environment causes firms to have little or no ability to pass costs on to the end user. This again places pressures on profitability. Both extremes—inflationary and deflationary environments—force companies to dramatically increase their investments in technology.

Statistical analysis of PPI and CPI prices shows a positive and significant relationship between pricing power and the small-cap cycle. The results are significant both in long- and short-term tests. Figure 6.19 presents the one-year performance of small- and large-cap stocks with

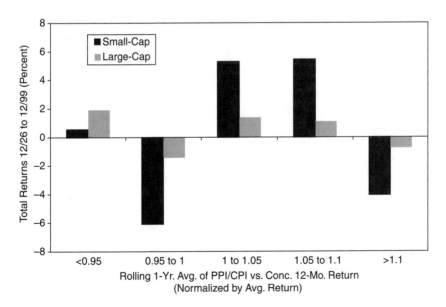

Figure 6.19 Small-Cap Cycle and PPI/CPI: 1926–99

respect to the expansion and contraction of the PPI/CPI ratio. An increasing ratio means an improved pricing environment; a decline in the ratio points to a difficult corporate pricing environment. Smaller stocks outperform large stocks by about 4 percent when the ratio is above 1.05 or when the PPI is above the CPI by 5 percent or greater; they lag severely by 5 percent when the PPI is at a discount to the CPI by 5 percent.

Relative Earnings Growth

One basic investing tenet is that prices appreciate to reflect the earning power of a company. If smaller firms are growing faster than larger firms, small stocks should outperform. Conversely, if large companies have superior profit results, they should outperform the small companies.

This principle can be difficult to verify, however, because long-term earnings for smaller firms cannot be easily determined. More specifically, many smaller firms are generally in the red. Biotechnology and Internet-related companies offer striking examples of companies for which profitability represents a distant hope.

As with cyclical firms, the aggregate earnings of small companies can be fleeting. One practical measure of company profitability by size, however, is median growth in earnings. Median statistics at least provide a picture of aggregate earnings.

This simple earnings measure offers a confounding perspective on size rotations, because smaller stocks outearned their larger peers during the 1990s. Figure 6.20 relates the median level of earnings growth for small- and large-capitalization stocks. If earnings did indeed drive share prices, though, small-cap stocks should have significantly outperformed large caps during the 1990s. Stock prices have not followed this type of profit pattern, however. There are several possible explanations for these surprising results. The measurement of small-stock earnings may be suspect because the benchmarks for smaller stocks are typically reshuffled annually to keep track of smaller firms. As companies migrate in and out, measurements of fundamental data, such as earnings, can become difficult to trace from one period to the next. It is also possible that longer-term earnings data for smaller stocks, if recovered, might refute the shorter-term results. If the numbers do indeed properly portray realized small-company earnings growth, then the earnings argument is perhaps missing a critical element—the market's need for certainty. It is not just a matter of how fast a company grows, but how consistent are its profits.

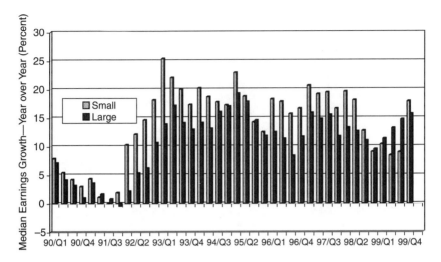

Figure 6.20 Earnings Growth: Small Cap vs. Large Cap

As the market becomes more concerned about the overall economy, its need for certainty increases. Hence, the absolute growth of earnings is perhaps only part of investors' criteria for buying a stock. Another criterion may be consistency of growth. The preference for small or large stocks may be more tied to a demand for the predictability of future earnings than to absolute growth.

This bias toward small caps in earnings growth is also reflected in earnings expectations or forecasts. The growth in earnings of smaller firms is always expected to be greater than that of large companies. Figure 6.21 summarizes the three- to five-year expected growth rate of small- and large-cap firms. Note that the expectations for smaller companies are well above those of large firms. Not surprisingly, smaller companies tend to offer aggressive growth. Over time, the data suggest a constant relationship; the expected growth rates for smaller firms are always greater than those of large-capitalization companies. The above-average growth that the small-cap universe exhibits is not surprising when one considers that small firms growing at a superfast rate are aggregated in this universe. If investors only paid attention to promises of growth, however, performance cycles would not exist. Small stocks would dominate the investment spectrum.

Ultimately, the need for certainty is dynamic. Depending on an investor's appetite for risk taking, the market can retreat toward bulletproof

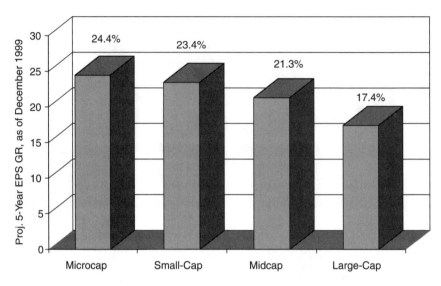

Figure 6.21   Projected Five-Year Earnings Growth Rates

earnings, which primarily reward megacap, blue-chip franchises. At other times, the fastest growing companies become dominant. For example, a biotech rally illustrates the market's demand for expected earnings rather than delivered earnings. Although growth may be an important factor in investing, market participants must also struggle with such complex issues as sea changes in the market's appetite for risk. The preference for more (or less) certainty determines swings in size preference, and a need for consistency is inversely related to small-stock holdings.

Figure 6.22a and b sets forth the uncertainty of small-cap earnings in the context of large-cap earnings. At times, delivered earnings can be more relevant than promised earnings growth. Note that small stocks exhibit a broader range of earnings results, which is considered typical of the small-cap market. A more confident economic setting allows investors to pin their hopes on longer-term expectations. In more troubled times, investors are forced to shorten their investment horizons and rein in their aggressive "bets."

How Valuations Offer Insight into Market Direction

Valuation of securities, as it affects the market pricing mechanism, also offers unique insights on size preferences. Share prices are based more

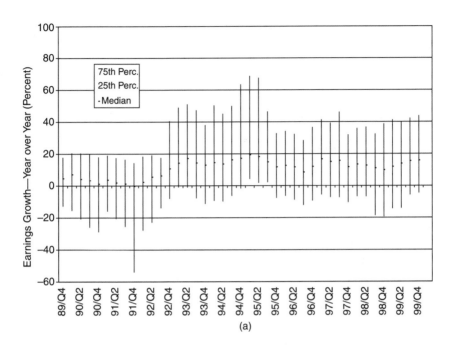

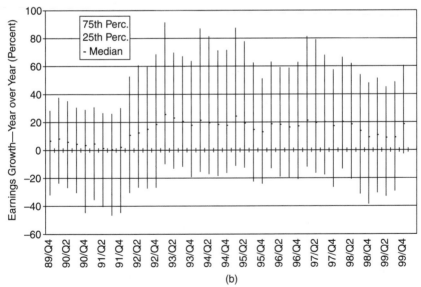

Figure 6.22 Range in Earnings Growth Rates: (a) Large Caps; (b) Small Caps

on expectations than on realized business results. For example, consider the economic landscape during the recession of the early 1990s. The economy did not emerge from the recession until 1991. Thus, small stocks might not have been expected to enter a bull market until 1992. Yet smaller stocks bottomed in November 1990 and then began to rise. The rebound occurred almost a full year before the economic signals turned favorable. Even though the U.S. economy was still technically in a recession, investors bucked the trend and began aggressively acquiring these broken fledglings.

Market participants may pay a severe price for safety in uncertain times. As the perceived need for safety dissipates, however, the preferred safe haven of the past period can become the overvalued albatross of the next. At some point in an investment cycle, trends can become exaggerated. A darling of the investment community is sometimes priced at a level on which growth expectations become fantastic. Similarly, investors can price risk, or a lack of risk, to extremes.

Small-cap investors do not initiate performance cycles; instead, the cycles ebb and flow because of the propensity of large-cap investors to migrate down to or out of small-cap issues. One way to measure this propensity is to assess the relative attractiveness of large-cap investments.

Investors do not simply look to purchase assets because they are believed to be safe. Expected returns motivate investors to flock toward certain assets. Valuations can provide discriminating evidence of potential returns that entice large-cap investors to shun their traditional confines. As market participants bid up an attractive asset, valuations become more extreme and the expected returns of the asset deteriorate. Relative valuations—simply, whether small caps are cheap or dear—are one way to assess the expected returns of large versus smaller companies.

Although valuations may be poor at offering market timing strategy or tactical solutions for size rotations, they can offer valuable long-term strategic insight into the size debate. If small-cap stocks are relatively cheap, the "security" premium that is traditionally awarded to such stocks might dissipate. In other words, depressed relative valuations among smaller stocks suggest that the risk premium typically associated with smaller firms might be too high. This extreme condition could cause small firms to outperform large firms as the market reassesses the small-cap risk premium.

Valuation comparisons can take many forms, such as relative price to earnings, cash flow, and revenues. These relevant measures give investors the ability to determine the relative merits of the small- or large-cap market. Ultimately, valuations help to determine whether all the good that is believed to be associated with an asset class has been fully discounted in current share prices.

Figure 6.23 presents the relative valuations of small and large stocks. The value relationship suggests that small stocks can trade anywhere from a 30 percent discount to a 60 percent premium to large stocks. This measure uses a price-to-cash-flow ratio to value both groups. At the peak small-cap cycle of the early 1980s, small stocks reached a 60 percent premium to the large-cap market before the cycle turned. The ensuing large-cap bull market that rolled through from 1983 to 1990 caused the valuation premium to shrink to 10 percent. In 1994 (the most recent peak in the small-cap cycle), small stocks nearly reached a 50 percent premium before they turned. The subsequent bear market for small stocks caused valuation multiples to collapse to a low of almost a 30 percent discount to the megacap sector by late 1998. Subsequent signals suggest that the large-cap market has been priced with extremely bullish expectations.

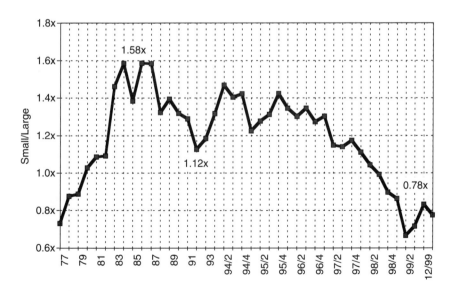

Figure 6.23   Relative Price to Cash Flow 1977–99

Increase in Corporate Activity as a Signal of Undervalued Assets

One of the difficult aspects of using relative valuation as a timing mechanism is that a cheap asset can become even cheaper. The more difficult question in assessing small-cap valuation levels is whether the asset is cheap on an absolute level. Because of the changing dynamics in economic growth and inflationary expectations, however, simple valuation metrics are difficult to use on an absolute basis. For example, in a world where inflation is at 2 percent annually, a stock trading at ten times current-year earnings is much cheaper than a stock trading at the identical multiple with inflation hovering around 5 percent. The corporate sector can offer supporting indicators of whether an asset class such as small stocks has been undervalued. If the small-cap market is really cheap, a wave of corporate activity should occur. Whether defined by mergers and acquisitions or by leveraged buyouts, corporate activity typically tends to increase as equity multiples fall. If the equity of a firm is cheap compared to the value of its tangible assets, an acquisition or buyout might be in order. If the entire small-cap market is compellingly cheap, a wave of corporate buying is likely to ensue to arbitrage this disparity in values.

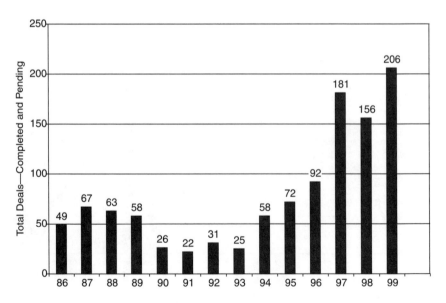

Figure 6.24 Mergers and Acquisitions Activity Among Smaller Stocks 1986–99 (Market Capitalization between $200 Million and $1 Billion)

Figure 6.24 represents the total number of small-cap deals for companies with market capitalization between $200 million and $1 billion in 1986–99. The number of mergers and acquisitions jumped to 206 deals through the end of 1999, from an average of 162 deals annually in the 1990s. Figure 6.25 represents the tally of the mergers and acquisitions activity among stocks under $200 million in market capitalization.

Ultimately, the pickup in corporate activity is driven by disparate equity valuations between small- and large-cap firms. This activity suggests that the corporate sector, not the equity investor, places a floor on the secondary market. Another significant implication of acquisition data is that equity valuations become more relevant when corporate acquisitions increase. Any asset can remain cheap for long periods; yet, if there is a buyer, prices are unlikely to remain depressed for long. Similarly, if the corporate sector finds the smaller capitalized firms cheap and begins taking them over, it is likely that equity investors will take notice.

Benjamin Graham and David L. Dodd, founders of the modern discipline of security analysis, have argued that undervalued assets eventually

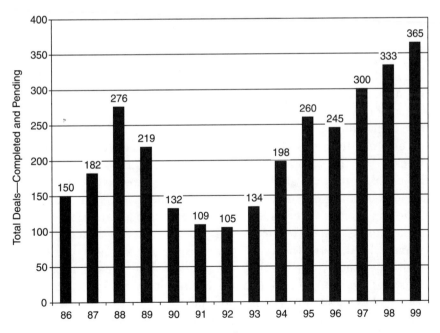

Figure 6.25   Mergers and Acquisitions Activity Among Smaller Stocks 1986–99
(Market Capitalization below $200 Million)

appreciate to a fair value in the marketplace. The corporate sector has the luxury of investing in companies and waiting for them to develop into profitable franchises. Professional equity investors, by contrast, are graded on a month-by-month basis. Thus, activity among small-cap firms offers Graham-and-Dodd-style signals from the corporate sector that can help investors hone valuation readings of these secondary stocks.

THE UNCERTAINTY PARADOX

Efficient market theorists, who believe that markets are perfectly efficient and that odd pricing behaviors cannot exist, have a very difficult time accepting the notion of a size premium. If the market is efficient, as they claim, how can such an obvious free lunch exist? The concept of a size premium places the efficient market advocates in a difficult bind. They can either accept the size premium and, in their eyes, relinquish the efficient market theory or refute the size premium and retain their position.

However, it is possible for a size premium to coexist within an efficient market frame. Riskier assets must offer higher expected returns compared with safer assets. As a result, the size premium does not represent a free lunch. Instead, it reflects the excess risk one takes when investing in smaller companies.

Another interesting phenomenon that supports the size premium is the inability for investors to predict periods of outperformance. Is it possible that the cyclical nature of the size effect prevents market anomalies from being arbitraged?

One can term this efficiency argument as the uncertainty paradox. According to this argument, the less predictable an odd pricing effect, the less likely it can be arbitraged. Simply finding an odd pricing effect or a market anomaly does not presuppose that the markets are inefficient. Unless an agent can consistently arbitrage some odd pricing effect, it is unlikely to dissipate. The small-cap premium is a great example of such an anomaly. Although the long-run returns suggest a positive bias toward small caps, there have been severe rotations from small- to large-cap firms over the history of the market. As a result, investors have been unable to arbitrage such an anomaly profitably.

If investors had taken the size premium calculations through the early 1980s and invested in smaller companies to capture the size premium, they would have significantly lost out on the incredible rebound of large-cap stocks and, more important, lost money attempting to arbitrage the size premium. Simply put, the size premium during the 1980s turned very negative, quite contrary to what might have been expected from the long-term returns.

According to the theory of rational expectations, as set forth by economists Thomas Sargent and Neil Wallace,[11] market participants learn from errors in estimating. This theory supports the old adage: "Fool me once, shame on you; fool me twice, shame on me." Because of the rational expectations argument, it is difficult to expect that market participants will truly miss out on an arbitrage opportunity or free lunch for too long. If the size premium were truly predictable and remained consistent, only then could one claim that the market is less than efficient. Hence, investors need to take the uncertainty of some pricing effects into account before market anomalies are valiantly proclaimed as evidence that markets are less than efficient.

The uncertainty paradox removes the perceived deadlock that efficient market theorists face when they consider the size effect. Ironically, the less certain the rotations in size, the more likely that such an effect remains. This theory might also account for other odd pricing behaviors, such as the unusually strong stock returns at the start of the year (the January Effect), which tend to be particularly prevalent among smaller stocks. (See Chapter 10 for a detailed discussion of this phenomenon.)

SEVEN

Market Timing Small Stocks

SHORT-TERM INDICATORS AND STRATEGIC FACTORS COMPARED

AN INVESTOR who was fortunate enough to have exited the small-cap market in May 1998 would have avoided a whopping 29.4 percent loss in the subsequent four months, during which the small-cap market collapsed. By properly timing an exit, the investor could have easily outperformed the majority of professional small-cap investors in that period. This chapter examines four specific risk indicators that allow investors to avoid short-term pitfalls in the small-cap market—volatility, earnings expectations, insider trading, and the issuance market. It explores their impact on the small-cap market and the performance signals they convey.

These indicators are in contrast to the strategic factors that influence investment behavior, discussed in Chapter 6. Such factors as cyclical growth and cost of capital have a longer term focus. For example, because the relationship between industrial production and smaller stocks tends to unfold over a lengthy period, it can be considered a strategic factor. Although broad measures such as industrial production may either climb or fall, they are unlikely to offer a strong signal today, turn weak the next day, and then rebound. Investing in education stocks based on changing demographic trends would be a long-term strategy. Similarly, overweighting energy stocks in a portfolio based on a bearish outlook for oil supply can be considered a strategic shift. Valuation-based decisions, in general, tend to be strategic, with a long-term orientation, because they focus on performance measures that change little from day to day.

But changes in long-term expectations are not the only event that can affect an investor's holdings. A sudden shift in the outlook for corporate profits or a jump in recent market volatility can have remarkable repercussions. In such situations, certain tactical or market timing indicators can help to guide decision making in the short term. For example, small-cap markets tend to come under pressure when volatility is high. By gauging volatility levels, investors can get a sense of how the small-cap market will fare. Analysis of other factors—earnings expectations, the trading habits of corporate insiders, and trends in initial public offerings—also provides useful market signals.

Volatility and Small-Cap Performance

Changes in the market environment influence the willingness of investors to take on or avoid risky investments. As discussed in Chapter 6, such factors as cyclical growth, the cost of capital, exogenous geopolitical events, and even valuations cause investors to become hypersensitive to risky assets. Changes in these factors can significantly affect the outlook of investors on the market and lead to an increase in market volatility. As concerns about the market heighten, investors demand more certainty. This relationship is evident in many different ways. Investors gravitate toward companies with more stable business lines. Investors rapidly bid up shares of Coke and Merck in 1998, for example, when investors feared the worst regarding the Southeast Asian economic collapse. They are more skittish about higher expectation stocks and emerging markets, and are more likely to shy away from less liquid assets. In such circumstances, smaller stocks lose their luster in the face of increased uncertainty. Under extreme conditions, Treasury bills or cash win out. Thus, changes in market volatility can have significant repercussions on a small-cap portfolio.

Figure 7.1 illustrates the inverse relationship between small-cap stocks and market volatility. A benign market produces a more constructive setting for small stocks, but secondary shares lose significant ground to large caps as market swings increase. According to the performance results, small stocks have approximately a 10 percent edge over large as volatility falls by 30 percent. Importantly, results appear to be especially muted for both large and small stocks as market volatility increases. The dramatic events overseas in 1998 well illustrate how an increasingly volatile market can wreak havoc on smaller, less liquid, assets. Market volatility, using the S&P 500 as the market proxy, jumped from 14 percent in May 1998 to 26 percent by year-end 1998. Small stocks went through a severe correction during 1998—at the darkest point small U.S. stocks lost nearly 30 percent of their value from April to October of that year.

An awareness of the size/volatility relationship arms investors with insight into possible sources of dislocations in the small-cap market. More volatility yields an increased demand for liquidity and therefore stocks with higher market capitalization. In a hypersensitive market,

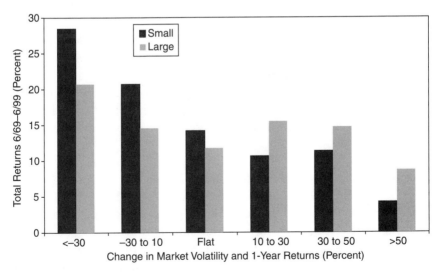

Figure 7.1 Small and Large Stocks vs. Market Volatility

investors no longer search for compelling investments. Instead, stocks that "won't go down with the rest of the market" are in demand. Stocks that appear to have easy exit strategies become a hot commodity. Small firms are greatly penalized as the liquidity premium in the market rises. Conversely, a more tranquil environment allows market participants to ignore short-term concerns and reach for more aggressive strategies. The latter is perhaps the ideal environment for a lower market capitalization bias.

Volatility in a Polarized Market

Forecasting market volatility is perhaps as elusive as forecasting the market. The numerous volatility forecasting tools that have been developed generally center on statistical modifications of realized volatility in the hope that it will offer insight into future volatility. This approach may not significantly differ from attempting to forecast future share prices based on past price trends.

A simple, more fundamental approach to modeling volatility is to determine if the market fancies a broad spectrum of companies or a handful of select companies. A market is said to be polarized when a favored few firms establish a peak level valuation relative to the rest of the market. A polarized market tends to forecast increased market volatility, reflecting a lack of breadth in the market. Such narrow leadership is undesirable because a market with only a few successful stocks is a prime setting for risk.

The collapse of a favorite name in a polarized setting is all it takes to create a shock to the system. The weakness of a single favorite stock is likely to cause sharper ripples across the market if the leadership is narrow rather than broad. When a handful of stocks leads the market, the market participants have obviously placed a great deal of confidence in these favorite ideas. This situation gives rise to greater volatility.

Momentum Stocks Defined

The hazard of a polarized market is vividly portrayed in the systemic relationship between market swings and momentum stocks, defined as stocks exhibiting sharp price gains with respect to the market. As seen in Figure 7.2, the direction of the market is accentuated in the momentum portfolio of stocks. The nature of momentum stocks, in this case price

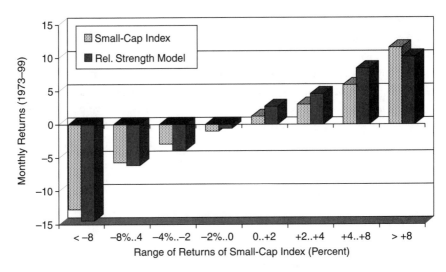

Figure 7.2 Relative Strength Model—Dispersion of Returns

momentum, makes them a particularly intriguing market segment, typically favored in a bullish environment. In this instance, momentum is defined as simply the best performing stocks over a 12-month period. Notice that momentum stocks outperform the market by 2 to 3 percent as the small-cap market is racing to new highs (for example, from a flat market to 8 percent price increases in a month). Conversely, momentum strategies lag the market as the small-cap market turns down with momentum stocks losing an additional 1 to 3 percent as the small-cap market sours.

With each market uptick, momentum shares are bid up to stratospheric valuations and thus become riskier. If the market then comes under pressure, such high valuation favorites can easily become an investment albatross. One can even argue that the market weakens because the high fliers have lost their luster, whether temporarily or over the long term. Taken as a basket, these stocks make up a high beta portfolio. By definition, increased market risks dictate more exaggerated momentum results.

Because momentum stocks, taken as a basket, reflect an exaggerated version of the overall market, carefully gauging the valuations of the stocks preferred in the market may be more useful than relying on overall market valuations. For example, a popular and common market risk metric is price-to-earnings ratio. An overall level of price-to-earnings ratios that is too high would argue for a lower risk posture. After all, if companies are selling well above some normal valuation band, the market may have priced in too generous a multiple for earnings growth. The flaw in this logic is that the market's multiple, or aggregate market valuation, is based on myriad stocks. Even though a more expensive market might appear riskier, the market's overall path need not take a negative direction. A market rotation into cheaper stocks could offset the risks of an inherently expensive market without a cataclysmic turn in the market averages.

Fine-Tuning Volatility Forecasts

Investors can fine-tune their forecasts of market volatility and small-cap risks by analyzing the valuation levels of momentum stocks. The relevant question is not whether the market is expensive, but whether the market's preferred stocks are too expensive. By applying a simple valuation model, such as price-to-earnings, to the stocks with the best trends, investors can gain more insight into swings in market volatility than by simply observing the valuation trends of the overall market. Valuation models are discussed in more detail in Chapter 6.

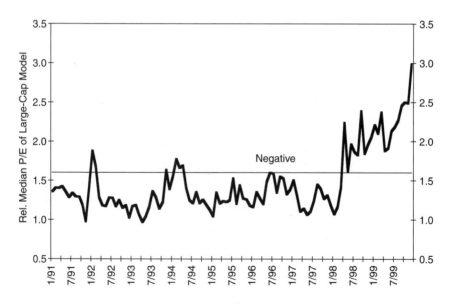

Figure 7.3 Valuation of Momentum Stocks

Stocks that are favored in the market are by nature unlikely to trade at a discount. Figure 7.3 represents the simple price-to-earnings ratio of the best performing stocks, on a one-year basis, versus the price-to-earnings level of the market. As the chart shows, momentum stocks trade at a premium to the market. A slight valuation premium of the relative strength candidates, or best performing stocks, to the market is unlikely to signal caution. However, stocks registering valuation readings at significant premium levels to the rest of the market are an indicator of increased volatility. As the valuation premium of fast-running stocks increases, expected volatility increases.

Figure 7.4 depicts the relationship between market polarization and increased volatility. The figure dissects market volatility levels based on ranges of the valuation premiums of momentum stocks. Although volatility levels appear unaffected, market volatility can range between 13 and 14 percent when the valuation ratio levels are below 1.4; and when relative valuation multiples reach high levels, say above 1.6, market volatility can jump to levels north of 17 percent.

Momentum stocks, by definition, have a devoted investor base. As the valuation disparity becomes more extreme, the divergence becomes sharper between the best performers and the remainder of the market. A sudden disappointment in the performance of only one of these smart picks can have a significant psychological effect on a broad base of investors.

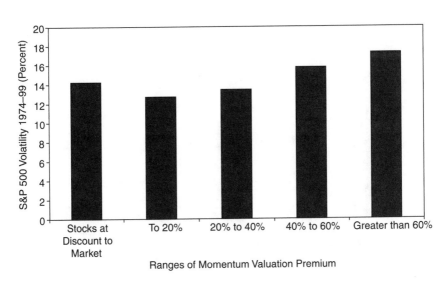

Figure 7.4 Momentum Valuation Levels and Market Volatility

Furthermore, such an effect can occur even if the change in environment is not particularly dramatic or significant. For example, assume the market is polarized because of a bull market in technology spending. If the market receives news about possible sluggish sales in the upcoming quarter for a single favored firm, a knee-jerk response is likely that will send adverse ripples across many related industries. The rash reaction occurs because market participants have grown to expect only good news from these firms.

A dramatic run-up in share prices can be telling, as a sign not only that business has posted successful profits trends, but also that market participants have become increasingly dependent on the company producing better and better results. Hence, only a slight miss can cause the stock to appear to have fallen from grace. The market's shaken confidence can lead to a jittery investment climate, which results in an increased risk premium for all stocks. The most illiquid shares are likely to be severely penalized as the liquidity premium widens. Figure 7.5 illustrates small-cap performance at varying degrees of market polarization. Note that the small-cap index has an expected return of a paltry 2 percent the subsequent 12 months when the valuation levels of momentum stocks are high, or above 1.6.

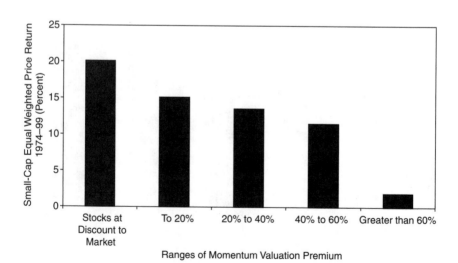

Figure 7.5 Momentum Valuation vs. Subsequent 1-Year Small-Cap Return

As these results imply, small-cap investors not only are bulls on smaller stocks, they also are bullish on lower volatility. These results effectively argue that small-cap investors are likely to find a more receptive environment when overall market volatility levels are benign. Simply put, secondary stocks appear to wither in a highly volatile market environment. Higher volatility indicates that investor emphasis should be more on large caps, with their greater liquidity.

EARNINGS SIGNALS

A basic tenet of investing is that earnings drive returns—that is, stock returns follow those companies that can grow their earnings the fastest. Because share prices discount expectations, investing in a company with increased forecasts is likely to be fruitful. In fact, as discussed in Chapter 8 on modeling stock returns, companies with the most significant earnings estimate increases produce the best returns. These excess returns are generally more difficult to find, however, as one tackles large stocks, the most efficient segment of the equity market. Nonetheless, increases in earnings estimates are generally beneficial for share prices. If earnings changes are positive for specific stocks, then it can be logically deduced that a significant increase in the number of smaller companies with improved earnings might also yield an improved outlook for the small-cap market.

But an empirical look at changes in the estimates of the total small-cap market indicates that the market has an inverse response to changes in positive earnings estimates. Figure 7.6 represents the proportion of smaller stocks with earnings estimate changes over time versus the entire small-cap universe. Intuitively, one would expect that improved profits forecasts, or the proportion of earnings estimates increases, would lead to higher share prices, whereas a noticeable decrease in earnings expectations would hint at downward price pressures. Yet tests on subsequent price gains of the small-cap market, alongside given changes in the earnings expectations of the small-cap market, indicate that the small-cap market tends to act inversely to aggregate changes in earnings estimates.

Based on data from 1985 to July 1999, a test of changes in the proportion of 3-month earnings estimate changes, or aggregate earnings changes, versus the subsequent 6-month small-cap return indicates a negative relationship that is statistically significant.[1]

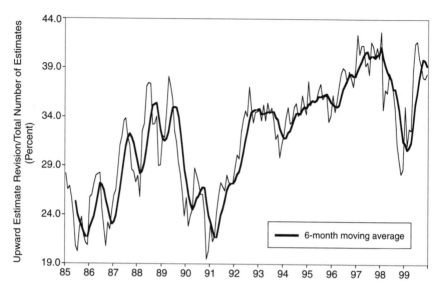

Figure 7.6   Small-Cap Earnings Forecast—Increase in Forecast
as a Proportion of Small-Cap Market

The perverse behavior of the small-cap market in response to changes in profits forecasts may largely be driven by the efficiency of the market. Although subtle changes in company estimates might allow astute small-cap investors to benefit from changes in earnings estimates for specific stocks, a groundswell of altered profits forecasts is likely to grab the attention of even the most distant observer. As analysts revise estimates, the market is likely to take notice and quickly act. When share estimates rise significantly, some investors who hold shares with an improved outlook promptly notice this effect and correctly turn more bullish. A more bullish stance is likely to cause a corresponding reaction (or overreaction) in share prices.

By the time most investors have stumbled on this phenomenon, however, it is usually too late to profit from such changes. Furthermore, the observed results suggest that a strong enough signal may cause a contrary effect. It is also reasonable to find a subsequent rebound in share prices if estimates have been cut to the bone. With such radically lowered estimates, share prices have likely followed suit. Because share prices tend to overreact, stock prices may have plummeted beyond a reasonable level that would reflect the fundamental changes in earnings expectations. As a result, any news that the company has stabilized may result in a bounce for its share price.

The contrary results of such tests are a constant reminder that the market is full of participants who scrutinize all sorts of changes in the marketplace. In the broadest sense, investors seeking to profit from inefficiencies are also agents of an efficient market. The less than intuitive results of earnings estimates and their impact on share prices affirm that the markets are more efficient than most believe.

TRADING INSIGHTS FROM INSIDER TRANSACTIONS

Successful investing is a game not of luck but of skill. In this contest, the winners are those who can best harvest kernels of knowledge from the vast pool of seemingly relevant information. Because of improvements in data technologies and more stringent securities regulatory requirements, investors are privy to a host of "new" kinds of investment data. Although some add to the noise of securities pricing, others are valuable in separating investment opportunities from investment fodder.

Investors have long attempted to ferret investment insights from a company's financial statements, management decisions, stated goals and strategies, corporate alignments, and other sources. They have expanded the search for a unique element or angle to an investment thesis that their research habits have become obsessive. It is not uncommon to find standing room only for the annual board meeting of Berkshire Hathaway, the company run by renowned investor, Warren Buffett. The town of Omaha, Nebraska, is overrun by thousands of investors who flock to listen to Buffet present his investment outlook. Many scrutinize his annual letter to investors for clues into Buffet's market outlook, investment opportunities, and, most important, possible insights into forthcoming investment decisions. This makes sense because studying an expert at his game can only help one in making investment decisions.

Thanks to new information releases, investors can take this approach to further extremes. Instead of listening to executives expound on the virtues of their company, one can look at how they invest their personal assets to measure their confidence in the company. If the executives had real faith in a new corporate strategy, they might purchase additional shares at the company's currently undervalued levels, before legions of investors snap up its shares. Or, if the market is condemning outstanding shares to a price well below their intrinsic value, company executives might take the opportunity to accumulate the oversold shares.

A criticism about the validity of insider insights might be that insiders are sometimes too close to a company to appreciate the simple truths about its situation. As a result, executives might miss out on a lost opportunity or let their emotions for the company cloud their judgment. Nonetheless, investors realize that it pays to heed not only the words or the body language of corporate executives but also their investment habits. This information is available via a regulation handed down by the Securities Exchange Commission (SEC). Under Section 16a of the Securities Exchange Act of 1934, insiders are required to report all trades of their underlying stock. The data is recorded in the Ownership Reporting System (ORS), which started in 1975.

FIRST CALL Insider Research Services and other sources have provided this data in easily screened format since the late 1980s. The data is also available in popular financial publications, including the *Wall Street Journal* and *Barron's,* as well as by electronic means via Bloomberg terminals and data and screening packages such as Factset. After carefully observing executives discuss their outlook for their company, serious investors can note if the executives' personal finance habits reflect an optimistic outlook.

Buying Habits as Useful Signals

Over the 1990s, several studies have concluded that share prices either react slowly or underreact to insider decision making. In a study by professors of banking and finance Josef Lakonishok and Immoo Lee,[2] a battery of statistical tests found that excess returns can result if an investor pays attention to the buy-and-sell habits of insiders. Unlike the SEC definition, which is limited to top officers and directors, "insiders" as defined in the study also include large shareholders (typically institutional investors) who own 10 percent or more of a company.

According to the study results, insiders' signals pertaining to purchasing habits are especially profitable. In fact, the sell signals do not appear to yield profitable short strategies. This distinction is interesting. The authors correctly assert that insiders sell for many reasons. For example, the compensation structure for executives has changed over the 1990s. A greater component of compensation is awarded in the form of stocks in an attempt to better align the shareholder interests with management interests. As these options and stock grants mature, insiders may be selling for a host of reasons, such as to cash in on compensation or to better diversify their assets. The least of these reasons might be to sell the stock because of impending adverse news. In contrast, executives who are purchasing shares are more than likely acting on an investment view, based on their perceptions of how the stock will perform in the future.

Application to Small-Cap Stocks

This study is especially interesting because it analyzes insider information by size. Not only did the results support exploiting of insider trading signals, they also revealed that the insider trading data produced more robust returns when applied to small-cap investing. As noted in the study, "Insiders are doing a better job in predicting aggregate movements of small companies than large companies."[3] Thus, the signals sent on small-cap stocks are useful market timing devices. In addition, the study concluded that such buy-and-sell signals of smaller stocks predict the direction of the small-cap market: Increased insider buying of smaller stocks also supports an upward bias toward the small-cap market. The study notes that "the biggest benefit in exploiting insider trading activity is in small companies."[4]

As argued throughout this book, the bias exists primarily because large stocks are much more efficiently priced than their small-cap counterparts. A glance at the sell-side or Wall Street analyst coverage of publicly held securities quickly confirms more robust coverage of large stocks, which have an average of 19 analysts covering each company versus 6 analysts for the average small stock. With expert opinions on large stocks well outnumbering those on small stocks, almost every interpretation of a blue-chip firm is expertly debated on a daily basis. With less material information available for smaller firms, it is understandable why the share buying habits of the executives for a neglected small stock would send more convincing and profitable signals than would be the case for large caps.

Another factor behind the linkage between insider trading habits and small-cap returns is that executives of small companies have more of a vested interest, at least on an aggregate basis, in the stock performance of their company. Figure 7.7 illustrates the average insider holding by size of the company. Note that the average holding for small- and microcap insiders, or companies below $1.5 billion in market capitalization, ranges

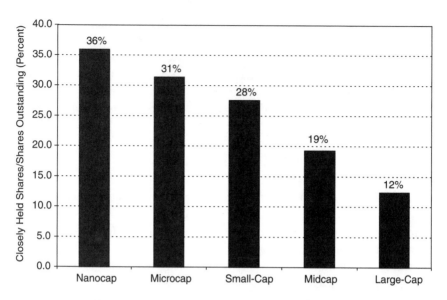

Figure 7.7   Average Insider Holdings as a Percent of
Total Shares Outstanding (*Source:* Worldscope)

between 28 and 36 percent versus 12 percent for large-cap firms. This finding suggests that small-cap executives are more closely tied to the stock performance of their companies than are large-cap executives.

The divergence between small- and large-cap insider holdings does not happen by mere chance. Holdings of smaller, younger firms are proportionately higher partly because managers expect significant price appreciation in their stocks. Moreover, the contracts of managers at these firms tend to include specific clauses that force managers to retain significant stakes in their firms for an extended period. This arrangement only creates a more robust basis for the positive relationship between insider buying and subsequent share appreciation. If insiders are forced to retain shares, they presumably would have a bias toward selling, and not buying, stocks. One can only assume that corporate insiders of a small-cap firm must have significant motivation when they decide to leverage up their corporate holdings.

NEW ISSUANCE MARKET AND SMALL-CAP TRENDS

Besides representing a financing event, the initial public offering (IPO) of a firm symbolizes the maturation of that company. It is a coming-out party for a company that has earned the right to compete with the "big boys." An IPO marks a new evolution in the progression of an enterprise. If the issuance is a success, the company gains access to much-needed capital, the executives monetize their worth, the underwriter makes a good profit, and the investor is able to obtain a sizable chunk of a solid company without market impact. Everyone wins.

Investors, especially institutional or professional investors, are never comfortable with the process, however. Each new deal that enters the market arena brings more foreboding to investors. Although no one ever issues a stock that is not expected to grow, not all deals are cut of the same cloth. Is this new growth company—and IPO candidates are always growth companies—a new Cisco Systems, or just another investment that will get lost in the investment shuffle?

The darker side of a new issue is that a seemingly healthy company may go amiss and drift aimlessly in an investor's portfolio. This said, a professional investor cannot afford to be out of the IPO game. If the investor's peers have bought into a deal that proceeds to mint cash for its holders, the investor who passed on this opportunity loses a sizable profit and, more significantly, falls several basis points behind the competition in the performance derby. As tense as the underwriting process is for the executives who launch and the bankers who broker a deal, it is just as complicated for the investor searching the prospectus for some prescient guidance. A professional investor needs to balance a keen eye for recognizing disaster in the making against the opportunistic edge that allows the investor to participate in the spoils of newfound success.

A popular truism about the IPO process is the more attendees to the ball, the less there is for those already there; an increase in the so-called deal flow is a contrary indicator for share prices. As the IPO pipeline gets clogged with upcoming deals, it is reasonable to believe that dollars originally earmarked for smaller stocks would be channeled to the new issuance market, partly because most new issues are smaller stocks. Figure 7.8 presents the issuance of small stocks, furnished by Securities Data Company, as a proportion of the small-cap market.

The increased supply of newly minted securities has generally been regarded as a contrary signal. As companies issue more stock in the marketplace, the belief is that increased supply in equities is likely to dampen subsequent share prices. From a supply/demand standpoint, this argument makes sense. Every extra share in the small-cap market represents increased supply and therefore more competition for the marginal dollar.

A hard look at the IPO market suggests otherwise. Underwriting appears to be positively related to subsequent price moves in the small-cap

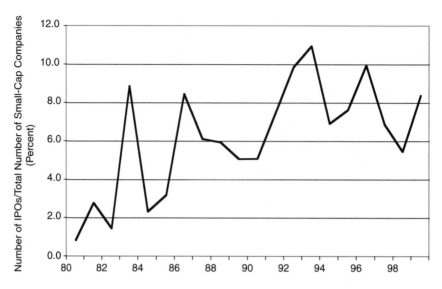

Figure 7.8   Small-Cap IPOs as a Proportion of Small-Cap Market

market. Contrary to an intuitive reading of IPO trends, smaller stocks appear to outperform large stocks when underwriting increases, but underperform as the pipeline slows. Figure 7.9 relates the performance of both small and large stocks with respect to three levels of the underwriting flow—weak, average, and strong. Figures 7.10 and 7.11 offer supporting snapshots of secondary offerings and IPOs dating back to 1970. Returns of small stocks are well above average and also superior to large-cap results only in a period of strong underwriting flows.

Based on data from July 1980 through August 1999, the regressed results between the rate of change of the IPO flow, on an annual basis, and the relative performance of small- to large-cap stocks are positively related.[5] More important, the underwriting trend appears to be positively related to the small-cap market the subsequent year. The trend in IPO activity is not only coincident and positive, it also appears to offer forecasting insight into the size puzzle.[6]

A look at the small-cap secondary issuance offerings (SEO) also supports the IPO results. Secondary issuance represents companies that are already public that return to the equity market for additional capital. Regression results based on data from December 1970 through August 1999 indicate that the overall relationship is positively related to the performance of smaller stocks. Furthermore, like the IPO

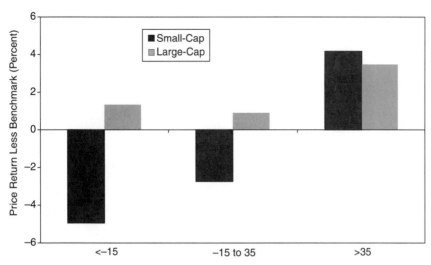

Figure 7.9 IPO vs. Small- and Large-Cap Returns

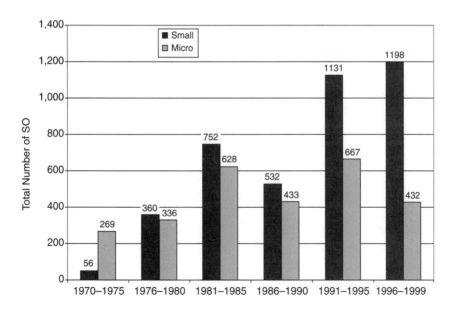

Figure 7.10 Total Number of Secondary Offerings by Size

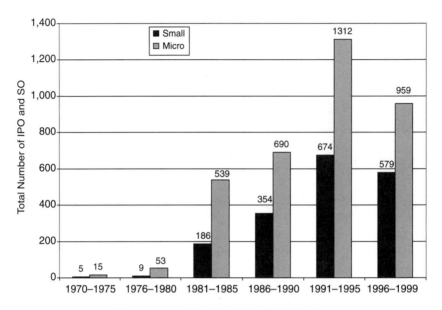

Figure 7.11   Total Number of IPOs by Size

relationship, the SEO data also offers strong forecast insight into the small-cap market.[7]

Why are the results so counterintuitive? The basic assumption is reasonable: an increase in the supply of stocks should place existing share prices under pressure. Yet it appears that the supply/demand argument is not sufficiently compelling to have an impact on the size equation. Thus, it is possible that the small-cap market is subject to broader forces than simply equity supply and demand. A successful IPO market implies that capital is flowing into more speculative issues. A risky environment not only closes the door on speculative IPO deals, it also generally places a great deal of strain on existing secondary issues, as discussed in Chapter 2.

This broader issue of risk taking appears to matter more to investors than supply and demand. The collapse of smaller stocks in 1998 is a good example of the market's focus on risk taking versus supply and demand. As investors became more concerned about global growth and liquidity issues involving the Long Term Capital Management hedge fund, investors flocked toward the safest haven situations—megacap ideas. The underwriting process came to a halt. Although 136 small-cap stocks went public in 1997, the deal flow in 1998 slowed to 98. In fact, only 13 issues came to market during the tumultuous second half of 1998. If IPOs had an inverse relationship to the small-cap cycle, the secondaries would have rallied to new highs. Instead, they came crashing down to even lower levels.

Simply put, the market needs to have an appetite for risk taking for the small-cap IPO strategy to pay off. In positive periods for the small-cap market, not only do existing shares outperform, the demand is so great that sufficient appetite exists for additional IPOs as well. If the proper setting is in place for a small-cap rally, the demand sustains existing share prices, along with a host of new companies about to enter the equity market. However, if investors are shying away from the market, the lack of competition from new entries plays no role in sustaining existing shares.

EIGHT

Stock Selection Models

IT IS perhaps simplistic to invest solely on the basis of rising price trends or shares that look cheap on some measure of valuation. Nonetheless, quantitative models that examine such factors allow an investor to pare away at the incredibly broad secondary market and thus, separate true investment opportunities from investment noise. Although single factors such as price momentum or earnings revision might fall short of offering a complete stock selection framework, they can be essential building blocks in a more extensive investing infrastructure.

INVESTING FRAMEWORK

An approach to modeling small-cap stocks, not unlike approaches for tackling the large-cap sector, is to model the investment process. What are the basic elements that investors look for in successful stocks? Ultimately, the hard work of investing boils down to two basic questions: (1) Are the company's earnings expectations improving or failing? (2) Have all expectations been priced into the underlying shares? When investors pore over a company's financial statements, they assess not only the financial data but also compare the company figures with those of its peers. More important, the investor needs to assess if the analysis leads to expectations that are below or above consensus.

Similarly, an investor attempts to assess how company management rates in the context of its competition to determine if the investor's outlook is above or below the consensus outlook. It is extremely important for investors to understand the company's position in the context of the market. Even though one is bullish on a company with solid earnings, this doesn't necessarily mean its share prices will appreciate. A company may report earnings ahead of an investor's optimistic estimate and paradoxically suffer weakening share prices. If the market consensus expected the company's earnings to fall well ahead of the investor's estimate, the earnings report may fall short of market expectations and a disappointing report can cause share prices to tumble.

Investors can minimize risk by understanding the market's outlook on a specific security and then gauging the shift in market expectations. Admittedly, it is difficult to distinguish the market expectations from one's own view for the stock. This analysis becomes more complicated when the portfolio comprises not ten, but one hundred, securities. It becomes even more complex when one considers that market opinions change frequently. Earnings expectation models can help investors make sense of this process.

The next step is to determine if you are paying too much for the asset. This component of the analysis involves assessing whether the market has already incorporated a very robust outlook in the share price. If this is the case, the company may report earnings well ahead of consensus but yield little change in the share value.

THE VALUE OF QUANTITATIVE MODELS

Assessing the value of a company is perhaps one of the most important tasks of investing. Assessing companies on the basis of expectations and valuations offers a formidable framework for investing. To this end, quantitative models can be useful tools. The models can be structured to generate a selection pool of stocks for conducting fundamental research or can be refined for a pure quantitative approach. Although it is difficult to quantify the ability of management for thousands of companies across multiple industries, there are many creative ways to back out expectations or the change in expectations. Price trends, earnings revision, earnings surprise, and earnings momentum are among the multitude of variables that may offer some insight into changes in expectations.

Contrary to popular belief, the use of models to generate stock ideas is not solely the realm of actively managed quantitative funds. Although modeling techniques are primarily used by numbers-oriented analysts, they are also a critical tool for the traditional kick-the-tire type investor. For example, a thesis on investing in energy stocks may be that energy stocks will outperform if oil prices rise. Simple backtests can offer some level of confidence on taking a position in oil stocks. More important, they can help determine if oil stocks outperform to the extent that warrants added exposure. These modeling studies offer investors a unique approach to assessing risk before they make an investment decision.

Given that academic journals and investment guides are filled with so-called cutting-edge techniques that beat the market, small-cap investors must evaluate if these factors or strategies offer an edge in the small-cap market. Although many studies offer a compelling argument that investors can benefit from investing in cheap stocks or in stocks with rising earnings or price trends, the question then is whether these strategies hold for the small-cap market.

Modeling strategies for the small-cap market can indeed yield more fruitful results than similar techniques applied to the megacap sector. The balance of this chapter examines several modeling variables and discusses their strengths and weaknesses in the context of the small-cap market. The factors examined are price trend, earnings changes, and valuations. These factors are extremely useful in assessing the quality of a stock pick. The sections that follow explore simple, but useful exercises that allow any investor to take a portfolio approach and apply prudence in making a sell or buy decision. Moreover, many tests applied and discussed in regard to the small-cap market do not require an advanced degree in statistics.

KEY CONSIDERATIONS IN SMALL-CAP MODELS

Stock models are powerful tools that help investors to manage an overwhelming sea of data. Yet quantitative simulations can offer misleading signals if the results are not properly stress tested. Ultimately, it must be confirmed that the findings are not a by-product of spurious relationships. If a factor yields unusually strong results without economic support for the findings, the results may be suspect.

To establish a model's significance, investors must examine the results of a strategy over an extended period. Beating the market for one marking period can be the result of simple chance. Multiperiod testing also allows a factor to be tested over several business cycles, both strong and weak economic cycles, as well as bull and bear markets. Model results can differ markedly, depending on shifts in overall market conditions.

Consistency of Results

The performance of any model should be examined for consistency of results. The more consistent the results, the more robust the model. Even if a model generates superior results, highly variable performance figures should be cause for concern. Investors can look at simple volatility statistics for insight into a model's consistency and also examine the data over several periods to control for this risk.

Model Bias

Properly accounting for inherent biases built into studies is one of the most difficult aspects of analyzing and interpreting backtest results. For example, the "look ahead" bias arises primarily when the model inadvertently selects investment ideas based on information that investors were not privy to in that past period although it was available in a backtest database. This might occur when an investor buys stocks with positive earnings surprises or companies report earnings well above the consensus level.

By calculating a surprise based on perfect foresight, or accidentally scoring the past results with data that was not available in real time but becomes available in a backtest database, a model can flag an earnings surprise before a company makes an actual announcement. This "look ahead" bias allows a model to magically forecast all positive surprises without error. Not surprisingly, a basket with perfect foresight generates spectacular results. Even though the pricing and earnings data are equally spotless, the measurement and timing process can cause models to generate terribly misleading results.

Although diligence and an eye for detail can prevent investors from falling into nasty backtest traps, most databases suffer from some degree of survivorship bias. When companies that fail or go bankrupt are deleted from databases, their removal causes the databases to have a good-company bias. This lowers the chance that a model will accidentally pick a failing company. If the database does not include shares that went to zero, the model results are likely to generate abnormally positive results. Although data suppliers have improved their quality control processes to minimize this problem, the historical archives cannot, of course, be neatly fixed.

Linearity

It is also important to test for significance between factors, or linearity. According to the linearity argument, if more of some trait is good, then less of such a trait should yield inferior results. Ultimately, robust factors tend to behave in a linear or near linear fashion. For example, if rising price trends forecast higher returns, then falling trends should similarly forecast weaker stock returns. Suppose, however, that the stocks with the best price trend performance, those in the first decile, or top 10 percent, lag those in the third decile. This result would be difficult to interpret. In this instance, it would be hard to accept that price trends are really a good forecast of stock prices. The best one could conclude is that stocks with slightly above average fare well, while those with extraordinary results lag. Simply put, "up is not up" and "down is not down." The less than predictable pattern of results in many equity market tests has forced financial engineers to study factors by using nonlinear solutions. They can correctly argue that financial market data do not always behave in a linear fashion.

Transaction Costs

When running simulations, investors must take transaction costs into account. Less liquid assets are more costly to trade. Because small caps are less liquid and therefore more costly to trade, the degree of turnover in a model or portfolio is crucial. Successful strategies may generate stunning results in a modeling scenario, but high transaction costs can marginalize even the best results. Is a strategy successful only because it relies on frequent trading? If so, the realized returns of a model based on less liquid investments might fall well short of the backtest returns.

Because transaction costs are difficult to estimate and vary according to the size of assets, a simple way to analyze the resiliency of a model in terms of trading is to change the frequency of the holding periods. Does a model still produce returns if the portfolio is rebalanced quarterly versus monthly? If model results dramatically weaken when the portfolio is rebalanced less frequently, its realized returns are likely to fall well short of the paper results.

Hit Ratio

It is also important to determine if a model functions better at generating an entire portfolio or selecting individual stocks. A model may generate superior returns when it selects an entire basket of stocks and yet function less well at selecting individual stocks. Such a model is regarded as having a low hit ratio.[1] The term *hit ratio* refers to a model's ability to pick stocks. A robust model not only generates superior aggregate results but also carries a high hit ratio.

A hit ratio is simply the percentage of stocks that outperform a given benchmark—the higher that percentage, the more robust the results. If the model outperforms its benchmark and a majority of its stocks outperform, it is considered robust and can be applied to stock selection, portfolio trading, or both. If a model has a high hit ratio but underperforms the benchmark, it is better suited for selecting individual stocks. A model that combines a low hit ratio with strong model performance lends itself more to portfolio trading strategy. Finally, a model that has a low hit ratio and underperforms the benchmark obviously should not be used.

Backtesting Pitfalls

Even if a model avoids the pitfalls discussed in the preceding section, it can be a challenge to keep the details and logic of the system free of error, thanks to the sizable amount of data and complex testing required.

Sometimes, minute details can cloud results. For example, modeling is carried out via computer programs that apply simple, compact lines of logic to modify mountains of data. These lines of code must be checked, however, for flaws in logic, which can occur in subtle, simple ways. In one company report, a company was curiously listed as "Junetag." By some accident, the company Maytag had been renamed Junetag. As it turned out, the month "May" had been replaced by "June" throughout the document. When the computer program correctly replaced all occurrences of May with June, it also changed the company name "Maytag" to "Junetag."

Thus, even after controlling for potential backtest flaws, model results may still stray from the real markets, whether in a relatively innocuous way, as with Junetag, or in a more serious manner. Although modeling tools for testing an investment hypothesis are powerful, the results they produce are nonetheless paper-based and must be carefully interpreted.

MOMENTUM INVESTING MODELS

Strategies for capturing price trends, also known as momentum investing, have always been a part of investment management. Price momentum strategy is simply an earlier form of earnings or revenue (topline) momentum strategies that have evolved over the past 15 to 20 years. The investment process is simple: buy the best-performing stocks based on the premise that changes in a company's situation will be quickly reflected in share prices. Although this sounds like a variation on the efficient markets principle, the argument for momentum investing is a bit more involved. According to its followers, the market typically exhibits a second-order effect. If a company has good news, it tends to ripple across several reporting periods. Similarly, declining business results are rarely singular events for a company. Key to momentum strategies is the belief that initial changes in a company's current operating environment are a telling sign of more profound change to come.

Because trend investing implicitly assumes that the market direction is generally correct, investors who follow this strategy are likely to quickly sell off shares at the first sign of a problem. A sudden and adverse turn of events for a company is a signal that its shares will exhibit weakness. Even if the stock's initial price weakness is commensurate with a company's performance shortfall, trend investors are still likely to sell a stock, based on the logic that such weakness forecasts additional turbulence and may signal the start of a multiperiod downturn.

Structuring the Model

Do past price trends have predictive value? Can an investor profit from buying the stocks that have performed the best over the past month? To answer these questions, we set forth a simple price trends model and perform a backtest based on the hypothesis that excess returns are a function of past price momentum. The assumption is that price behavior is serially correlated—that prior price movements indicate subsequent direction. The momentum backtest is designed to answer a few simple, related questions:

- Can I make money by investing in this strategy?
- Can such a strategy consistently beat the market?
- Did I trade away my gains?

Assume Investor A measures the one-month price performance of all stocks in the small-cap market and then purchases the best-performing 10 percent of the market. Can A make an excess return above and beyond the entire market or a relevant benchmark in subsequent periods? As one approach to backtesting this strategy, A can pool the performance of all small stocks into buckets or deciles ranging from best to worst one-month price performance. Although there are no absolute rules of measure, deciles are often used as an industry standard in such models. Assume that the best results are in the 90th decile or first bucket. The next decile contains the second best 10 percent of the small-cap market, and so on. At the end of the list, the worst-performing small stocks fall in the 10th decile.

The stocks in each group or decile are purchased at the beginning of a period and sold at the end. If the period tested is January 2000, each group or decile is purchased at the start of the month and sold at the end of the period. In this case, assume that the holding period is one quarter. The simulations are then run through the first quarter to determine if the first decile, or best-performing, stocks from the prior one-month period outperform the market or the remaining deciles in the rest of the quarter. If so, then the factor being tested, price trends for a one-month period, becomes more relevant. The excess returns generated over the sample period define the robustness of the model.

In the example illustrated in Figure 8.1, the price momentum model is based on a sampling period dating back to 1973. A sample of best-performing stocks is taken from the small-cap market and compared with a benchmark; here, the hurdle of success is the small-cap market. The model is relevant only if it can outperform the market in the stock selection process.

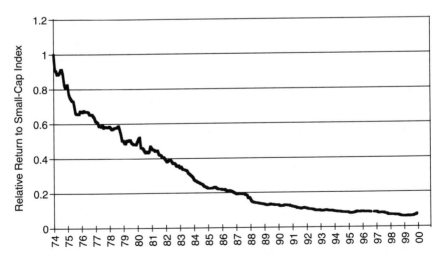

Figure 8.1   Small-Cap Relative Strength Model—One-Month Price Change

The model is structured on an equal-weighted basis. The equal-weighting method helps an investor establish the model's ability to identify stocks that outperform the market. Performance can and should be measured on a market- or sized-weighted basis as well. By examining the results on a market-weighted basis, an investor can better deal with the liquidity aspects of trading a basket of stocks. Market-weighted results, however, might overstate a model's effectiveness if larger companies outperform smaller companies because the largest stocks hold the most significant weight in a market-weighted portfolio.

Figure 8.1 illustrates the performance results for this simple one-month price momentum strategy. A declining line suggests that the one-month price momentum model is underperforming the small-cap market. An upward trending relative performance line would indicate a strategy that is outperforming the market. As can be seen, the one-month strategy severely lags the overall small-cap market. This price momentum model, as defined by a one-month period, appears to behave perversely on a short-term basis.

The results might lead to the conclusion that the strategy of momentum investing is sadly unproductive. The results in Figure 8.1 suggest that one would have gained a paltry 0.5 percent annually from January 1974 to December 1999 investing in small stocks with the strongest prior one-month price performance. The small-cap market generated 11.4 percent annually over the same period. However, other measures of momentum variables or relative strength support the popular contention that these factors can be useful.

The dilemma in relative strength models lies in the measure, and not the concept. In fact, the concept is quite simple: the trend is your "friend." The burden involves properly defining a trend, as the permutations of a price momentum or relative strength model can be daunting. Is a short-term price move significant? The test in Figure 8.1 involving one-month price change does not appear useful. Is a long-run move more significant? If so, how long? These questions become compounded once you consider other derivative measures of momentum, such as accelerating price trends (stocks that are racing to new highs at an increasing rate).

In fact, if one were to thoroughly study the merits or demerits of relative strength strategies manually or anecdotally, this exercise would become incredibly tedious and in fact untestable without tidy pricing databases and the number-crunching abilities of a computer. The power of quantitative methods is that they enable one to properly conduct simple experiments to validate or strike down popular investment theories.

Refining the Model

Refining the model is an iterative process to determine whether a better model is based on a 3-, 6-, 12-, 18-, or 24-month performance period. Table 8.1 presents six possible relative strength measures. Although the list is not exhaustive, running such a sample series can help investors to refine the search for a better measure of relative strength. According to the performance results for these interval definitions, a simple 12-month (or 1-year) performance period appears to produce the most positive results. The short-term variations tend to act in a contrary fashion; stocks with abnormal short-term price bounces tend to reverse in subsequent periods.

Because price changes can be volatile, smoothed variations—price changes "smoothed" by moving averages of the price trends—are also worth testing. Although some of the definitions appeared improved, the overall results were marginal in this series of tests. Because the smoothing overlay yields only marginally improved net results and can make it more difficult to interpret the definitions, the raw or simple relative strength definition of a 1-year trend produced the most compelling results among the backtested models.

The results support the general hypothesis that price momentum over the short term, such as a 1-month interval, is less of an indicator of future price moves than long-term periods or, as noted previously, is merely a contrary indicator. By extending the period to 12 months, relative strength models add value to the investment process.[2] Figure 8.2 represents the relative performance of the 12-month price momentum

Table 8.1 Sample Price Momentum or Relative Strength Models

1-Month Price Change = Selection of the top 10 percent of the small-cap market with the best 1-month price performance.

3-Month Price Change = Selection of the top 10 percent of the small-cap market with the best 3-month price performance.

6-Month Price Change = Selection of the top 10 percent of the small-cap market with the best 6-month price performance.

12-Month Price Change = Selection of the top 10 percent of the small-cap market with the best 12-month price performance.

18-Month Price Change = Selection of the top 10 percent of the small-cap market with the best 18-month price performance.

24-Month Price Change = Selection of the top 10 percent of the small-cap market with the best 24-month price performance.

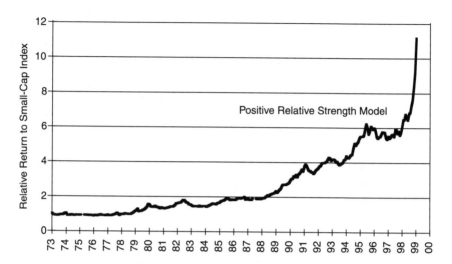

Figure 8.2   Small-Cap Relative Strength Model—12-Month Price Change

model versus the small-cap market. The upward trending relationship implies that the momentum model is outperforming the small-cap market. The results suggest that a relative strength model based on a 12-month price momentum generated an annual rate of return of 22.3 percent versus 11.4 percent for the small-cap market. The momentum strategy based on a 12-month definition outperformed the small-cap market by a sizable 10.9 percent annually. These results are based on the 1974–99 period. Even if one were to remove the spectacular run-up among momentum stocks in the 1999–2000 market, the long-term results remain quite strong. Curiously, the performance edge of a momentum model appears to deteriorate as periods extend beyond one year. The 18-month definition is not as compelling as the 1-year measure, and the 24-month definition lags the 18-month measure.

The conclusions reached in these tests are supported by other finance-related literature. In his book *How to Make Money in Stocks,* William O'Neil[3] suggests that stocks with a strong relative-strength rank (percentile) of 80 or better in a 6- or 12-month price change seemed to be the best performers. In quant terms, this means that the top 20 percent, or the first quintile, of price momentum stocks appear to add value to a portfolio.

In other research, Narasimhan Jagadeesh found that "the negative first-order serial correlation in monthly stock returns is highly significant.

Furthermore, significant positive serial correlation is found at longer lags, and the 12-month serial correlation is particularly strong."[4] Stocks with strong returns over a 12-month period appear to outperform. Furthermore, the results of short-term relative strength models, such as a 1-month price change, tend to generate perverse results.

Utility of Long-Term Price Trends

It is possible that longer-term price trends are more useful than short-term trends because investors need time to separate investment noise from tangible and solid opportunities. Longer periods give investors the chance to assess the merits of a company. It is difficult to argue that the valuations of some companies should significantly rise because of a short-term bounce in share price. If, however, a company reports unexpectedly strong business results and can consistently beat street expectations, its stock is likely to trade at a premium to its peer group. As investors become more interested in the stock, it is likely to continue its upward trend. A rising stock that evinces sound business results gives rise to an increasing price trend with ample liquidity. A short-term jump in share price is not enough to sustain the interest of the investment community.

Stress Testing the Model

Variability

In addition to the performance merits of each definition, the model should also be tested for its level of variability. The less variable the results, the more robust the model. Assessing the robustness of a model or factor depends on not only the raw performance results but also their uncertainty or variability quotient. If the variability is notably high, the predictability of the model falls. These momentum models can be incredibly volatile. Figure 8.3 relates the performance results of the benchmark and relative strength models of various asset classes with the corresponding volatility of each.

Even a momentum model that produces superior results, such as the 12-month price trend model, carries an annualized volatility of 24.9 percent. The annualized volatility of the small-cap market is only 19.2 percent over the same time. Despite the high level of volatility, the risk-adjusted returns of the 12-month price trend model remain compelling.

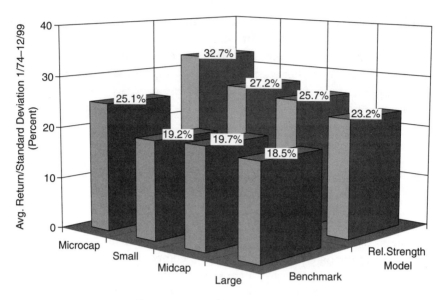

Figure 8.3   Risk-Adjusted Returns

Linearity

As discussed, investors also look at the linearity of a model to determine its robustness. Figure 8.4 illustrates the linearity of the models discussed here. As can be seen from the decile breakdown of risk /return levels for the 12-month price change model (panel d), the results are mostly linear. The first decile outperforms the second, which outperforms the third, and so on. This, however, is not the case for many of the variations.

An example of a model with less than linear results is the accelerating trend 1- to 6-month price change models (panel c). This approach groups the stocks with the sharpest acceleration over the past month relative to the past 6 months. Not only do the performance results lag compared with those of other simple models, the results of the mid-deciles, such as the third and fourth deciles, are more compelling than those of the first decile. When results are not linear, they are difficult to interpret.

The argument could be made that it should not matter if a model is less than linear; the best returns are the goal and not the best accountable results. The problem is that a nonlinear result is difficult to justify because there is no underlying theory or logic to support the observed result. For example, the results of the 1- to 6-month accelerating trend price model are hard to interpret. According to the results, stocks that exhibit moderate acceleration in share prices are the best investments. Conversely, stocks that sharply accelerate or decelerate tend to be laggards. Even for the less mathematically inclined, such logic is difficult to accept. If a model yields nonlinear results, this may indicate that the underlying theory requires more work. Although statistical transformations, such as nonlinear solutions or neural networks, can improve the statistical soundness of any structure, a model grounded in solid economic theory ultimately yields the best results.

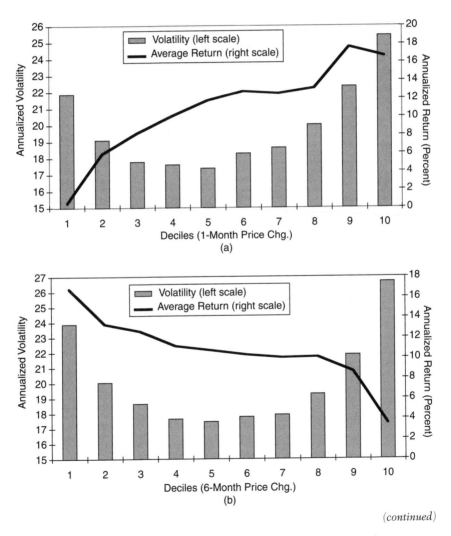

(continued)

Figure 8.4 Small-Cap Relative Strength Model—Decile Results

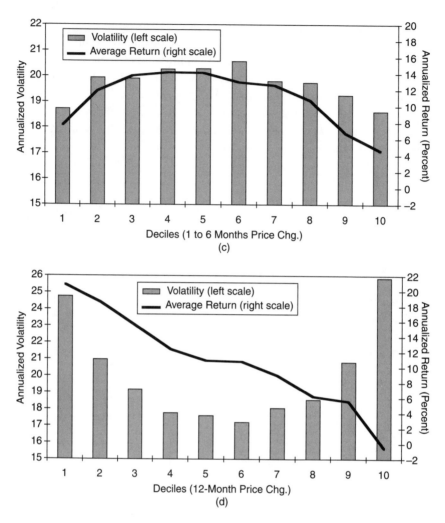

Figure 8.4 Continued

A relevant implication of linearity for trend investing models is that failing price trends indicate subsequent price weakness for a stock. Besides identifying high-performing stocks, this model appears to offer some insight on which securities to avoid. The net rate of return for the weak performers in the tenth decile significantly lags that of the first decile and of the small-cap benchmark. This finding is in line with the general theory that rising price trends reflect rising expectations for such stocks. A similar argument could be made that declining share prices reflect stocks with deteriorating expectations and therefore are a signal of subsequent price weakness. Downward trends not only offer some support for a sell discipline, they also bring more credibility to price momentum factors.

Hit Ratio

A close look at relative strength results suggests that the intraportfolio returns are fairly consistent and robust. The relative strength model has a high hit ratio. The above-average returns of this trend model are not a by-product of unusual price jumps for a few names but stem from the results of the majority. To test this idea, compare the average result of the model with the benchmark. If the average returns of the model beat the benchmark more often than less, the model is said to be robust from a portfolio standpoint. If a majority of the stocks in the portfolio participate in the periods when the model outperforms, the model is also useful in the stock selection process. As shown in Table 8.2, the relative strength models not only outperform their benchmarks a majority of the time, they also have compelling hit ratios.

Table 8.2 relates the proportion of times that the model outperforms the market and the corresponding hit ratios or the proportion of stocks that tend to outperform the benchmark. The higher the ratio the more consistent the model. For instance, the small-cap 12-month momentum model outperforms the small-cap market 62.8 percent of the time (these tests are based on results between 1974–99). The hit ratio based on the small-cap results is strong at 81.1 percent. This means that, on average,

Table 8.2   Positive Relative Strength Model

Median Summary	
Midcap	
Model beats benchmark	60.9%
Hit ratio	80.5%
Small-Cap	
Model beats benchmark	62.8%
Hit ratio	81.1%
Microcap	
Model beats benchmark	62.8%
Hit ratio	57.7%

81 percent of the stocks in the momentum portfolio outperformed the market, in this instance the small-cap market, each month the model outperformed the market. Thus, a majority of the stocks in the model generally outperformed the benchmark, which allowed the model to register compelling gains. This is important because it implies that one does not benefit from a momentum strategy by simple chance or dramatic jumps in singular stocks; instead a majority of the portfolio appears to drive the net results.

Transaction Costs

Transaction costs and portfolio turnover are paramount when stock selection processes are being modeled for a less liquid universe of stocks. Nonetheless, transaction costs can be difficult to model; the combination of the bid-ask spread and market impact factors determines the total cost of trading. These factors are dependent on several dynamic variables, such as market conditions (e.g., bullish or bearish sentiment), market and stock volatility, and the size demanded of the order.

Active investment is an attempt to arbitrage market inefficiencies. A delayed reaction to an investment opportunity can result in terribly expensive opportunity costs. Yet overall performance can suffer if the investor too aggressively trades a less liquid subset of stocks. Ultimately, active management results are determined by a delicate balance between opportunistic trading and strategic rebalancing.

In simple terms, a model is more robust when lower turnover only marginally erodes returns. Momentum measures, such as the one-year trend model, require a good deal of maintenance. As shown in Figure 8.5, a significant slippage occurs in returns from a one-month holding period to a one-year holding period—the portfolio rebalanced monthly outperforms the annually rebalanced portfolio by 6.0 percent on a yearly basis. Holding period represents the amount of time a portfolio is held without updating the constituents. In fact, the average performance of the model noticeably shrinks as the holding period extends beyond six months. Yet the results of the semiannual and annual holding periods still handily outperformed, by more than twofold, the small-cap market over the sample period.

Market Risk

Surprisingly, a simple price momentum model appears to withstand the rigors of most stress tests. It yields risk-adjusted returns that are superior

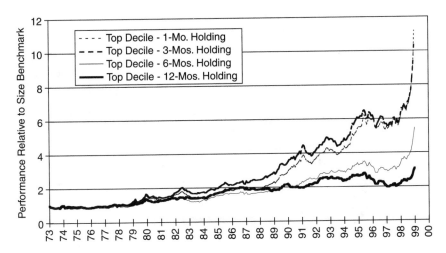

Figure 8.5 Small-Cap Relative Strength Model by Varying Holding Periods

to the small-cap benchmark. Not only does it score well as a portfolio strategy, it also functions well as a stock-picking mechanism, and holds up even after taking trading costs into account. On the surface, this model appears flawless, except for its one observed Achilles heel, market risk. The model produces superior returns but relies heavily on overall market trends. A rising market yields exceptional model returns, while a declining market wrecks havoc on a momentum strategy.

Figure 8.6 illustrates the returns of the 12-month trend model with respect to market direction. When the small-cap market is flat to rising, the model results are superior. The difficulty arises when the market begins to weaken and even correct. As the market weakens, momentum factors stumble and produce performance figures much weaker than those of the small-cap averages. The relative strength model lost approximately 21.7 percent of its value between June 1996 and April 1997, while the small-cap market lost approximately 11 percent over the same time frame—only half of the loss suffered by momentum strategies. The results are a sobering reminder that trend models require a very bullish outlook on the market. As Figure 8.6 demonstrates, when small-cap stocks lost beyond 8 percent in a given month, momentum strategies on average lost roughly 14.5 percent compared with the small-cap market losing 12.8 percent.

Most momentum factors may test well because many of the tests are taken over a bullish market backdrop. A quick look at the results during

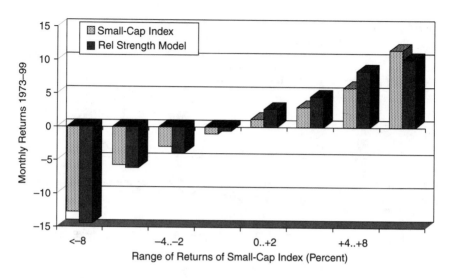

Figure 8.6   Relative Strength Model—Dispersion of Returns

the mid-1970s indicates that momentum investing was then a losing proposition.

EARNINGS EXPECTATIONS MODELS

Profits and the outlook for corporate profits are critical to the pricing of securities and also play a critical role in most investment decisions. When investors purchase the shares of Company A over those of Company B, their primary motivation is the belief that A can grow profits faster than B. Investors traditionally have held that the faster a company can grow its profits, the better the outlook for share prices. In fact, the pricing environment for Internet securities suggests that current profits are meaningless and expectations are all that matter. Although the existing assets for such companies are negligible and most operate at a deficit, their market capitalizations soar well above the levels of many Fortune 500 companies.

A critical task for financial analysts is to determine the forward cash flows of a prospective investment. If the expectations are improving, the value of the firm is said to increase; as the outlook sours, however, so go the shares. It is paramount for investors to keep a pulse on the outlook for earnings. Thanks to current technological and data delivery innovations, investors can apply more intensive earnings forecast models to their decision process than in the past.

Investors no longer are limited to their own individual analysis and outlook for a company. In an instant, they can access the views of several analysts and all their prospective figures on a company. The forecasts for thousands of companies are collected and summarized on many competing data systems. Not only can investors poll the figures of their favorite analyst, they can get, in time series form, the changes in estimates over the past few weeks or months. These changes also are offered in real time. Vendors now capture and resell the intraday estimate changes that occur in almost every stock covered by analysts.

Structuring the Model

Given the investor focus on earnings expectations, the question becomes whether models based on changes in expectations add value to the investment process. To answer, one can structure an earnings model that simulates investing based on changes in earnings expectations. If an investor were to buy a basket of stocks with the best earnings forecasts, would the returns of such a basket be superior to the market?

Simple backtests suggest that earnings estimates models lend value to the stock selection process. Figure 8.7 represents the relative performance of small stocks based on positive earnings forecasts, covering the period from January 1980 to December 1999. The lines in the chart represent the equal-weighted returns of the top decile comprising stocks with the best earnings forecasts versus that of an equal-weighted small-cap index. An upward sloping line indicates that the model is outperforming the small-cap market.

The backtest stratifies changes in earnings estimates by deciles. The group with the best earnings revisions fall in the first decile, the next best batch in the second decile, and so on. The revisions or changes in estimates are based on the prior three months. The top 10 percent of small stocks with the strongest estimate changes for that period are then priced at the end of the current month. The performance of the top earnings estimate candidates are then aggregated for that period. As with the relative strength model, defining an earnings estimate model can be tedious. In looking at earnings estimates, should investors examine the change over one week, one month, six months, or a year? Because of the many permutations, it is difficult to decide which period is most relevant. The test

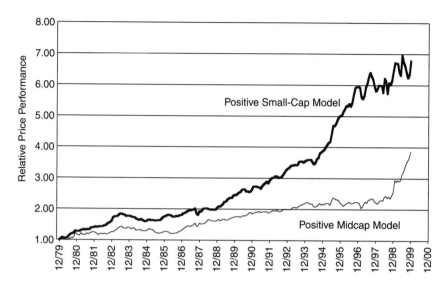

Figure 8.7   Power Estimate Revision Model—Relative Cumulative Price

could also be run on many types of estimate changes—the change in year two, the change in the next quarter, and so on.

Stress Testing the Model

The results of the earnings revision model show that an earnings revision strategy has yielded an annualized return of 22.2 percent versus an 11.0 percent gain for the small-cap market over the same period. Because some of the excess returns in this model are generated at the expense of high turnover, they are less likely to be replicated in a real-world portfolio setting where trading costs would be incurred. Nonetheless, such models offer a simple and compelling approach to modeling the expectation of stock performance. While the investor should not use only earnings revisions as a stock selection model, they can play a crucial role when combined with other factors.

Variability

Earnings revision models tend to be more growth-oriented. Like many growth models, the level of volatility for earnings revision models is likely to be higher than that of their respective benchmarks: the rate of return for positive earnings estimate models may be more volatile than its comparable size benchmark. Figure 8.8 represents a comparison of the underlying volatility or standard deviation of returns of an earnings revision models with respect to the volatility of their respective benchmark. The results are based on data ranging from 1980 to 1999. Although the model's rate of return is approximately 11 percent above the small-cap index, volatility is roughly 3 percent in excess of the small-cap market volatility.

This is not a surprising result because securities with the best earnings outlook tend to carry a significant valuation premium with respect to the market. The associated volatility of high expectation stocks thus tends to be well above average. Nonetheless, as shown in Figure 8.9, the risk-adjusted figures support the superior performance of the models over their benchmarks. Returns of the models are compared only after the results are normalized by their respective volatility levels.

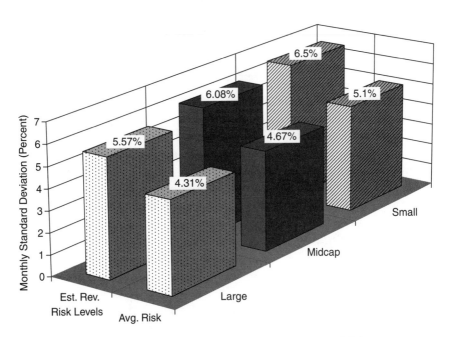

Figure 8.8   Risk Levels of the Earnings Estimate Models

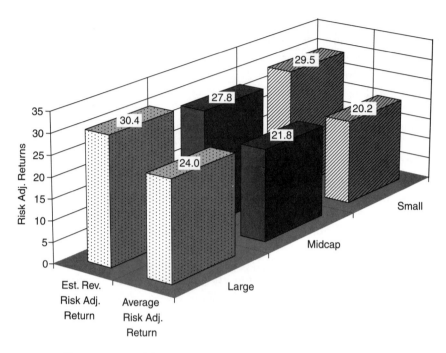

Figure 8.9 Risk/Reward Levels of the Earnings Estimate Models

Linearity

Based on the earnings revision model, rising profit expectations appear to lead to increasing share prices. The earnings revision model, for the most part, generates linear results; the stocks with the sharpest rise in forecasted earnings outperform the group exhibiting the next best forecasted earnings.

As with many equity puzzles, not all the performance groups support a linear pattern. The performance of the tenth decile, which covers the stocks with the weakest earnings change, is in line with that of the small-cap market.[5] If the earnings revision factor were completely linear, however, the tenth decile stocks should severely lag the small-cap market. Figure 8.10 represents the relative performance of the bottom decile or groups with the weakest earnings forecasts. While the tenth decile of earnings revision stocks (those stocks with the sharpest cuts in earnings estimates) underperform the small-cap benchmark, with an absolute rate of return of 7.9 percent, the results nonetheless, are much better than those of the ninth decile, or stocks with slightly better earnings outlook.

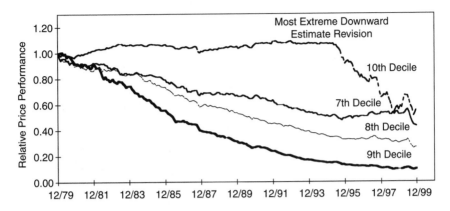

Figure 8.10   Small-Cap Downward Estimate Revision Models

Small stocks with weak estimates that fall into the ninth decile significantly underperform the small-cap market and the tenth decile with an average loss of 1.1 percent per year. This is confounding—companies with the weakest earnings outlook are not necessarily the weakest stocks.

Intuitively, the same reasoning that supports the positive model should apply, in reverse, when revising earnings downward. Why does this logic fail to hold with earnings revision data? If investors are willing to believe that rising earnings estimates are good, why then do cuts in estimates yield such perverse effects? These dichotomous results may stem from a behavioral bias in investors, who have become desensitized to buy recommendations from analysts. Upgraded stocks tend to well outnumber those downgraded, partially because the marketing of researched ideas usually is tailored toward buying stocks, not selling them. This bias may lead managers to be more critical and deliberate in acquiring shares with rising profit expectations. The managers may even wait for a confirming signal, such as a rise in share prices, before they make a move.

Conversely, managers may be attuned to weakening signals or areas of risk within their portfolio. Because of the lack of selling signals and their vested interest as holders of these securities, investors may be much more inclined to listen to damning information, and in fact, sell at the first hint of weakness. Thus, managers may react more rapidly to bad or initial downward earnings estimate revisions than to positive news. As a result, the eighth or ninth decile of earnings revision candidates may weaken more so than the tenth decile downward revision candidates. It is quite possible that the stocks would have been sold off well before analysts lowered estimates. Hence, models that test stocks on the extreme changes of upward earnings revisions may be more useful than signals offered by significant downward revisions.

A valuation parameter, such as price-to-earnings ratio or price-to-cash flow ratio, might control for this shortfall. If share prices already reflect a more concerned investor sentiment, then the valuation of the security is already likely to reflect a muted outlook. Although simple earnings revision models cannot detect if prices already reflect investor concerns, a valuation perspective can nicely compensate for this shortcoming.

Transaction Costs

Like other fast-moving expectational variables such as relative strength or earnings momentum, an earnings revision model must reflect random and dynamic change and thus relies on frequent updates to generate powerful results. Figure 8.11 represents the performance of an earnings revision model with and without trading constraints. The thick dotted line represents the monthly rebalancing portfolio versus quarterly reconstitution as represented by the solid line. If the model is rebalanced less

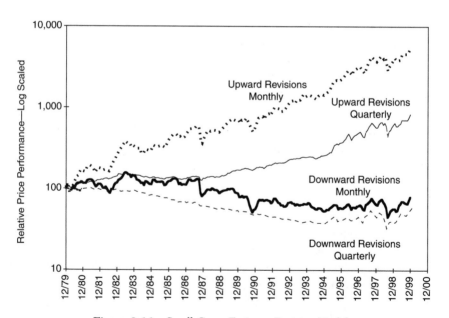

Figure 8.11   Small-Cap—Estimate Revision Models

frequently, for example, quarterly rather than monthly, this costs the investor a hefty 11 percent in expected returns on an annual basis. Results deteriorate even more as one goes to a semiannual or annual rebalancing. This pattern implies more aggressive trading as one employs an earnings revision strategy. More frequent rebalancing leads to expensive trading costs, however. The downward revisions models, stocks with severe cuts in earnings estimates, suggest similar degradation: downward revision models rebalanced less frequently also deteriorate, as seen in the lower half of Figure 8.11. The solid line represents monthly rebalancing results versus quarterly performance results as shown by the thin/dashed line.

All investors, especially small-cap investors, who are forced to deal with liquidity issues (discussed in Chapter 2), need to strike the proper balance between opportunity costs and trading costs. The less than compelling results from the earnings revision model that is rebalanced infrequently suggest that investors need to temper their attempts to arbitrage market opportunities. Furthermore, the decay in earnings revision returns in the wake of less frequent rebalancing suggests that real-world portfolio returns might fall well short of the paper results. This is a dilemma for small-cap investors.

Because current investment technologies offer a wide array of timely data, the temptation is to aggressively pursue new strategies that promise to arbitrage potential opportunities. The critical question then becomes whether this information is worthy of increased trading. Even with evidence that a factor will generate excess returns, the issue becomes at what cost? Can an investor afford to trade on market signals that change every minute? A manager must address these difficult questions before increasing portfolio turnover.

The earnings revision model, without trading constraints, produces compelling results that warrant the attention of investors. Because of the relatively short life span of these changes in earnings signals, however, investors must exercise much caution before implementing this model.

Market Risk

Swings in the market are accentuated in the earnings revision model. Thus, candidates with rising earnings revisions tend to perform exceptionally well in an upward market, but significantly underperform in a downward market. To some extent, most strategies that focus on stocks with high expectations behave in extremes relative to the markets. This

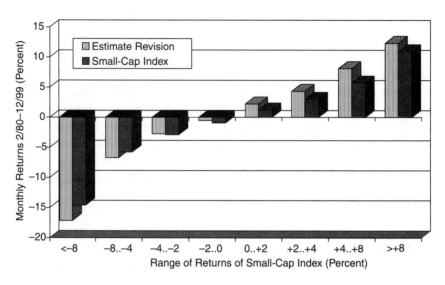

Figure 8.12   Dispersion of Returns—Estimate Revision

applies to the relative strength model discussed previously. As shown in Figure 8.12, the favored earnings candidates generate an excess 1.4 percent if the market takes an upward trend. Conversely, in a declining market, those stocks decline 2.6 percent more than the already weakening market.

When the overall market is weak, concerned participants are likely to subject stocks with rising aggressive expectations to special scrutiny. Market uncertainty is likely to hamper the performance of the favored glamour stocks. As a result, portfolios based on high earnings expectations models, including relative strength models, are more likely to act perversely.

VALUATION MODELS

A popular investment strategy is to buy undervalued stocks. The belief is that the market can overprice concerns into stocks. As a result, otherwise sound companies can exhibit unusually discounted market values, in turn creating investment opportunities. If the stock is really beaten down, its downside risk may be below normal. The argument behind investing in deeply discounted securities is that, as long as a company is generating positive earnings, cash flow, or free cash flow, the investor is, in a sense, being paid to wait. Buyers of deeply discounted securities are likely to be less concerned about a volatile equity market than momentum investors, who are playing a musical chairs game that requires them to nimbly exit ideas.

Valuation models identify undervalued stocks and compare their performance to that of stocks with high valuations. For smaller companies, the potential definitions of cheapness can be unending; for example, low price-to-earnings ratio, low price-to-sales ratio, or low price-to-book value ratio. Although it may be appealing to base a model on more robust definitions of value as in a dividend discount model that discounts future cash flows to the present using a risk-adjusted required rate of return, such models can require many earnings and interest rate assumptions. Because of the vagaries in smaller, less mature, firms, the simpler or fewer the assumptions required in the modeling process, the better. This is especially true when one is attempting to model a broad cross-section of stocks. It is advisable to reduce the study to the most practical scope.

Company Valuation Measures

In a simulation of several valuation measures, a cash flow or a price-to-cash flow model emerges as the most robust method of distinguishing cheap from expensive small stocks. Figure 8.13 summarizes the risk-adjusted

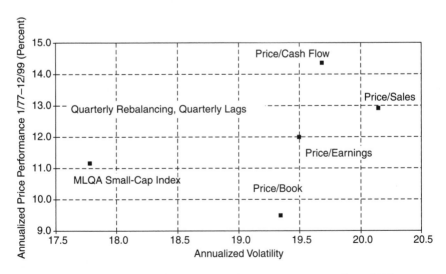

Figure 8.13 Risk/Return of Small-Cap Value Factors—Sector Adjusted Valuation

performance of several valuation measures, including price-to-earnings, price-to-cash flow, price-to-sales, and price-to-book value ratios. Each approach is plotted in terms of returns, along the y-axis, and risk, along the x-axis. Results plotted in the upper left quadrant are most compelling because returns are highest and volatility levels are muted in this quadrant. Conversely, model results found in the lower right quadrant are inferior because returns are lagging and volatility levels are high. All the valuation factors are based on quarterly reported financial data from December 1977 to December 1999. For example, the price-to-earnings ratio is based on the month-end price divided by the trailing four quarters of earnings. For the price-to-cash flow ratio, cash flow is based on earnings plus depreciation and amortization, or gross cash flow.

Surprisingly, a price-to-earnings valuation model for small stocks falls short of other simple models. The price-to-cash flow model generates a strong 14.5 percent rate of return annually versus 12.0 percent using a model based on price-to-earnings. In the same time frame, the small-cap market only offered 11.1 percent. The price-to-earnings ratio is one of the most popular measures of a firm's value. Yet the simulations suggest that a simple, low price-to-earnings model produces inferior results compared to a gross cash flow model.

A possible explanation is that many small-cap companies may simply be running earnings deficits. Unlike the blue chip segment, a good portion of the small-cap universe tends to consist of fledgling companies that are attempting to turn a positive cash flow. As a result, much of the small-cap universe is typically earnings deficit and therefore cannot be graded on a simple price-to-earnings basis. A price-to-earnings model might produce more relevant results if a greater proportion of the small-cap market could be sampled. Earnings not only account for a company's margins, they are also influenced by its capital structure and tax effects. Factors such as cash flow and sales fail to account for some or all of these considerations.

The investment world has focused much attention on the top line or revenues over the past few years. Although revenues are an adequate measure of stratifying small-cap stocks on a valuation basis, a close look at the price-to-sales results provokes concern because of the high level of variability. A price-to-cash flow model edges out the price-to-sales model on a returns basis but offers more predictable returns.

The shortcomings of revenue models might relate to the cyclical bias of price-to-sales ratios. At the peak of an economic cycle, cyclical stocks can appear cheap on a revenue basis. The sensitivity of such stocks to swings in the economy can cause a price-to-sales strategy to backfire, however. A good means of testing this theory would be to examine the valuation models on the basis of economic sensitivity. Economic sensitivity tests can be as useful to the modeling process as market sensitivity tests, which attempt to determine the level of sensitivity a factor has to an up or down market.

Structuring the Model

Valuation models stratify small stocks by their respective valuation levels and then group them by deciles. For example, a low price-to-cash flow simulation measures the performance and variability of returns for the cheapest basket or the cheapest 10 percent of the small-cap market. To arrive at the best valuation model, simply select the model with the best performance and minimal variability.

In addition, the valuation level of each stock is adjusted for the sector in which it resides. Adjusting a stock's valuation level for its sector removes a possible bias among sectors, which tend to trade at varying multiples. For example, the average technology stocks sell at several multiples of the average financial stocks. One can reasonably argue that technology stocks offer much higher growth prospects and therefore deserve to carry a higher multiple. Without attempting to correct for such a bias in the stock level data, a low valuation portfolio may consistently overweight deep cyclical and financial sectors, where stocks typically sell below the valuation levels of the market. Adjusting the valuation data by sector creates a somewhat more level playing field.

In addition to sector adjustments, it is necessary to incorporate lagging financial statement data. This helps minimize look-ahead bias that can be unknowingly embedded in one's backtest process. The four simple measures included here incorporate one quarter's worth of lagging financial data. To accomplish this, the denominator of the ratio, whether it be earnings or cash flow, is lagged by one quarter. For example, a price-to-earnings ratio of January 1999 is based on the price as of December 1999 and the full year's earnings ending third-quarter 1998.

Although financial statements are reported promptly to financial databases, there may be a lag between the reporting of the data and the end of the quarter. There also tend to be lags in updates to databases. The smaller the firm, the greater the reporting lag. Hence, when screening for a low price-to-earnings portfolio on a trailing 12-month basis, the current database is likely to lag by more than one quarter. Unlike screens for current data, screens for past performance data require investors to pay careful attention to reporting lags.

For example, fourth-quarter earnings for a company, assuming they are calendar based, are not available until weeks or even months into the first quarter of the next year. A simple query of a historical financial database is likely to yield the fourth-quarter data as of the end of December. Although this sounds trivial, if the firm reported earnings well above the norm and the stock immediately jumps, a backtest could easily and incorrectly credit the returns. If a time stamp is available for the data, some of these concerns become negligible. Curiously, a backtest that does not account for financial reporting lags results in a sizable low price-to-earnings effect. However, many of these excess gains are whittled away after lags are introduced to the data. Figure 8.14 represents the upward bias that can result in one's backtest without appropriate data assumptions. The simple price-to-earnings results suggest a whopping 21.3 percent rate of return without any lags and monthly rebalancing. A price-to-earnings model that takes into account the issues of lags and quarterly rebalancing only offers 12.0 percent rate of return. This is crucial—a price-to-earnings model that does not take into account properly lagged data and quarterly rebalancing can inflate one's results by roughly 9.3 percent.

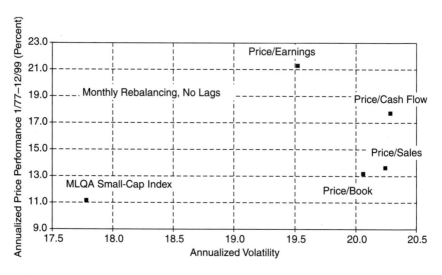

Figure 8.14   Risk/Return of Small-Cap Value Factors—Sector Adjusted Valuation

Stress Testing the Model

The price-to-cash flow model generates fairly robust results compared to many valuation measures within the small-cap market. In terms of risk return, rebalancing, and market sensitivity, this model yields positive results. Interestingly, the results are somewhat questionable when examined for linearity. The cheapest stocks fared well; yet the most expensive shares were not the laggards, as would be expected from the model's basic premise.

Variability

When the price-to-cash flow model is adjusted for variability, its returns remain superior to those of the small-cap market. The model outperforms the small-cap market by 6.9 percent, with only 1.9 percent in excess volatility. Not only is the variability of the model close to that of the small-cap market, which is a more diversified small-cap proxy, the uncertainty of the model's outcome is well below that of other models, such as the relative strength and earnings revision models discussed previously.

Simple value strategies usually offer a more conservative market profile, because they focus on neglected securities. These undervalued securities tend to trade less frequently and often reside in the backwaters of the market.

Linearity

Although a price-to-cash flow model appears to be a useful tool for investing in the small-cap market, its linearity results suggest caution. The cheapest "bucket," or the tenth decile, nicely outperforms the small-cap market, but numerous decile groups are more inconsistent. Figure 8.15 presents the returns and variability of each decile of small stocks ranked by price-to-cash flow levels. The most expensive group, or the first decile, underperforms the basket of cheapest stocks (annualized gain of 9.9 percent), but fails to offer the weakest results, as would be expected. Oddly enough, the second decile, not the first decile, appears to underperform all other groups—it only generates a 9.3 percent annual rate of return.

These results are difficult to interpret. If one can argue that the cheapest stocks offer the best returns because the market has overpriced risks, it might logically follow that the most expensive stocks

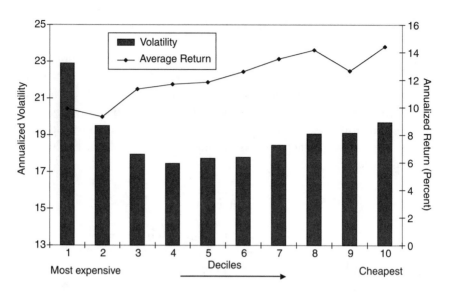

Figure 8.15   Small-Cap Value Factor: Price to Cash Flow—Deciles 1–10

should subsequently generate inferior results because the market has overpriced a bright outlook.

It is difficult to accept the logic that cheap stocks outperform and average multiples tend to be weak, while the most expensive stocks generate par results. The difficulty of explaining these results points to the complexity of the valuation process. The best value stock is not always the cheapest candidate, as measured by price to cash flow, price-to-sales, or any other standard. Valuations must also take into account the expectations that investors have for the stock. It is possible that a high-multiple stock will continue to generate above-average returns. If the stock's outlook continues to be revised upward, its already high multiple may reach even higher valuations.

Even though the valuation of smaller firms requires more than simply calculating a single price-to-cash flow multiple, the results of price-to-cash flow models are sufficiently compelling to warrant their use in distinguishing cheap from expensive stocks.

Transaction Costs

With an eye toward turnover and trading costs, the price-to-cash flow model remains fairly robust even when the model is rebalanced less frequently. Figure 8.16 relates the performance of a price to cash flow model with varied rebalancing periods. Given fewer rebalancing periods, the annualized rate of return on a quarterly basis is roughly 14.5 percent, slightly better than the monthly variation of 13.8 percent. Overall volatility is slightly higher for the quarterly variation—19.5 percent versus 19.4 percent annually. These results suggest that a value model is not penalized for less rebalancing, in fact the results suggest otherwise, and therefore are less likely to diminish as one attempts to minimize trading costs.

The results appear to support the long-held belief that strategies with a value tilt exhibit less turnover. This makes sense, as investors tend to ignore cheap and beaten down securities and focus little attention on the cheapest group of stocks, which make up the first decile of price-to-cash flow stocks. If there is less investor interest, the chances of revised expectations rapidly go down. This is in stark contrast to the fast-changing relative strength and earnings revision models.

High expectation ideas, epitomized by Internet stocks, typically receive much attention from the investment community. Because all eyes are on the next move of these potentially stratospheric growth stocks, it is easy to find opinions on them. For every new investment concept, a new expert is born. With newfound experts come rapidly changing opinions. By contrast, a down-and-out furniture maker is likely to receive little attention. Few "experts" are willing to offer their opinions on such a

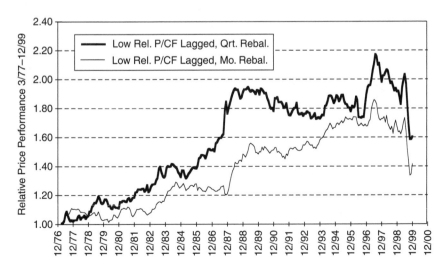

Figure 8.16   Small-Cap Value Factor—Rebalancing Monthly vs. Quarterly

downtrodden stock. Hence, neglected securities are less likely to ebb and flow than their more glamorous counterparts.

Market Risk

Downside risk is perhaps the area of critical distinction between the small-cap valuation model and the momentum models. Even though the momentum model produces positive long-run results, this investing style appears to weaken in down markets. On the other hand, the small-cap valuation model holds up well. Small-cap value and momentum models lead the market when the market is flat to rising, but their results begin to diverge in down markets. Although momentum models tend to weaken more severely than the small-cap benchmark in a down market, the value models appear to weaken only as much as the small-cap benchmark. Hence, value strategies appear to protect on the downside, while momentum strategies accentuate market risks.

Figure 8.17 presents the range of returns for the small-cap benchmark. The value model, as represented by dark bars, outperforms the benchmark, represented by gray bars, in a better flat to rising market, while the basket of cheap stocks weakens slightly more than the market in downturns. In an extremely weak market (e.g., when small-caps are

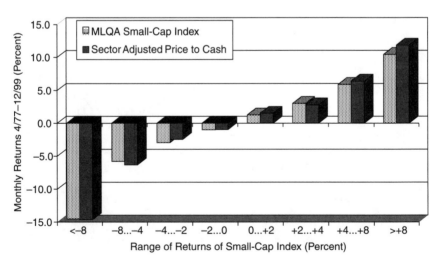

Figure 8.17   Dispersion of Returns—Small-Cap Value Investing

losing more than 8 percent), the value approach only loses an incremental 0.13 percent or 13 basis points beyond the small-cap market.

Cheap stocks can be seen as the ultimate low beta securities. Because of this trait, undervalued stocks are less likely to swing with market vagaries. For the most part, these securities are truly neglected. They do not participate in the rise of the market, which explains their laggard status, and are likely to remain stagnant as the market trades down.

THE SIZE EFFECT

Although each model discussed in this chapter displays unique characteristics and varied performance figures, they all exhibit one striking similarity, a significant size effect. Each model outperforms the small-cap benchmark and the corresponding large-cap model. Even when the large-cap model is adjusted for the size effect, the small-cap models offer a considerable advantage over the large-cap segment.

As a case in point, the small-cap relative strength model generates a strong 22.3 percent rate of return versus 15.9 percent for the large-cap proxy—almost a 7 percent annual bias that favors small-cap models. In simple terms, there is a compelling performance bias toward the secondary market.

Figure 8.18 relates the performance differential between size-defined relative strength models. The results of the earnings revision

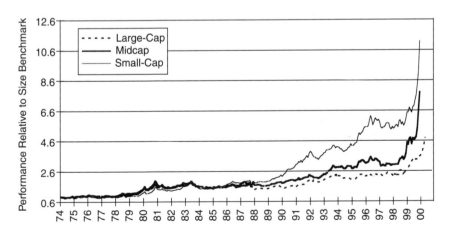

Figure 8.18 Positive Relative Strength Models by Size

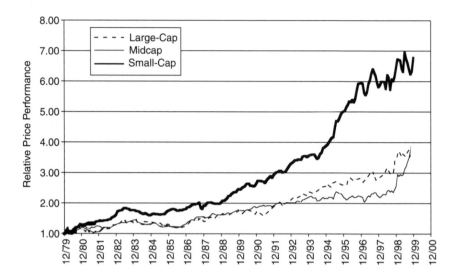

Figure 8.19   Positive Earnings Estimate Revision Models

model point to the same conclusion. Figure 8.19 represents the relative performance of the earnings revision model, stratified by size. The small-cap earnings revision model yields an excess 2.3 percent return over the large-cap model annually.

Likewise, the valuation framework yields similar results as illustrated in Figure 8.20. A large-cap valuation model that exploits pricing ineffi-ciencies among the large-cap shares falls short of its small-cap counter-part. The small-cap value model outperforms its large-cap counterpart by 1.6 percent per year.

Small-cap models should yield returns that exceed those of their cor-responding large-cap models, an advantage that can be attributed to the lack of information flow among secondary stocks. Because the large-cap market is terribly efficient, it is difficult and perhaps even futile to arbi-trage large-cap price discrepancies. As pointed out in Chapter 2, however, the small-cap market is underfollowed and thus less efficiently priced. Large-cap shares are covered by an average of 19 analysts per name, whereas the small-cap universe has an average of 6 analysts. This dispar-ity in research coverage may lead to investment opportunities.

One might well question whether a model based on price momen-tum should really offer an investment edge. Probably not. Yet if a small stock is not being followed by twenty or thirty analysts or is a neglected stock, then a jump in price might call attention to such a lesser known

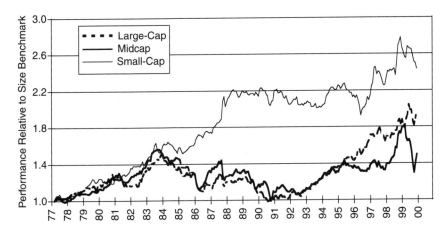

Figure 8.20 Price/Cash Flow Model by Size

small firm. In this instance, price becomes information. This argument also holds for the earnings revision framework. Because investors are well briefed on earnings estimates and management goals for most of the megacap companies, a shift in the consensus estimates for these stocks might be only reactionary. However, applying an earnings revision model to smaller stocks allows the small-cap investor the opportunity to quickly focus on possibly changing fundamentals.

The disparity in information flow, which is a by-product of the current market emphasis on large caps, is further compounded by the law of large numbers. Even if investors wanted more thorough coverage of the secondary market, the 10-to-1 ratio of small to large stocks prevents small caps from being covered at a level comparable to that of large caps. Furthermore, the valuation model is no exception to this information flow argument. Cheap stocks are likely to remain unnoticed in the small-cap market. A worthy small stock may remain cheap for some time before it is exploited, in contrast to a large-cap stock. It is extremely difficult to find large-cap value stocks.

The performance disparities between small and large stocks relate not only to the lack of information on smaller stocks but also to the difficult financing environment that smaller firms typically face.[6] As a result, the prices of small-cap value candidates can remain in a depressed state much longer than their large-cap, well-financed counterparts.

The performance results previously discussed indicate not only that quantitative methods can help investors "beat" the small-cap market but also that active management style participants might profit by taking aim at the small-cap market. These results should not, however, dissuade investors from making qualitative decisions. Because of the information disparities in smaller firms, pure modeling systems should not be the only logical approach to small-cap investing. A great deal of the data on small caps are never recorded and thus cannot by used for modeling purposes. Although databases have significantly improved since the 1980s, they have much further to go.

Evaluating a management team can add "alpha" or excess returns to an investment approach: Is a great stock purely the result of industry trends or does it partly depend on the talented individuals who have carved out a market niche? Until databanks can offer some of the subtle insights into a company and industry that only an individual can offer, the best approach might be to combine quantitative techniques and qualitative insights to obtain the maximum analytical leverage.

A Multifactor Small-Cap Model

All the models discussed in this chapter can form the basis of a multifactor small-cap model. A stock selection model can be structured to combine, for instance, a simple earnings revision model with a price-to-cash flow model. The change in earnings forecast can be a proxy for the change in expectations for the stock, while the valuation model allows investors to determine whether the improved outlook has already been priced in the stock.

Such a structure allows investors to grade a large subset of stocks in a highly efficient manner. By focusing on securities that rate well or on stocks with high expectations and low valuations, investors can systematically screen out investment noise in the small-cap market. Furthermore, the results can also identify risky securities. Stocks that rank poorly, that have falling expectations and high multiples, are likely to introduce more risk to an investor's portfolio.

An investor can determine which variables to emphasize by running simulations. The emphasis of the variables should also depend on one's investment style, as discussed in Chapter 9. Is the goal of the portfolio to find terrific small-cap ideas? Or is the goal more specific, for example, to invest in smaller growth stocks? In this instance, the portfolio should focus more on stock expectations. After all, growth stock investors are unlikely to start their investment search with rigid valuation targets. By contrast to a growth stock approach, a value-based portfolio is more likely to emphasize valuations over expectations.

Not only can models enable investors to focus on core ideas, they can also be engineered to focus on style-specific constraints, such as those discussed in Chapter 9. This new financial technology offers investment tools that simulate complex relationships in a workable framework. Not surprisingly, data modeling has become another competitive factor among investors. It is especially relevant to small-cap investors because small-cap models appear to produce more fruitful results than similar large-cap models.

NINE

Style Investing

INVESTMENT STYLE—GROWTH, VALUE, AND THE STYLE CYCLE

THE GROWTH or value orientation of a stock selection process, known as investment style, has become a common part of the investment landscape. One's style bias can account for significant variation between an investor's realized returns and the market. The issue is no longer simply if the market is rising or falling, but rather which one of its components is deteriorating or rebounding. A market can generate sub-par results, yet components such as growth stocks may be in the midst of a bull market. As a result, identifying whether it is more opportune to be invested with a growth or value bias has become relevant to market performance.

The research on investment styles is extensive. Discussions range from asset allocation of growth and value to tactical shifts between one and the other, cause and effect linkages, and measurement of investment styles. For greater insight into beating the market or lowering their risk profile, market participants have found style distinctions are a way to focus on their own competencies, label their process, and identify their approach for existing and prospective clients. As a result, the search to distinguish performance differentials between growth and value has become especially keen. Furthermore, this demarcation of growth and value styles has become increasingly institutionalized as active managers attempt to distinguish their approach, and clients, including the consultant community, in turn struggle to categorize and evaluate investment managers.

Style Rotations

Style rotations can create severe performance disparities for small-cap investors. Small-cap market participants need to be aware of the investment-style implications of their underlying bets. This is especially true for those investors who do not consider themselves to be aggressive growth or deep-value bettors. The performance swings between growth stocks and value stocks can create a difficult backdrop for even the most talented investor. By being aware of the possible style bias in one's portfolio, one can be proactive in responding to the market's vagaries.

Smaller capitalized firms tend to exhibit greater swings in style rotation than do large-cap stocks. For example, the period from June 1994 to May 1996 was a phenomenal period for growth investing: growth funds posted a whopping 66 percent gain compared to a 35 percent gain among value investors. The Russell 2000, a popular small-cap index, appreciated by 53 percent over that period. The sharp run-up in these small-cap growth stocks made the careers of many up-and-coming investment managers.

This was a period in which investors chased after wonderful smaller growth firms. Even though the small-cap bull market had begun to exhibit signs of sluggishness, these new, tiny, sexy growth companies had captured the fancy of the investing public. A coffee/coffee bar company could make a plausible case that secular earnings growth in the coffee and coffee bar business was worth over 50 times current earnings. Starbucks started 1995 with an earnings multiple of 62.5, yet a punch-drunk market continued to swallow up such aromatic blends of growth at an alarming rate. Starbucks managed to rally roughly 53 percent over the course of that year, and stocks such as Starbucks led the market.

A boom in the capital spending cycle and investors' fetish for technology stocks fueled this dramatic rally among aggressive growth stocks. During the 1994–96 period, the small-cap technology sector gained a whopping 40.8 percent. As a result, technology companies went to high and extreme valuation multiples. In similar fashion, drug and biotechnology-related shares also captivated the investment community in 1995. The secondary shares in drug-related ideas rallied 51 percent, while biotechnology stocks jumped 82 percent.

This era marked a period of misery for the value hunter. The 1994–96 bull market for growth stocks represented a 24 percent shortfall for value investors. The best performing stocks were not being priced to some reasonable level of comparable earnings, cash flow, or even revenue by the market. Yet the shares of these high-priced stocks continued to roll over even the most compelling value situations. The underperformance of value funds was severe enough to shake even the staunchest value investors during the 1994–96 period.

Those who approached the aggressive growth segment with caution were finally rewarded in the summer of 1996. The period that immediately followed was much more favorable for value investors. Small-cap value funds generated a gain of 3 percent from June 1996 to April 1997–98. While 3 percent appears meager for the stock market, emerging growth funds lost on average 15 percent over this same time frame creating an 18 percent gap between value and growth. The Russell 2000 lost 3 percent during this period.

Traditional groups that value investors commonly examine such as transportation stocks gained 37 percent, credit cyclicals such as building material stocks appreciated by 42 percent, and basic material stocks gained approximately 37 percent in 1997. Even energy stocks, a long-time laggard, led the technology sector that year. This sea change in the market environment was especially difficult for the aggressive growth manager.

The Polarized Small-Cap Universe

The small-cap universe is polarized in terms of investment styles. Because of the extreme swings in performance between growth and value styles, small-cap investors have to be mindful of where they are in the style cycle. Figure 9.1 illustrates the divergence of performance between growth and value styles. Each line represents the relative performance between growth and value. The solid thick line depicts small-cap style results, and the dotted line represents large-cap style results. An inclining line represents growth stocks outperforming value stocks. A declining

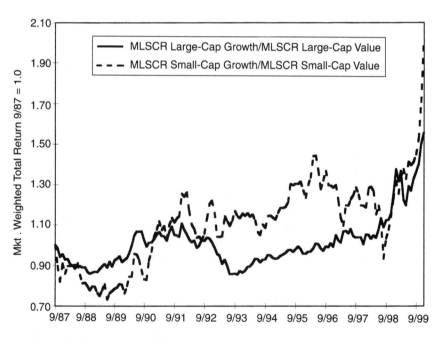

Figure 9.1   Investment Style—Growth vs. Value and Small-Cap vs. Large-Cap

line indicates that value-driven strategies are outperforming growth stocks.

Notice how much more extreme the rotations of style are among the secondary stocks (solid line). Large capitalization rotations in growth and value are simply not as significant as they are for smaller firms.[1]

If one is searching for value, truly deep-value situations can be found in the small-cap market. After all, the more the price of a stock collapses, the lower the market capitalization. Likewise, truly aggressive growth stocks are much more abundant within the small-cap market. Expectations can be especially high among smaller firms. Even though firms that deliver 50 percent growth in earnings per annum are rare, the odds of finding a 100-million-dollar corporation growing at 50 percent per annum are far greater than the likelihood of finding a 100-billion-dollar corporation growing as fast. As a result, the drivers of investment styles, while playing an important role in the equity market generally, play a critical role within the small-cap market. The dramatic variation in the success of one investment style versus another among stocks, especially smaller companies, can profoundly add to or detract from investment performance.

Growth and Value Compared

In simple terms, growth stock investors look for companies with above average, sustainable growth. "True growth is organic and comes from within," according to economist Peter Bernstein.[2] Growth investors look for companies that can capture higher growth due to some advantage based on advanced technology, can generate above-average profit margins, and face minimal price competition. Growth companies are viewed as likely to be better insulated from swings in the economic cycle than commodity-based organizations that accentuate the ebb and flow of the economy. The search for growth typically places the investor in a higher multiple subset of the market. Fast growing companies are likely to attract interest and are more likely to be accompanied by higher valuation levels than more economically sensitive firms.

The level of aggressiveness a growth investor can assume varies. Some growth investors look for firms with strong positive profit comparisons, yet take into account some metric of valuation levels. In the extreme case, such investors are likely to avoid firms with triple-digit valuation figures. Other extreme growth investors aggressively search out the fastest growing companies with little regard for valuation yardsticks.

Such firms, they believe, can generate superior results over the long term. The logic goes that the market can overlook real opportunities because the earnings of a start-up appear depressed. However, investing in assets with skyrocketing potential invariably demands grit and internal fortitude that few investors may have.

Value investors, by contrast, look for companies that offer compellingly low valuations. They hope that the market has overpriced existing concerns about a company and believe that market participants cause security prices to overshoot and undershoot intrinsic values. If a company is experiencing above-average growth, the market chases the stock above reasonable levels. If a firm hits adverse business conditions, the market tends to severely punish its shares. To value investors, a precipitous drop in a security's share price can suggest that the market may have overpriced its concerns. The value investor looks for companies that are severely down in price terms, so low that adverse news could not cause further price erosion. Stocks whose riskiness has been overpriced are more likely to offer reasonable risk/reward comparisons.

The nature of growth stock investing suggests that an investor who follows this style will be willing to ride out the vagaries of the market if a firm's business is sound. Conversely, a value investor may prefer to ride out the vagaries of the economic cycle to avoid the market's volatility. Style-based investing may be defined in terms of preference for different types of risk taking. A growth investor can assume considerable market risks, while the value investor appears to be more confident taking on business risks.

Because holding companies with extreme valuations can lead to sudden price fluctuations, growth stock bettors tend to participate in a riskier segment of the equity market. At the first hint of business concern, the market reaction can be swift. The caveat for those holding securities with extreme valuations is that such companies typically exhibit few signs of business erosion. In fact, the business outlook for most growth stocks tends to be positive.

Conversely, a value candidate may exhibit less share price volatility than its growth counterpart yet reflect greater business risks. The market is fairly efficient at pricing these perceived risks. If a stock is trading at a significant discount to its peers, then it is likely that concerns exist about the business outlook of the firm. An investor who purchases cheap stock might minimize the potential for market risks, but increase exposure to the business risks of the firm in question.

Focusing on investment styles as a means of besting the competition and the market has garnered as much interest as that of traditional sector-based investing. However, sector tilts or bets are more easily defined than portfolio positions based on investment styles as well as being simpler to recognize and model. While investors have taken into account their sector position with respect to the overall market for the past 60 years or more, understanding one's style bias has only become prevalent over the past two decades. If a company is in the paper business, it is easy to determine that it belongs in the basic industries sector and is probably more cyclical than, for argument's sake, a food company. Most investors can follow this argument to the next logical step and conclude that by holding the paper company, one is implicitly betting on a robust economic backdrop.

Classification according to investment styles is complex and variable. Companies do not necessarily remain in any particular category, growth or value, over the long run. Depending on perceptions, market direction, and company strategies, a full-fledged growth stock can quickly become a value stock. Oxford Healthcare is a good example of a growth stock of the early 1990s. Investors saw the managed care business as a fast-growth industry and aggressively bid-up Oxford and most of its peers. The stock rocketed in two years. As the client base broadened, so did the expense ratios for the industry. The rising costs of the industry started to slow the growth rates of the companies, and investors began to shy away. In a six-month period, Oxford and many of its peers exhibited a collapse in share prices. Thus, in a short time, a segment of growth stocks fell out of favor and began to shrink from growth investors' holdings. As share prices continued to tumble, value investors began taking notice. The industry provided a necessary service—rationing much needed resources. At some price, these companies make good investments.

An emerging growth company that has fallen on tough times may stumble with a product rollout and raise serious concern in the marketplace. Investors may reevaluate the firm and question its potential for growth. If expectations fall, causing the selloff of the stock to levels well below intrinsic value, a firm that was only recently perceived as a growth bet can quickly become a value candidate. At this point, value investors may assess the damage, question whether the market's wrath was an overreaction, and decide whether this "fallen angel" is a good value.

Similarly, a beaten-down value candidate can, by design or accident, launch a successful product or campaign and become a high expectation candidate. Price level alone, therefore, may not be the best indicator of the inherent style of a stock. Nevertheless, most simple valuation parameters of style benchmarks are primarily driven by price changes. Although most simple value metrics tend to contain some measure of value from the income statement, the balance sheet, or both, the share price of the value measure is by far the most volatile component. As price swings occur, the style assignment of a stock, be it growth or value, can easily bounce between deep value situations to severely overbought conditions.

Drivers of Style Investing

Attempting to benefit from the timing of growth and value rotations in the small-cap market is difficult and often ephemeral. Nonetheless, investors need to grasp the primary drivers of each style because the performance divergence between growth and value stocks is significant. Investment styles are interrelated and appear to perform inversely. As growth comes into favor, it tends to be at the expense of value, and vice versa. What events or economic conditions signal these shifts?

Three groups of indicators offer insight into investment style rotations. The first category includes proxies for economic trends. Relationships such as changes in industrial production, corporate profit forecasts, and changes in earnings estimates appear to be useful for tying together the economic cross-currents to investment styles. The second category is based on interest rate relationships. Changes in short- and long-term interest rates appear to be useful. Other useful measures include the slope in the yield curve. A third group of indicators that offers some guidance is derived from the equity market. Changes in equity market volatility and in the valuation of growth versus value stocks, for each example, are also useful in determining the market's preference for one style or the other.

The definitions of growth and value offer useful insights into the turning points for investment styles. As described previously, style-based investing may be defined along the lines of a preference for particular types of risk taking. Growth investing reflects an investor who is much more willing to ride out the vagaries of the market with a stock if the firm's business is sound. Conversely, a value investor may be more willing to ride out the vagaries of the economic cycle with his investment to avoid exposure to the swings of the market. This critical distinction implies a demarcation along the lines of economic cycle. As suggested by market strategist Richard Bernstein, factors such as the abundance of earnings on the one hand, and economic sensitivity on the other, tend to drive the preference for growth or value.[3]

Against a robust economic backdrop, even marginal companies with less than optimal business strategies may prosper, and the equity component of such firms may thrive. This happens not merely because investors believe that past woes are forgiven and a wobbly corporate strategy has become acceptable overnight, but because such stocks have most likely suffered significant corrections as investors questioned the corporate profit cycle. An improved economic outlook forces market participants to revisit those shares that encountered severe overreaction. As the economic outlook improves, marginal companies with depressed valuations are more likely to be rewarded.

Growth stocks are less likely to outperform in such a scenario. If marginal companies are beginning to reach or surpass consensus estimates, why should an investor pay a significant premium for growth that appears to be similarly attained by marginal companies carrying half the equity valuation premium?

Even though economically sensitive stocks such as paper, steel, and retail come to mind, value stocks can also represent marginal companies in fairly stable or economically insensitive groups. These companies may be value-based simply because of poor implementation of corporate strategy, questionable corporate practices, lack of a clear corporate strategy, poor communication with the investment community, or a host of similar factors that cause such companies to remain laggards and appear to carry a valuation discount.

Growth stocks are more likely to prevail as the economic cycle becomes uncertain or shifts downward. The companies with a well-established franchise and a tendency to generate more consistent earnings or cash flow are more likely to remain a smoothly flowing operation in difficult times. Such companies are likely to maintain or expand their valuation multiple as the range in the overall market multiple compresses. Hence, as the outlook for economic profit growth is muted, companies less likely to stumble, or growth companies, are more likely to lead value investments.

Even though the valuation levels for most growth stocks tend to be well above average, investors are less likely to question such levels if economic activity is expected to slow. Companies that traditionally appear too expensive become attractive if they can successfully dodge developing worries about the economy. Valuation levels play a less significant role in the investment process as growth becomes scarce.

Economic Activity and Investment Styles

Changes in patterns of economic growth tend to drive the cyclical shifts between growth and value stocks. Measures such as industrial production, forecast in market earnings, and earnings revision support this phenomenon.

Industrial Production

The inverse relationship between investment styles and the economic backdrop is depicted in Figure 9.2. The chart represents the performance of small-cap growth versus value stocks (solid line) in the context of changes in the industrial production data (dotted line). If industrial production data suggest a stronger economic backdrop, valuations become more relevant to investors. As a result, value strategies outperform growth. Figure 9.3 represents the subsequent 12-month style results. Notice that growth strategies handily outpace value as industrial production remains below an annual growth rate of 3 percent. The statistics that relate the change in industrial production and style are significant.[4]

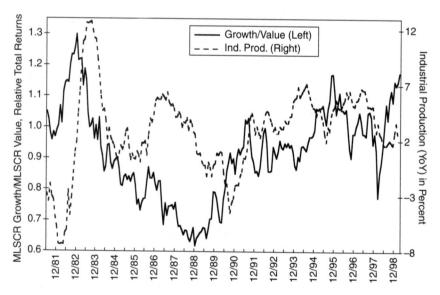

Figure 9.2   Investment Styles and Economic Activity

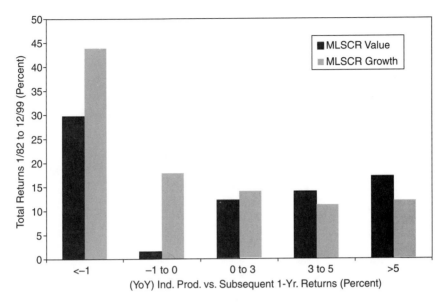

Figure 9.3   Change in Industrial Production and Style Results

Corporate Profit Forecasts

Forecasts in corporate profits also support the apparent connection between economic strength and style rotations. The changes in profits and economic growth tend to be correlated. The forecasts are, one hopes, more forward-looking and potentially more sensitive to inflection points than signals derived by traditional economic growth measures. Figure 9.4 reflects the performance of small-cap growth versus small-cap value (solid line) with respect to the rise and fall in corporate profit forecasts (dotted line). Although the relationship is not perfectly correlated to the swings in style, dominant growth markets are more evident in periods that exhibit slower growth expectations. Conversely, value appears to outperform as expectations for the profit cycle accelerate. Thus, style swings are inversely related to profits expectations.

The regression results of a change in forecast S&P 500 earnings, using consensus I/B/E/S estimates, and the style results are not as strong as the industrial production data but still compelling[5] (see Table 9.1 for a comparison).

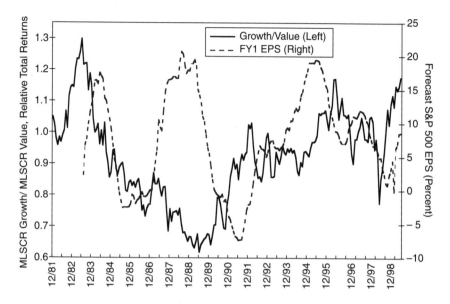

Figure 9.4   Investment Styles and Profit Cycle

Earnings Revisions

A look at earnings revision data in Figure 9.5 offers supportive signals on style transitions. In this instance, the positive earnings revisions for growth stocks, using the Merrill Lynch Small Cap Growth Index, are compared to the level of positive revisions for the value constituents. An increasing ratio suggests that small-cap growth stocks have marginally improving earnings forecast compared to their value counterparts. The coincident relationship between earnings revision and style is positive and somewhat useful as a predictive model.

Surprisingly, this relationship appears more robust as a leading indicator than as a coincident (i.e., concurrent) indicator. The one-year change in earnings revision, with a one-year lead, appears to have good predictive ability. However, the results suggest a contrary indication (see Figure 9.5). As revisions become more compelling for growth stocks, for example, the statistics suggest that such stocks are likely to lag value 12 months hence.[6] Curiously, the 6-month lead relationship does not appear significant.

Other measures of change in economic trends, such as earnings surprise or companies posting unexpected earnings results, do not appear to generate similarly convincing statistics. This might be partly attributed to fewer observations having been available during the test sample period.

Interest Rate Effects

The theory that growth stocks are also longer duration, or more interest-rate sensitive, is especially useful in analyzing market swings from growth to value stocks. The typically higher valuation levels that accompany

Table 9.1   Regression Analysis

	Beta Coef	T-Stat	Correlation	R-square
Economic Indicators				
Industrial Production	−1.90	−6.75†	−0.44	0.19
Profit Cycle (Forecast EPS)	−0.70	−5.61†	−0.38	0.14
Profit Cycle (Forecast EPS)—				
12 mos lead	0.05	0.35	0.03	0.00
Currency (Trade Weighted Dollar)	−0.06	−0.64	−0.05	0.00
Equity Relationships (Market Sensitivity)				
Relative Valuation (Growth to Value)				
P/BK	0.62	14.15†	0.71	0.51
P/BK—12 mos lead	−0.25	−3.59†	−0.26	0.07
P/CF	0.09	2.14*	0.15	0.02
P/CF—12 mos lead	0.09	2.16	0.16	0.02
P/S	0.36	6.93†	0.44	0.20
P/S—12 mos lead	−0.31	−5.19	−0.36	0.13
Relative Strength Risk Indicator	0.10	2.91*	0.20	0.04
Relative Strength Risk Indicator	−0.21	−6.3†	0.42	0.18
Volatility	−0.02	−0.86	−0.06	0.00
Relative Estimate Revision				
(Growth to Value)	0.12	3.5*	0.24	0.06
Relative Estimate Revision				
(Growth to Value—12 mos lead	−0.19	−4.17†	−0.29	0.09
Interest Rate				
Short-Term Interest Rate	−0.14	−3.68†	−0.25	0.06
Long-Term Interest Rate	−0.16	−2.51*	−0.18	0.03
CPI	−0.20	−0.19	−0.01	0.00
PPI	2.20	2.58*	0.18	0.03

Growth and Value Returns are based on the Merrill Lynch Small-Cap Research (MLSCR) Style indices, 1/82–5/99. The recession analysis is based on 1-year change of the variables.

* = T-Stat is significant at the 95th percentile level of confidence.

† = T-Stat is significant at the 99th percentile level of confidence.

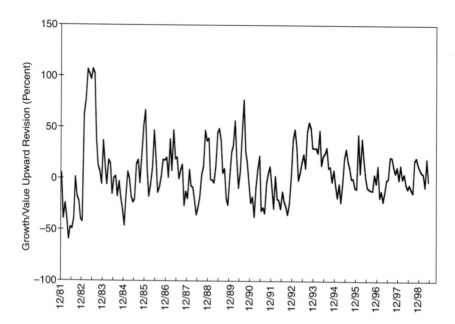

Figure 9.5 One-Year Change in Three Month's Earnings Revision

growth stocks suggest that a great deal of growth is discounted well into the future. Few assets benefit from a rise in interest rates, but the impact is most severe among the highest expectation, highest multiple subset of the equity market. Small-cap growth stocks tend to carry the highest valuation premium in the U.S. equity market and as a result face the most significant obstacles as bond yields rise. As interest rates rise, future earnings prospects are thought to deteriorate. Because the price of a growth stock is predicated on an earnings stream reaching far into the future, the discounting effect has a greater impact on it than on a value stock. Value choices have much more reasonable earnings multiples and therefore have less to lose as interest rates rise.

Falling interest rates are generally positive for most asset classes—especially growth stocks. Each tick down in bond yields causes the discounting effect to dramatically increase the present value of such firms. Because the future cash flow stream of value ideas is not as back-ended as that of growth stocks, a fall in interest rates has less material impact.

The relationship of interest rates and growth stock is also critical from a financing standpoint. Although most small-cap firms are fairly starved for capital, growth stocks, by nature, tend to demand capital for ongoing operations. In some instances, the expected growth of a firm is predicated on a furious acquisition track. This need to finance growth is humorously portrayed in Michael Wolff's *Burn Rate,* which chronicles the unending need to raise capital in the Internet industry.[7] The book's title refers to the number of days remaining before a firm runs out of cash.

Generally, the cost of capital follows the trend in interest rates. As rates rise, the cost of capital increases (for illustration, see Figure 9.6). The acceptance rate for projects is inversely related to the cost of capital. If the cost of money goes up, the hurdle rate, or the minimum expected rate of return on investment, also goes up. Hence, the companies with the most need for cash are most severely penalized and in the most extreme circumstances, are locked out of the market. Predictably, growth companies, not value, tend to react most violently as interest rates rise.

The change in both short-term Treasury yields—using 3-month T-bills—and long-term government bond yields—using 10-year Treasury notes—can be examined against investment style results. Generally, increases in either long- or short-term instruments offer cautionary signals for growth stocks. Figure 9.7 relates the inverse relationship between interest rates and small-cap growth stocks. It appears as though the short-term signals are more robust than changes in long-term bond yields.[8] This might be partly caused by the manner in which short-term instruments

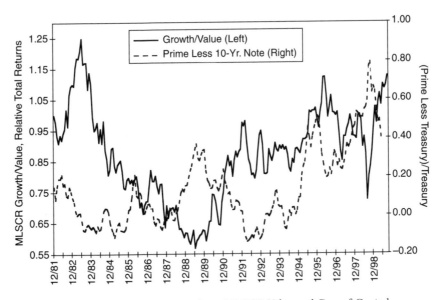

Figure 9.6   MLSCR Growth vs. MLSCR Value and Cost of Capital

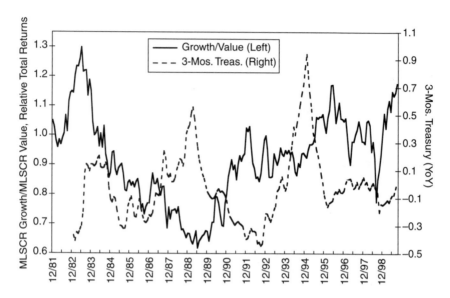

Figure 9.7   Investment Styles and Short-Term Interest Rate

change versus long-term bond yields. Because long-term bond yields tend to drift more than short term, and short-term changes tend to be more policy driven, short-term Treasuries may offer a more compelling signal.

Factors such as economic activity and interest rates are related. If the economy strengthens or is expected to strengthen, growth becomes more widespread and therefore the demand or competition for capital increases. As a result, interest rates rise. Hence, value can outperform growth because of an expected pickup in economic activity and the concurrent increase in interest rates. Conversely, as the economy softens and interest rates subside, longer-duration, higher expectation growth stocks are more likely to lead value.

The slope of the yield curve can be argued as a predictor of economic growth. In this instance, the steepness of the yield curve appears to offer quite useful signals in timing style rotations. Figure 9.8 relates the subsequent 12-month performance of growth versus value stocks in the context of the slope of the yield curve. The flat yield curve indicates a growth stock bias.

Other measures related to the changes in interest rates are the Consumer Price Index (CPI) and Producer Price Index (PPI). Surprisingly, both variables appear to offer anemic signals at best. The data

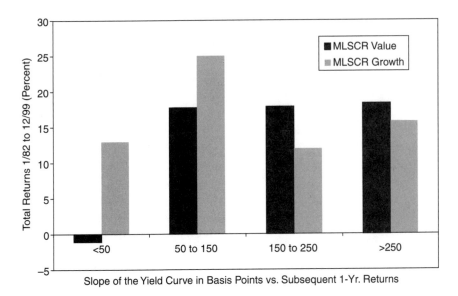

Figure 9.8 Slope of the Yield Curve and Style Results

suggests that growth stocks appear marginally healthier in a more flexible pricing environment or when the rate of change in the PPI increases (see Table 9.1 for details).

Equity Market Signals

Valuations and Style Turns

Equity-driven relationships also appear useful in understanding and predicting style rotations, especially factors such as relative valuations of growth versus value shares and market volatility.

Looking at the valuation level of growth stocks with respect to the price of value stocks appears useful. Simply put, growth stocks generally trade at a significant premium to value situations, yet a valuation premium should range within some reasonable band. It appears as though style rotations occur at the extreme valuation points.

Growth outperforms value coincident to the relative valuation reading. Using the relative valuation reading as a leading indicator offers a fairly contrary signal, however. This makes sense—an outperforming style is likely to exhibit higher relative valuation multiples. Yet, as those valuations get rich, it is more likely that the performance of those stocks reverse or lag their counterparts.

The statistical tests suggest price-to-book measures offer some of the more compelling coincident signals. A look at the predictive ability in such models, however, suggests that the price-to-sales relationship offer a more consistent signal than the price-to-book relationship. Figure 9.9 relates the valuation of growth stocks to value stocks (see Table 9.1 for the regression summary).[9]

Market Polarization and Style Turns

A look at the concentration of stock market returns appears useful in determining a style bent (see also Chapter 7 for a detailed discussion of this topic). This measure indicates the level of polarity of the equity market. Figure 9.10 represents yearly change in valuation premium of momentum stocks. Simply put, a polarized market leads to a more turbulent equity environment. As a result, higher-multiple stocks are likely to face added pressures. An increasingly polarized or concentrated market reading suggests that growth stocks are outperforming their value counterparts.

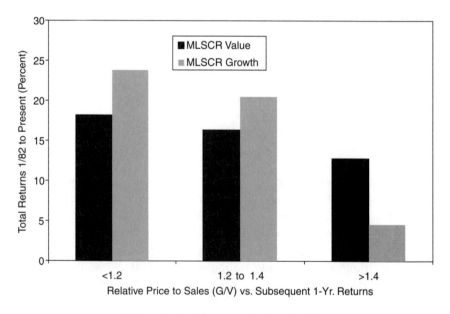

Figure 9.9 Valuation and Style Results

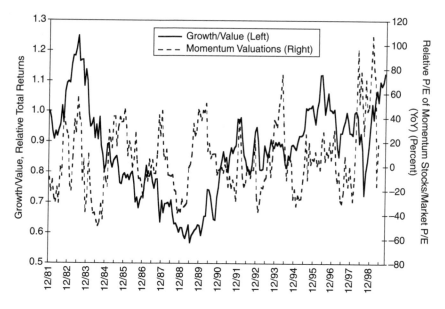

Figure 9.10   Investment Styles and Momentum Stocks

Interpreting the polarized readings as a lead indicator offers a solid contrary reading. An increase in the relative multiples over a one-year trend suggests that value strategies are likely to outpace their growth counterparts in subsequent periods. The regression statistics for investment style in a polarized market are inversely related and statistically significant.[10] Table 9.1 summarizes the statistical relationship between investment styles and market driven signals.

GROWTH OR VALUE ORIENTATION: THE PSYCHOLOGICAL FACTOR

Product proliferation can easily occur in the throes of a bull market. Investors have witnessed the birth of thousands of new investment funds over the past decade. With share prices rising over the past 15 years, it has become much easier for successful fund families to cross-sell their expertise. Hence, as share prices continue to trend upward, it is common to see traditionally U.S.-focused investors introduce international funds, long-time large-cap managers market small-company funds, and growth investors parlay their skill into the value camp. Competition among funds to grow their asset bases drives equity managers to develop creative approaches to attracting capital. Such a proliferation of investment vehicles has caused the investment audience to question whether all the available choices make sense for their long-term holdings or are simply a fad spawned by a fast and furious bull market.

The marketing success of investment style products—for example, those sold as growth funds, growth at a reasonable price, aggressive growth, and many other variations on growth has been illuminated by research in psychology and in management development showing that individuals have marked preferences in analyzing, interpreting, and assimilating information. These leanings appear to be powerful and a fairly permanent component of an investor's personality. To the extent that style investing stems from individual preferences, then style distinctions in the equity market, such as growth and value, are probably long-standing and not a fad, even though the investment community has only recently learned to label such distinctions.

Psychologist Carl Jung proposed that our preferences for particular ways of identifying and evaluating information are developed at an early age.[11] Behavioral researchers such as Stephen Stumpf and Thomas Mullen, and the Myers-Briggs team in the field of management development and organizational learning have applied these basic personality traits to better understand the motivations behind corporate managers.[12] In the context of investing, these inborn preferences in an individual may cause one to migrate toward a more growth-focused orientation or a value bent.

The research on individual preference suggests that investment styles are not solely born out of objective factors in the marketplace. Style investing is also based on individual preferences for different decision-making modes or comfort level at making an investment in an asset depending on the available information. Style investing exists partly as a result of the variety of companies within the investment landscape but also partly because of the natural preferences of the individual when buying and selling stocks.

Decision-Making Styles

A set of personality dimensions has been formalized in the so-called Myers-Briggs Type Indicator (MBTI), a diagnostic test aimed at identifying an individual's preferred way of thinking and making decisions. The four dimensions are:

1. Methods of identifying information (sensing or intuition).
2. How one initiates a search for information (introversion or extroversion).
3. Preferences for making decisions (judging and perceiving).
4. Methods of evaluating information (thinking or feeling).

These dimensions exist along a continuum. Hence, individuals are likely to fall somewhere on the continuum for each dimension rather than at either of its polar extremes.

There are two distinct approaches to identifying information—through sensing or through intuition. Sensing dominance refers to individuals who prefer to examine available hard data. A value investor is sensing dominant. The need to work in an investing environment with some metric to observe an asset class and make decisions places one more on the side of value. In most instances, the intrinsic value of fast-growing firms can be terribly difficult to model or quantify. A person with a preference for sensing is less likely to chase after a biotechnology or Internet stock. Such ideas tend to stretch the assumptions of most intrinsic value models.

Conversely, individuals with a predisposition to use intuition tend to adopt less conventional approaches to analysis. An individual who is comfortable with innovation might simply be bored looking for value stocks. An individual closer to being intuition dominant is likely to be a growth investor. The capital market with a booming calendar of initial public offerings offers a wealth of innovative, future-thinking stories in which to invest. Such an environment is more suited to someone who needs less structure or quantifiable evidence to make decisions. An intuitive reading of management's hopes and dreams may be more compelling to such an individual than, say, the cost of capital or the current economics of the industry. Hence, an unstructured world of fast-growing firms might be a difficult place for managers who require an abundance of deliverable metrics but ideal for someone with a bent toward intuition for identifying information.

Individuals also appear to have a preference in the way they arrive at conclusions—one may be predisposed toward judging or perceiving. Individuals who are judging dominant tend to live in an orderly and decisive manner; perception dominant types tend to be more spontaneous and flexible. The preference for judging points to an investor with a value bias. An attempt to pin down the intrinsic value of a stock requires an individual with a need for an orderly world. An investor with a leaning toward growth is more of a perceiving type, needing less structure and more flexibility to arrive at a conclusion. Small-cap growth stocks generally do not offer a wealth of evidence of current profitability, with much of their luster coming from the expectation of wealth projected far into the future. Modeling such long-term hopefuls requires an investor with a chemistry for spontaneity.

Biotechnology firms are a great example of an industry that offers limited insights into the future prospects of share returns. The probability of a new drug being successful in the marketplace is fairly low. Yet portfolio managers and analysts have to grapple with some construct that allows them to take on a view. Because many of these young firms have limited history, there is little one can model from an historical standpoint. In addition, numerous uncertainties exist regarding the success of the drug, including prospective demand, pricing elasticity, margin assumptions, and of course regulatory approval. These are but a few of the analytical issues an investor needs to resolve to formulate the value of such speculative shares. Individuals with a preference for sensing and less structure can only find such an exercise in financial analysis invigorating. The appeal of this challenge may be what ultimately allows them to formulate a novel approach to valuing terribly uncertain prospects.

Jung also theorized that individuals have a preference for where they initiate their search for information—whether from an inner world of concepts or ideas in a process called introversion; or from an outer world of actions, objects, and people in a process called extroversion. Value investors by nature are more likely to be introversion dominant. They tend to have a more fixed rule on what an earnings or cash flow stream is ultimately worth, with a bias to long-held beliefs in asset valuation. Conversely, an individual prone to look outward for new paradigms is more likely to hold a looser view of the traditional return on investment concepts. Such an individual is likely to look for growth stocks, not value scenarios.

The fourth personality dimension of the Myer-Briggs Type Indicator identifies two forms of evaluating information, thinking and feeling. Thinking-dominant individuals prefer to make judgments objectively and impersonally. They tend to be analytical and rely on logic. An individual prone to evaluate information with feeling tends to make decisions based not only on the information, but also on abstract and qualitative dimensions. Investors, in general, tend to be analytic and therefore thinking dominant. It is rare to see an investment manager attempt to rely simply on instincts in evaluating an asset. Yet, certain investors prefer to select assets with far-reaching goals and far less quantifiable information. To this extent, the feeling-dominant investor may be more growth-driven.

A Long-Standing Phenomenon

Style investing is not a fad. Because the preferences for different ways of interpreting information and making decisions are intrinsic in human nature, the demarcation of style investing can be viewed as long-standing and not a current fancy of market participants. Perhaps at some level, investors have always acted according to their instincts; only recently have researchers and market participants been able to label the differences along the lines of growth and value.

Are top-rank growth stock managers simply buying fast-growing firms? Even though investing requires a unique skill set, one can also argue that exceptional managers tend to hold other intangible skills that allow them to better their peers. Like a jump shot by Michael Jordan in the heat of a game, the successful growth stock investor's analysis of fundamentals is only part of the skill set that allows him or her to stand out among a fairly talented cast. In similar fashion, better growth managers not only are equipped with solid investment skills, but also carry an innate ability to distinguish new concepts and unique business models that make good investment sense. That innate sense of finding better growth stocks or a value investor nimbly avoiding the so-called value trap, purchasing seemingly cheap stocks that continue to get cheaper, may be linked to basic individual traits or personal preferences.

An individual with a leaning toward the use of hard evidence, a need for existing rules and measures to be applied in a consistent manner, could not be comfortable investing in "high flying," aggressive growth situations. In similar light, an individual with a bias toward creative valuation models, a tendency to look beyond the conventional, may be severely challenged in a value box. Such individual traits may offer an investment manager a distinct advantage over her peers who are less in tune with their own unavoidable tendencies. Individuals have unique tendencies that can create a predisposition to examine the market with a "growthy" style or a value, contrarian skew.

Measuring Investment Styles

Most existing benchmarks and measures for investment styles typically zero in on a valuation frame. Popular style indices such as the Russell 2000 Growth and Value, S&P/Barra Style, and Wilshire Next 1750 Growth and Value share a common trait—each approach relies heavily, if not completely, on valuation disparities among stocks in determining the style assignment. They rank stocks from cheapest to most expensive. Those with the lowest valuations can be thought of as "value" ideas and those that are most expensive or "nonvalue" can be called growth. The basic premise is that value candidates are likely to be cheaper, whereas growth stocks tend to be more expensive.

Limitations of Valuation-Based Models

Even though the general approach seems reasonable and has in effect become the industry standard, such methodologies in effect only model "symptoms" of growth and value. Low valuations are symptomatic of low expectations, not necessarily a primary driver of value. Valuation factors can lead to false signals. Is a cheap stock merely oversold because it is representative of low expectations? Or is a beaten-down stock that appears cheap reflecting greater market concerns in subsequent periods? If the evidence points to the former, then a valuation variable may appropriately lead to a value opportunity. However, if the latter scenario is more descriptive, then a valuation-based signal could lead one into a deteriorating situation.

The case against using simple valuations is even clearer when applied in defining growth stocks. Most growth managers will adamantly argue that in searching for good growth stocks, they are not necessarily searching for expensive ideas. While higher valuations are generally associated with faster growing firms, they are not necessarily a precursor of growth.

The relative performance between growth and value investors is distinct and cyclical. A better benchmark should capture a good deal of the variation among the market participants. Figure 9.11 represents the style results of active small-cap managers in the mutual fund benchmark versus a simple valuation-based style model. The valuation-based proxies of investment styles do not resemble market participant results; the comparisons are not even similar. The thick line represents the relative

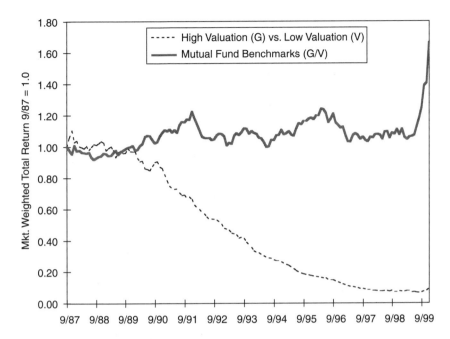

Figure 9.11   Investment Styles—Small-Caps: Growth vs. Value and Valuation

performance of the average active manager. As the line advances, growth managers are beating value, and as the slope retreats, value managers are outpacing growth investors. Valuations do not offer reasonable proxies for investment styles. They simply suggest that simple measures of cheap stocks tend to outperform simple measures of expensive stocks.

The dotted line in Figure 9.11 represents the relative performance of two baskets of stocks. The first basket is the top 10 percent of the most expensive stocks in the small-cap universe. This is used as a simple proxy for growth. The second basket is defined as the top 10 percent of the cheapest set of stocks in the small-cap universe. Stratifying a subset of smaller companies by valuation, or cheap versus expensive companies, is defined by the price-to-cash flow of a company, adjusted for the sector valuation. Cash flow has tested out to be a useful variable in valuing smaller firms (see Chapter 8 for more information on modeling small-cap stocks).

The relative performance of the two baskets, in theory, should offer a similar curve traced by the results of active managers. Yet Figure 9.11 portrays no such relationship. In fact, there appears to be little in common between the competition among growth and value investors and the relative performance of expensive and cheap stocks.

The relative performance of cheap stocks versus expensive stocks is more representative of terribly overvalued stocks underperforming stocks with high levels of intrinsic value. If valuation measures are good measures of style, the curves between the active fund managers and a simple value model should be more closely related.

The 1997 S&P Directory—citing a Richards & Tierney, Inc. presentation, notes the following features of a better benchmark. It should be unambiguous; be an investable, passive alternative; be measurable; be appropriate for the manager; reflect the manager's current investment opinions; and be specified in advance. For the most part, investment managers are not satisfied with the common method among popular benchmarks for defining investment styles. A close look at the data supports concerns among active managers that valuations do not fairly represent the subtleties of investment style.

Key Characteristics for a More Complete Style Benchmark

To better model style benchmarks, it is necessary to identify traits that can uniquely discriminate style characteristics. Four key characteristics or categories help to better define and segment stocks by investment style. A priori, growth stocks should exhibit the following:

- Higher growth expectations.
- Greater systemic risk.
- Higher visibility.
- Higher valuations.

Table 9.2   Defining Traits of Investment Styles

Traits	Factors to Model Such Traits
Expected growth	Forecast in sales and earnings growth
Systemic risk	Beta
Information flow	Analyst coverage
Valuations	Sector-adjusted price-to-cash flow*

* = Sector-adjusted price-to-book value for large caps.

Conversely, value candidates are more likely to reflect the opposite features:

- Lower growth expectations.
- Less systemic risk.
- Lower visibility.
- Lower valuations.

These defining traits and the associated factors by which they can be modeled are displayed in Table 9.2.

Expected Growth

Higher growth expectations can generally be described by some measure of profits or revenue growth. Simple measures of historical or forecast earnings and sales growth rates should suffice. Furthermore, long-term growth rates should minimize the cyclical influences of short-term estimates. Figure 9.12 relates the performance of growth versus value

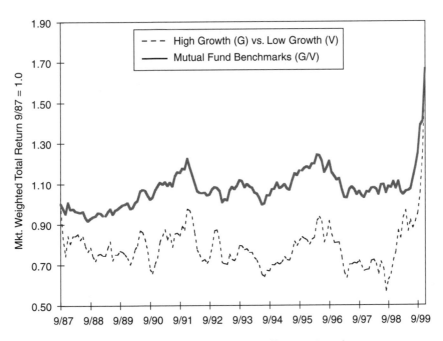

Figure 9.12 Investment Styles—Small-Caps: Growth vs. Value and Expectations of Growth

investors. Notice that the relative performance of high expected growth rate firms versus low expectation firms (dotted line) appears to trace a similar path as the benchmark for active small-cap investors. Thus, expectations appear to capture significant variation in style results.

Systemic Risk

Systemic risk reflects the level of riskiness of an asset as compared with the equity market as a whole. In theory, if a company has higher expectations than the market, then it will most likely reflect above-average market risks, as measured by beta, which represents the relative riskiness of assets in the equity market. Growth stocks should reflect higher betas. If value ideas are truly out of favor, then they are likely to reflect lower systemic risk and therefore exhibit lower betas. Figure 9.13 suggests that stocks stratified by beta mimic the relative performance of growth versus value investors. Thus, beta or systemic risk appears to offer some insight into style measures.

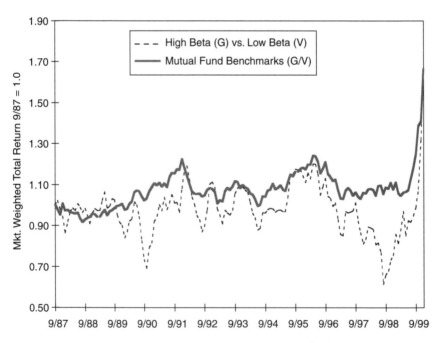

Figure 9.13   Investment Styles—Small-Caps: Growth vs. Value and Beta

Information Flow

Growth stocks tend to be more visible than their value counterparts. Higher-expectation growth stocks tend to be the ideas that are more often discussed at cocktail parties. Wall Street finds it easier to raise capital for fast-growing firms. Not surprisingly, sell-side analysts tend to follow growth stocks more than value ideas. Hence, the level of information flow helps to better identify growth from value candidates.

Valuation

Finally, valuations can certainly be useful in distinguishing a cheap, low expectation idea from an expensive, high expectation candidate. The factor is most useful in finding cheap stocks, not in merely determining the difference between growth and value stocks. As noted, exhibit 5.11 suggests that stocks stratified purely by valuation poorly represent observed investment style results.

STRUCTURING A STYLE MODEL

Are the expectations of growth more relevant than beta in stratifying a growth stock from a value stock? Even though each element nicely describes the polarized nature of growth and value styles, which of the four factors that define stocks by investment style matters more? While each variable reasonably traces the variation in investment style results, a noticeable level of drift remains. Each factor discussed in the preceding section and illustrated in Figures 9.11 through 9.13 appears to capture some of the variation between growth and value, but fails to completely explain or account for the style variation.

Naive Equal-Weighted Model

The initial assumption, or naive, approach places equal emphasis on each of the four traits. Expected earnings/sales growth, beta, analyst coverage, and valuations are considered equally important in stratifying value ideas from growth. This equal-weighted model appears to capture major rotations between growth and value. For instance, growth managers peaked in their outperformance versus value investors in 1991 and began to lag their value counterparts subsequently. The naive model aptly captures this sea change in style preference; the top decile of the small-cap market defined as growth stocks, placing an equal emphasis on each of the four factors, similarly underperforms the value portion over the same time frame. Figure 9.14 relates the results of the naive model versus the relative performance of active managers in the mutual fund benchmarks. The chart shows placing equal emphasis on expectations of growth, valuations, beta, and information flow to stratify investment style yields only marginal to fair results on a generalized basis.

While the equal-weighted model appears to properly capture key inflection points, or major turning points, between growth and value, the results can deviate severely from actively managed portfolios. The 1996–98 period shown in Figure 9.15 is a good example of the deterioration between the simulated data and active returns. Much of this appears to have been caused by the growth composite lagging the actual returns of small-cap growth managers (see Figure 9.15 a and b). It appears as though the value segment of the naive model generally leads the active

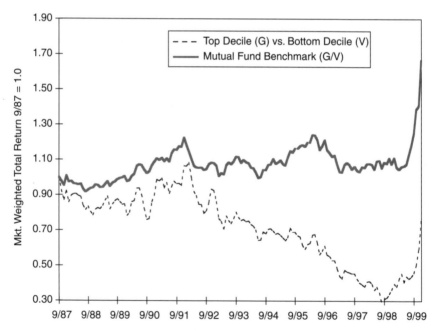

Figure 9.14   Investment Styles—Small-Caps: Growth vs. Value and Equal Weighted Model

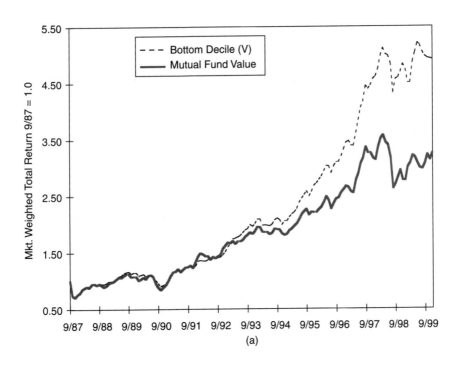

(a)

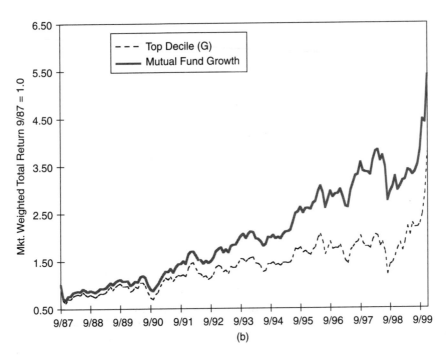

(b)

Figure 9.15 Small-Caps Value and Growth: Equal Weighted
Model vs. Mutual Fund Benchmark

results. Conversely, the growth model perennially lags the active fund results.

Delving deeper into this issue, in an equal-weighted model even though each of the four variables appears to reasonably represent growth and value traits, the factors considered together are somewhat correlated or interrelated. For instance, higher earnings growth rates also tend to exhibit higher valuations. Because of the interrelatedness of expectations of growth and valuation, either growth expectations or valuations may suffice in the modeling process. In fact, excluding certain variables may improve the modeling results because including highly correlated factors in a model is akin to double counting. The simple backtest results suggest that expectations of growth, rather than valuations, are more relevant in defining style.

Similarly, systemic risk, or beta, may already be reflected by the information flow and outlook for profits. Higher expectation stocks can generate significant price swings when earnings come in above or below expectations, even when the differential is only pennies. Furthermore, stocks in the spotlight are more likely to fluctuate with the ebb and flow of the overall market. As a result, beta does not appear to add much to one's decision framework for growth and value. Including valuations and beta as modeling variables may in fact detract from a better defined style benchmark.

An Optimal Model Based on Expected
Growth and Information Flow

Forecasts in earnings and information flow are key factors that can account for significant variation in rotation from growth to value and vice versa. Companies with high expected earnings growth and high analyst coverage constitute a reasonable proxy of growth stocks, while those companies that offer slower or sluggish growth and are underfollowed by Wall Street analysts tend to characterize value stocks.

Figure 9.16 represents the comparison of growth and value style results of active small-cap managers versus a model structured on growth expectations of a firm and number of analysts covering the stock. The benchmark results (thin dotted line) not only trace closely the relative performance of growth versus value managers (solid line), but also do so on an absolute performance basis, as in Figure 9.17(a) and (b).

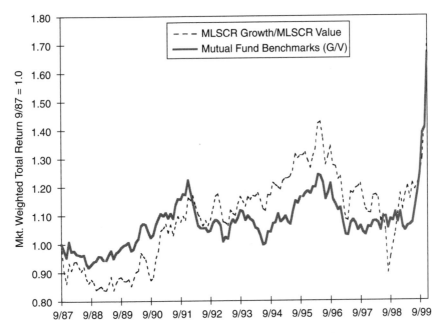

Figure 9.16 Investment Style—Growth vs. Value:
Optimal Benchmark vs. Mutual Funds

Figure 9.17(a), represents the absolute performance of the small-cap value model with its active manager counterpart. Notice how closely the simulated performance of the value model traces the realized returns of active value investors. Similarly, the results of the growth model capture most of the variation exhibited by the results of actual small-cap growth investors, as depicted in Figure 9.14(b). Thus, a model based on expected growth and information flow better defines growth and value style distinctions.

The model results not only appear to mimic the behavior of growth and value funds, but also reflect some of the basic traits believed to accompany investment styles. The benchmark appears to correctly group more economically sensitive, less liquid, lower-valuation, and less volatile issues into the value bin. Importantly, the value benchmark also reflects a seasonal bias, the unusual jump in share prices at the start of the year, typically found in small-cap value stocks. Conversely, stocks with high earnings growth, more liquidity, higher valuations, and high volatility appear properly to drift into the growth compartment.

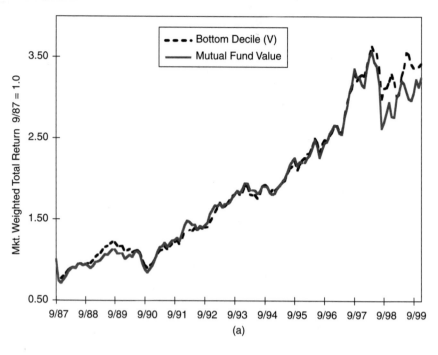

(a)

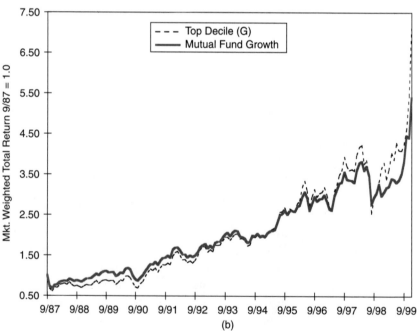

(b)

Figure 9.17 Small-Caps Value and Growth:
Optimal Model vs. Mutual Fund Benchmark

Figure 9.18(a)–(c) illustrates how traditional style traits are manifested among the stocks in the benchmarks over the period from September 1987 through December 1999. Figure 9.18(a) presents the performance of growth versus value using the style benchmarks in contrast to changes in industrial production. Value appears to lead growth in times of a healthy economic backdrop, while growth appears to lead value in times of sluggish or slowing growth. The style benchmark returns support the argument that growth stocks are likely to be more volatile than their value counterparts. Figure 9.18(b) reflects this divergence in price volatility. The growth index has an average volatility of 27.8 percent per annum compared to tame 13.2 percent for the value index.

Growth stocks offer more liquidity. Value stocks may be less volatile, but also less liquid than growth, for several reasons including failing or falling expectations, less focus from analysts on sell-side, and less glamour. It is not uncommon to find aggressive growth companies promising to grow their earnings by 30 percent or 40 percent on an annual basis. Such growth companies generally offer business models that can appear revolutionary and are likely to garner major interest among market observers. Figure 9.18(c) suggests that the value proxy has an average daily

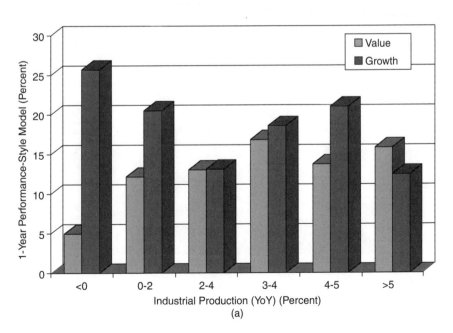

Figure 9.18 Style Investing and Economic Activity, Volatility, and Liquidity

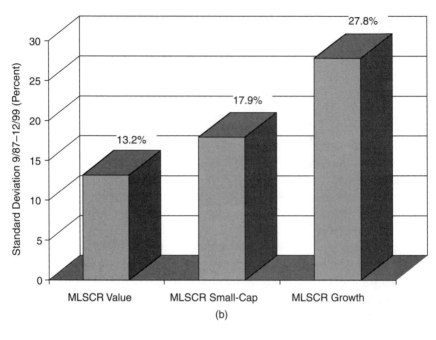

(b)

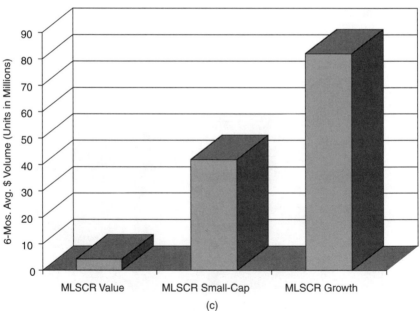

(c)

Figure 9.18 Continued

dollar volume of only 4.2 million versus 82.0 million for the growth stock bogey.

Seasonal Bias and Valuation Disparities

The January effect refers to a marked jump in equity returns in the month of January. More important, this effect appears to be more pronounced in smaller stocks. Chapter 10 has a complete discussion of the January effect and style investing. One of the curious findings in the seasonal effect studies is that small value stocks appear to reflect the most pronounced seasonal jump in price returns. In other words, this effect is also related to investment styles. Properly defined style benchmarks should reflect the seasonal disparities.

The benchmark results support the thesis that the January effect is not only a small-cap effect, but also a small value effect. Furthermore, as investors attempt to bid for smaller stocks prior to January, they are more inclined to buy "broken" growth stocks that have severely corrected during the year. Hence, the seasonal bias is twofold: small-cap growth outperforms in December, and small-cap value wins in January. The data in Figure 9.19 supports the seasonal bias embedded in the style results.

To no surprise, the style benchmarks also reflect the valuation disparity that should exist between growth and value stocks. The growth

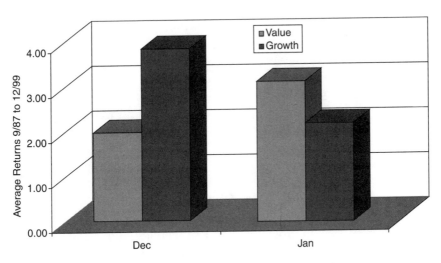

Figure 9.19   Style Investing and the January Effect

stock index has an average price-to-earnings ratio of 693 versus a multiple of 34 for the small-cap value index. The growth benchmark also sells at a premium to the value benchmark on a price-to-book value (5.1x versus 1.7x), price-to-cash flow (33.1x versus 10.8x), and a price-to-sales basis (1.9x versus 0.8x). Furthermore, the value model offers a significant yield premium to the growth model: 3.0 percent versus 0.2 percent respectively.

Sector Disparities

The sector details of the style benchmarks reveal the distinct sector bias between growth and value styles. The results portray the financial overweighting typically found in value-driven strategies. Similarly, the technology overweighting is severe in the growth benchmark. The technology component in the growth proxy makes up nearly 40 percent of the total benchmark. Its value counterpart only holds roughly 9 percent. Tables 9.3 and 9.4 provide a detailed look at the style benchmarks by sector.

Large-Cap Style Results

The large-cap investment universe also is stratified along the lines of investment styles. To no surprise, properly defining growth from value is also relevant for large-cap investors. Applying the small-cap methodology to the large-cap market also yields fruitful results. For the most part, tests run for large stocks have generated similar results. That is, valuations and beta do not appear to enhance or better define style results. A combination of expected growth and information flow or analyst coverage handily models the twists and turns of large-cap growth and value investments. Figure 9.20(a), relates the similarities between the large-cap style swings and the model results.

Even though the results for large caps are fairly strong, they are not as compelling as the smaller capitalized sector results. Some of this is explained by more subtle style distinctions that may exist among large companies. Pradhuman[13] and Crosby have argued that larger companies, with their improved access to financing and higher visibility, more easily reinvent their corporate identity. The advantages of being large imply that a large-cap value idea may be more successful than its

Table 9.3 Growth Model—Economic Sector Distribution

	Equity Characteristics										
	Valuation Characteristics					Earnings Growth %			6 Mos $	%	Number
	PE	P/BK	P/CF	P/S	Div Yld	5 Yr	Curr Yr	Next Yr	Vol (Mil)	Weight	of Cos.
Economic Sectors											
Credit cyclicals	9.69	1.83	7.26	0.44	0.46	15.6	46.5	14.5	3.7	0.48	3
Consumer services		5.43	30.18	2.25	0.02	34.7	15.5	26.3	171.3	9.88	54
Consumer cyclicals	27.86	2.36	11.59	0.65	0.29	23.2	22.3	23.8	7.9	8.15	79
Consumer staples		5.26	18.87	0.56	0.00	19.7	23.3	21.1	6.5	0.88	9
Healthcare/drugs		5.67		1.82	0.02	31.0	33.3	48.1	30.7	9.67	78
Capital goods	25.84	2.46	13.92	0.92	0.08	28.8	33.5	39.1	12.1	4.80	40
Technology		11.49		5.93	0.01	40.0	53.5	51.8	114.4	49.28	155
Energy		2.17	13.28	1.23	0.42	20.3	75.8	40.1	14.6	5.01	31
Basic industrials		1.98	21.29	0.96	0.31	27.7	3.1	134.8	8.6	1.74	14
Financials	30.78	2.98	19.89	2.65	1.13	25.1	-16.4	18.9	51.9	5.72	37
Transportation	20.65	2.55	6.27	0.65	0.54	18.7	16.4	21.2	6.0	2.17	15
Utilities		125.91		0.87	0.32	26.5	27.9	66.9	17.9	2.21	13
Small-Cap Growth	692.94	5.12	33.12	1.91	0.15	33.6	37.5	43.4	82.0	100.00	528
Small-Cap Growth Ind		5.34	36.64	2.03	0.07	34.7	42.4	45.5	87.4	89.90	463

283

Table 9.4 Value Model—Economic Sector Distribution

| | Equity Characteristics | | | | | | | | | | |
| | Valuation Characteristics | | | | | Earnings Growth % | | | 6 Mos $ | % | Number |
	PE	P/BK	P/CF	P/S	Div Yld	5 Yr	Curr Yr	Next Yr	Vol (Mil)	Weight	of Cos.
Economic Sectors											
Credit cyclicals	14.76	11.84	6.91	0.42	0.99	12.6	15.7	14.3	0.9	0.84	6
Consumer services		2.64	33.91	0.94	0.93	14.5	34.5	54.5	5.4	7.18	24
Consumer cyclicals	17.22	1.62	6.91	0.49	1.35	13.8	26.9	23.7	1.5	10.53	53
Consumer staples	51.98	1.26	11.17	0.19	2.71	11.5	11.5	17.0	1.0	4.52	23
Healthcare/drugs		3.26		1.11	0.27	17.0	11.9	25.7	15.9	6.72	20
Capital goods	18.90	1.61	9.03	0.53	1.74	11.9	15.9	15.0	1.1	4.76	25
Technology		2.34	21.91	1.01	0.74	12.5	16.2	17.4	9.0	5.29	27
Energy		2.24	9.31	0.49	4.62	9.9	39.4	35.9	1.6	3.27	12
Basic industrials	25.56	1.88	8.97	0.79	2.05	10.9	58.2	57.1	1.0	10.15	32
Financials	20.34	1.43	9.65	1.75	4.86	9.5	10.8	17.5	4.7	36.45	151
Transportation		1.70	10.68	0.63	1.57	10.7	78.5	12.8	1.7	2.48	8
Utilities	17.93	1.94	8.12	1.21	4.45	5.7	33.5	17.9	1.4	7.51	26
Conglomerates	12.12	1.08	4.10	0.52	10.47	13.5	0.0	-18.8	4.8	0.29	1
Small-Cap Value	33.97	1.72	10.79	0.78	3.01	10.9	25.9	26.0	4.2	100.00	408
Small-Cap Value Ind	68.14	1.96	12.24	0.56	1.62	12.7	29.4	31.9	4.4	53.56	223

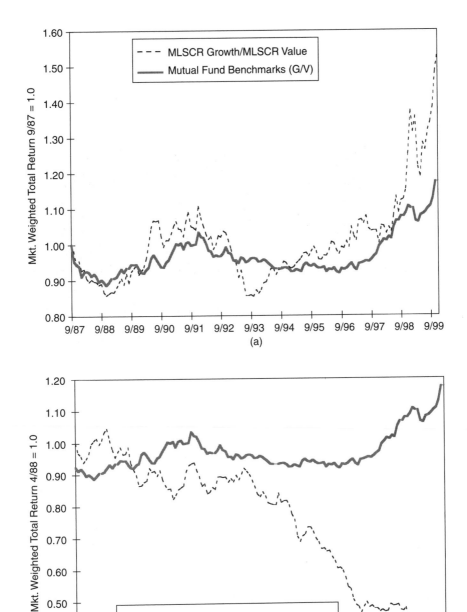

Figure 9.20 Large-Cap Investment Style: (a) Growth vs. Value;
(b) Optimal Benchmark vs. Mutual Funds

small-cap counterpart in capturing and creating interest among traditional growth managers. As a result, large-cap style-based distinctions may appear less distinct than style results found in the small-cap market.

To better model investment styles, one needs to segment the various sizes that exist in an equity market. After all, smaller stocks behave quite differently than large stocks. The secondary market, as described in Chapter 2, exhibits more erratic earnings results, projects more aggressive growth, is terribly underfollowed, and is far less liquid. Because of such distinctions, the small-cap section of the equity market reflects a market where data tends to be much more varied than that for large caps. Furthermore, small caps tend to have less available data. Combining such varied data can lead to mixed results. By segmenting the equity market first by size and then by style, investors may avoid many difficulties in categorization.

METHODOLOGY CONSIDERATIONS

Poor implementation of even sound economic and investment theory can lead to poor results. There are many reasonable paths to take when modeling such a broad set of variables. Two general methods considered in structuring the model are discriminate analysis and a nonparametric approach. To avoid the assumption that the equity market behaves "normally," a nonparametric approach is appropriate.

Discriminate Analysis

In using discriminate analysis, specifically cross-sectional regressions, one can calculate the stock sensitivity to each of the four factors. Then the sensitivities or the beta coefficient is combined with the stock's current levels of each factor (earnings growth, beta, analyst coverage, and valuation level). Once combined, the list of securities can then be ranked from growth to value. Although this is a sound and fairly popular approach to modeling multifactor models, it assumes that the data behave "normally" from a statistical standpoint. This assumption may or may not be appropriate. Current research in finance generally tends to question the assumption of normality within the equity markets.

Nonparametric Approach

Instead of using a discriminate analysis, a nonparametric approach, using a ranking scheme to dissect growth from value was used to create the style models discussed. This approach assigns a rank for each of the relevant variables. The factors are then combined by assigning a certain weight or probability. This leads to the iterative or optimized portion of the analysis. What is the optimal combination or optimal weighting for each factor? Is it 35 percent earnings growth or 65 percent valuations? Or, is it some other combination? Because there are four factors, one can imagine the permutations.

Narrowing the Selection Pool

Table 9.5 relates a series of basic combinations among the four variables under examination (see Table 9.1 for a description of the data). By looking at the permutations that closely match the performance of the active fund manager results, one can narrow the selection pool. Figure 9.21(a)–(b) portrays the performance spreads between the model results and those of the active managers for many of the tested combinations.

Table 9.5 Investment Style Permutations

S1	25%#, 25%G, 25%B, 25%V	S12	75%#, 25%G
S2	25%#, 15%G, 25%B, 35%V	S13	25%#, 75%G
S3	25%#, 35%G, 25%B, 15%V	S14	75%B, 25%V
S4	35%#, 25%G, 15%B, 25%V	S15	25%B, 75%V
S5	15%#, 25%G, 35%B, 25%V	S16	100% Valuation
S6	35%#, 15%G, 15%B, 35%V	S17	75%#, 25%V
S7	35%#, 35%G, 15%B, 15%V	S18	50%G, 50%V
S8	15%#, 35%G, 35%B, 15%V	S19	75%G, 25%V
S9	15%#, 15%G, 35%B, 35%V	S20	25%G, 75%V
S10*	**50%#, 50%G**	S21	100%# of Estimate
S11	50%B, 50%V	S22	100% Growth
		S23	100% Beta

* = Optimal model
B = Beta
V = Valuation
# = Number of estimates
G = Long-term proj. growth rate

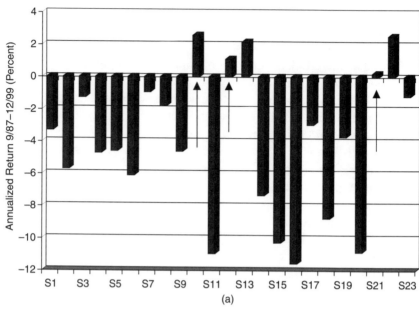

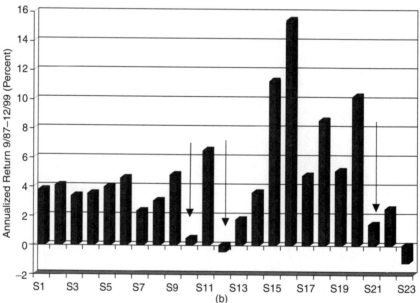

Figure 9.21   Growth and Value Stock Investing—Deviations from Benchmark

The selection pool was considerably narrowed once combinations that significantly deviated from active or realized returns were removed. The decision was not difficult; only three combinations closely match the fund results. Both approaches 10 and 12 are defined as combinations of expected growth and analyst coverage. The analyst coverage variable, or 21, also appears reasonable but does not appear to track the fund manager results as closely. There is also an implementation issue with analyst coverage: the data is clustered, much of it around no analyst coverage. To develop a relevant time series of low coverage, a pool of companies of zero coverage is created. That portion is far greater than the top decile (top 10 percent) of companies with high analyst coverage.

Only a handful of combinations become relevant after accounting for return drift. The summary statistics in Table 9.6 supports the contention that style benchmarks are more robust when expectations and information flow are combined. The statistics become more robust as variables such as valuations and beta are removed. Models without

Table 9.6   Regression Statistics—Proprietary Style Models vs. Active Fund Returns

	T-Stat	Correlation	R-square
Optimal[†]			
Growth/value vs. fund returns	15.35	0.80	0.64
Growth model vs. fund returns*	15.45	0.80	0.64
Value model vs. fund returns*	7.75	0.56	0.31
Naive or Equal-Weighted Model			
Growth/value vs. fund returns	16.03	0.81	0.66
Growth model vs. fund returns*	14.09	0.77	0.60
Value model vs. fund returns*	6.00	0.46	0.21
S12			
Growth/value vs. fund returns	10.50	0.67	0.45
Growth model vs. fund returns*	12.21	0.73	0.53
Value model vs. fund returns*	5.23	0.41	0.17
Analyst Coverage			
Growth/value vs. fund returns	4.12	0.34	0.11
Growth model vs. fund returns*	5.17	0.41	0.17
Value model vs. fund returns*	3.56	0.29	0.09

The regression statistics are based on data from Sept. 87 to Nov. 98.
* = Excess returns are regressed.
[†] = Optimal Model = Expected growth (50%) and analyst coverage (50%).
S12 = Expected growth (75%) and analyst coverage (25%).

growth expectations and information flow significantly drift from results of the benchmark mutual fund active managers.

NOTES

The data used to develop the stock-specific style benchmarks throughout this chapter are based on Compustat for financial statements and I/B/E/S for forecast information. The expected growth rates are based on the average of historical sales and consensus forecast earnings growth. Both variables when combined offer a better sense of a company's prospects. The analyst coverage variable is simply the number of analysts that submit a forecast for the current year.

Valuation is an open-ended topic. In many ways, finding the proper valuation model is simply work in progress. Recent work on valuing firms suggests a sector-adjusted price-to-cash flow variable appears to best value smaller companies. For a full discussion, see Chapter 8. Conversely, a sector-adjusted book value model generated superior results among large firms. As a result, the tests developed for large-cap firms used a book value model instead of cash flow.

The active manager returns discussed throughout this chapter were based on the funds listed in Tables 9.7 and 9.8.

Table 9.7   Small-Cap Funds by Growth and Value

Emerging Growth Funds	Small Value Funds
Acorn Investment TR	Pennsylvania Mutual
Kemper Small Capitalization EQ	DFA Investment Dimensions Group Inc.
PBHG FDS Inc.	Evergreen Micro Cap FD
United New Concepts	FPA Capital FD Inc.
Putnam OTC Emerging Growth Funds	Heartland Value
Safeco Growth FD Inc.	Pioneer Mid Cap FD
Scudder Securities TR	Prudential Small Companies FD Inc.
T. Rowe New Horizons FDI	Babson Value FD Inc.
Vanguard Explorer FD Inc.	Winthrop Focus FDS

*Note: Babson Value replaced Royce Value and PBHG (Pilgrim Baxter) replaced Keystone American Hartwell in September 1997.

Table 9.8 Large-Cap Funds by Growth and Value

Growth Funds	Value Funds
American Century Select	Dreyfus Co.
T Rowe Price Growth Fund	Investment Co. of America
American Capital Fund	Putnam Growth and Income
Fidelity Destiny	American Mutual
Nicholas Fund	Pioneer II
Growth Fund of America	Lord Abbett Affiliated Fund
Smith Barney Appreciation Fund	Mutual Shares
Van Kampen American Capital Pace	Washington Mutual
GE S&S Program	Vanguard/Windsor Fund

TEN

The January Effect: A Seasonal Premium

JANUARY EFFECT DEFINED

SINCE THE early 1980s, the so-called January effect has caught the interest of the investment and academic community. Cited in 1980 by professor of finance Donald Kiem,[1] this effect generally refers to the substantial appreciation of share prices in the month of January. As shown in Figure 10.1, which presents market returns on a monthly basis, stock returns are generally more pronounced not only for the month of

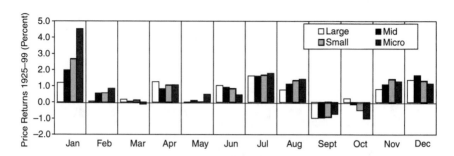

Figure 10.1 Seasonality of Returns by Size

January but also for the entire first quarter. In this instance, market performance is defined by the microcap, small-cap, midcap, and large-cap benchmarks dating from 1926 to 1999. But this odd effect has been recorded for other asset classes also, such as high yield or junk bonds.[2]

The dramatic spike of returns in January suggests an equity market enigma. Small stocks in January of 1991, which started the rebound of small stocks in the early 1990s, jumped 6.9 percent. On an annualized basis, this gain would produce a full-year return of 123 percent.

This January bias is especially mysterious because the effect appears to be more pronounced for smaller companies. As shown in Figure 10.1, midcaps outperform large caps, small caps beat out midcaps, and microcaps outperform small caps. This steplike performance supports the argument that the January seasonal bias is a function of size.

Although the January effect can produce compelling returns at the start of the year, it is a fleeting and complex effect to exploit. Like most market anomalies, the January effect is not a stable event that occurs on a consistent year-after-year basis. The uncertainty of the figures is a strong reminder that "there ain't no such thing as a free lunch." Nonetheless, the effect has significant implications for equity participants, most notably for small-cap investors.

More important, there appears to be a fairly pronounced distinction between growth and value stocks, with value stocks outperforming growth stocks during this period.[3] Because of the bias toward value investing in the data, small-cap investors need to be especially aware that the generally favorable swings in small caps at the end of the year have marked style implications.

Many efficient market theorists argue that pricing anomalies such as the January effect are likely to dissipate because the financial markets are thought to be efficiently priced. Unusually large returns are unlikely to remain as investors become aware of such unusual price swings and aggressively chase them down. As one investor attempts to take advantage of an unusual price discrepancy, another investor attempts to preempt his competition, and so on. This cutthroat behavior tends to marginalize most unusual pricing situations such as a January effect, or so efficient market theorists would maintain.

However, an alternative argument can be made that the January effect is likely to continue in future years. It is unlikely that this effect will dissipate because much of it is predicated on the unique preference curves of investors, the unpredictability of the effect, and possibly the illiquidity of the secondary market.

A MARKET ANOMALY

The beginning-of-the-year effect has been a prime topic of research journals since the early 1980s. Although one might expect increased awareness of this phenomenon to dilute its effect, the rates of return for small-cap stocks still continue to show a January bias.

This effect does indeed seem somewhat anomalous given an efficient market. Abnormal excess returns should be arbitraged in such a market, diminishing the effect over subsequent periods. Arbitrageurs, acting in their best interest, tend to stamp out the existence of any abnormal excesses carried by any asset class. Armed with the knowledge that stocks bounce in January, investors should attempt to purchase shares in December and thereby profit in the subsequent period. Such actions in turn should spur prices to rise a month earlier, which would force the January effect to surface in the month of December. The shift to an earlier period should motivate yet more arbitrageurs to act in the preceding month of November, causing the effect to be pushed back to an even earlier period. This feedback loop of investors attempting to profit from the January effect, as they do with most investment opportunities, should theoretically reduce and eventually eliminate any traces of a seasonal premium.

The existence of an anomalous effect does not necessarily force an arbitrage, however. Odd pricing effects are abundant in many markets. The jumps in price for snowblowers in early winter or for air conditioners in the dead of summer are good examples of pricing inefficiencies that exist annually. If the market for air conditioners were perfectly efficient, the price of air conditioners should not surge in the months prior to the summer and trough in the fall. After all, buyers of home appliances, as well as market participants, have good insight into demand and when they will need air conditioners. Although weather forecasters still struggle to pinpoint temperature fluctuations from day to day, the summer months are generally warm and the winter months predictably cold. Given this information, prices should remain somewhat constant, or without a seasonal surge. Yet the surge in prices remains.

This inefficient pricing suggests that consumers lack savvy shopping instincts, which leads to anomalous pricing of seasonal equipment. Yet another explanation may be that an interest in air conditioning is very much one of personal preference. In theory, if all individuals viewed the ability to keep cool as a primary need or had identical preferences for air conditioning, pricing disparities might wane. Additional factors that may account for the seasonal surge in pricing relate to slippage in the raw material costs for producers, transportation and storage costs, and supply and demand imbalances at regional levels.

In the same light, investors tend to trade stocks based on their own preferences and priorities. All investors enter the market with the same goal—to make money by buying stocks that go up and by selling them before they go down. But investors vary greatly in the priority with which they view their investments and how diligently they manage their portfolios. Because of these individual investor differences, pockets of inefficiencies can easily exist in the market.

More important, the sheer unpredictability of the January effect may contribute to its continued existence. There have been numerous periods in which the January effect failed to materialize. For example, large stocks outpaced their small-cap counterparts from 1994 to 1999 in the month of January; put another way, the January effect was dormant for five years.

Arbitrage typically refers to attempts to capture a "sure thing." Because of its somewhat random nature, the January effect is far from a sure bet. As a result, arbitrageurs may be less zealous in their attempt to capture this effect. To continue with the analogy of the air conditioner market, the uncertainty of a heat wave is likely to cause consumers to be more passive in their behavior. If such an event were more predictable, consumers might be much more hawkish in their purchasing habits. Similarly, arbitrageurs might attempt to capture January returns if they were more predictable, but this, in itself, could diminish the January effect.

Potential Drivers of the Seasonal Effect

Numerous theories have attempted to account for the January effect. It may have psychological roots, while some research points to a neglected stock effect, which arises when a spate of information is released at the end of the year on otherwise generally neglected stocks. Tax and accounting issues have also been cited as a factor in the January effect, and it has been attributed to a reflex action stemming from a turbulent marketplace.[4] Although each argument appears to support the existence of the effect, each has gaps in its approach. Taken together, however, these factors provide a compelling explanation for this unusual market phenomenon.

Behavioral Influences

One behavioral explanation for the January effect relates to the human impulse to start afresh with the new year. Whether by making New Year's resolutions, or starting a new business venture, the turning of a year spurs individuals to take action.

Because of this behavioral impulse, it follows that investors would generally look to the beginning of the year to focus on new investments. Although certain investors frequently manage their portfolio with market timing in mind, some reluctantly approach this as a tedious task. This reluctant segment of the investment community is more likely to act at the start of a year. Typically, tax and accounting issues force the most unwilling estate manager to revisit his financial affairs. The January bounce could be partly attributed to this group of "infrequent" investors who are "forced" to revisit holdings once a year. Because of the "new" marginal buyer, the buying pressure increases as they act, whether through direct purchase, mutual funds, or retirement fund contributions.

The business world reflects similar seasonal tendencies. Traditionally, the success of a business is measured in annual terms. Although some companies have fiscal years that begin in months other than January, the fiscal years of many more companies are still defined on a calendar basis. Not surprisingly, a great deal of information is released to the public as a firm closes its books. This implies that a slew of corporate decisions or signals are released to the public at the beginning of a new year. For example, a company may release information that suggests its results are better or worse than expected, or it may convey the prospects of tackling new ventures or cementing old relationships.

These waves of information enter the market in a "lumpy," uneven fashion. To some extent, the announcements are also likely to have a positive bias. The beginning of the year is a highly visible period that receives attention and publicity. A company would likely delay the release of inauspicious news or information to a quieter period. Thus, if information is disseminated in a lumpy manner and the data has a positive bias, not only are prices in the beginning of the year bound to jump in a seemingly anomalous manner, they will also reflect a positive drift.

Neglect Theory

The release of new information at the close of a year might account for a surge in prices across the equity market. But why do small companies experience greater surges in share prices than large companies? The neglect theory offers an elegant argument on why small-cap stocks tend to exhibit a greater January surge. Unlike their large-cap counterparts, small firms tend to receive less attention from the market and general media. Much research has attributed the superior performance of small stocks to their less efficient pricing. As suggested by Avner Arbel and Paul Strebel (1982)[5] (1983)[6] and (1985),[7] the small-stock effect may be attributable to neglect and not simply size.

Because of the year-end reporting structure of most companies, investors are more likely to revisit existing investment decisions or consider new courses when a company releases fresh information. This is particularly evident for those investing in companies that issue little or no information during the year. When a neglected pool of stocks issues a seasonal surge of information, most likely with a positive spin, these stocks are likely to bounce at the start of a year.

A simple scan of the business news reinforces the sharp contrast between the press coverage of larger and smaller firms. Being small also means being undiscovered, a bias that is reinforced by the advertising medium. Large companies tend to dominate advertising, especially television. For example, because football's annual Superbowl attracts millions of viewers, it has also become a gala event for megafirms to showcase their brand names. The hefty price for a thirty-second commercial slot immediately removes the majority of marginal firms from the running. The regional nature of some smaller companies also makes the national or international stage of the Superbowl an inappropriate forum.

This bias in information flow exists on the institutional investing side as well. The focus of Wall Street generally is on large companies. As discussed in Chapter 2, the average number of research analysts for large companies far outnumbers those for small companies.

Tax/Accounting Effects

The pressure to sell tax losses has also been cited as a contributor to the January effect, as noted by researchers Dan Givoly, Avie Ovadia (1983),[8] and Marc Reinganum (1983).[9] Stocks that have fallen in price throughout the year are subject to selling pressure toward the end of the year. The logic goes that a substantial drop in share prices is more likely to induce a rebound at the beginning of the year. If investors face significant losses, selling can at least offset some of the tax pinch on current or past capital gains. Thus, investors might want to sell simply because they have incurred losses in their portfolio. By selling out to offset taxable gains, however, investors increase the chance that most stocks and benchmarks will face added downward pressures. Ironically, the pressure to sell can exacerbate a difficult period in the market.

In a compelling argument for the tax-selling hypothesis, finance professors Josef Lakonishok and Seymour Smidt[10] have examined the relationship between trading volume and stock trends. According to their theory, higher trading volume is generally correlated to positive trends in stocks. This relationship reverses in December, when losing shares exhibit increased trading volume. Tax-loss selling is a compelling reason for this sudden swing in the trading volume of failing shares.

This theory goes only so far, however. In fact, seasonal effects have been observed in other countries where the tax year does not coincide with the calendar year (see Tinic and Barone-Adesi, 1983).[11] Researcher Marc Reinganum also found evidence of a January effect, even after the tax bias was removed.

To arbitrage this effect, investors could hold onto fallen shares and wait for a bounce in January, thus saving the transaction costs and possibly gaining a more significant payoff. If the January effect fails to materialize, they could then sell out of the shares and minimize the impact of their prior error in investment judgment.

Rebound Effect

The January effect also appears related to market swings. It appears that much of the time small companies have either a very good year or a very bad year. Figure 10.2 shows that the rate of return for small-cap stocks during an average January is 2.6 percent. The January results are even more impressive by focusing on the January results immediately after small stocks had lost ground. The average January bounce after a poor year jumps to 3.7 percent. In contrast, the rate of return after a good year, or a year in which small stocks gained in value, was decidedly lower—only 2.0 percent.

On closer inspection, the January effect appears especially compelling at extreme levels of market weakness. Figure 10.3 stratifies the small-cap January results in ranges of prior year returns. For instance, the January effect appears even more robust after a very weak year in the small-cap market, say a 5 percent correction or more. In fact, the January returns climb to an expected return of 4.8 percent after extremely weak years showing that a strong relationship exists between poor performance over the prior year and subsequent January results. In this instance, it is

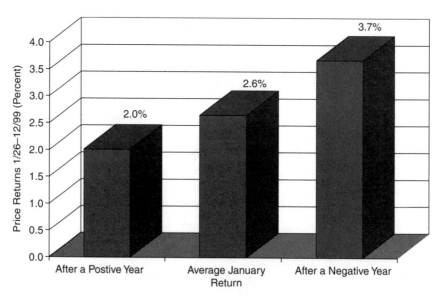

Figure 10.2 January Effect—Market with Gains vs. Losses

Average January Returns

	<-5%	-5..0%	0..5%	5..10%	10..15%	15..20%	>20%
→	4.8%	0.3%	-0.4%	-0.9%	2.8%	2.8%	2.6%
							-8.1
							-3.9
							-2.9
							-2.3
							-2.1
	-7.4						-2.0
	-4.6						-2.0
	-2.3						-1.2
	1.2						0.7
	1.4						0.8
	1.7						1.0
	2.5						1.8
	2.5						2.5
	3.8						2.5
	4.4						2.6
	5.9				-5.5		2.9
	6.2				-3.3		3.1
	6.3				1.2		3.3
	6.9	-5.3			1.4		4.7
	7.5	-4.0			1.9		5.1
	8.1	-2.4			2.6	-1.0	7.2
	8.8	0.7		-6.3	2.9	2.4	7.2
	9.8	1.1		-5.2	5.2	3.3	7.4
	11.5	4.4	-1.2	1.2	9.1	3.4	15.9
	22.8	7.8	0.3	6.6	12.8	5.9	20.7

Actual January Observations (1926–99)

Range of Prior Year's Small-Cap Return

Figure 10.3   January Returns and Prior Year's Results

almost appropriate to suggest that poor past performance is indicative of better future returns.

Small-cap January statistics appear most relevant immediately after extreme years, whether good or bad. Because of the competitive environment among professional money managers, and the average investor's hunger to hit the jackpot, a sudden collapse in any asset becomes a bull's-eye for opportunists to take aim and bring down their game. This is especially true for the more overlooked secondary market.

Furthermore, the seasonal jump in the secondary markets represents the entry of the less traditional buyer. Serious small-cap investors are already invested in the secondary markets, so the more casual buyer becomes the catalyst that creates a bounce in the secondary markets. What are typical signs that draw such an investor to a new segment of the equity market? More directly, what could cause a terribly overlooked asset class such as small caps to get onto the menu of available choice items? One noticeable signal, or "bell ringer," is a drastic shift in share prices. A dramatic increase or collapse in share prices typically draws an audience.

This behavior is not terribly different from the motivations of an individual who happens into a tag sale. You may not really need or be in the market for an extra set of golf clubs or that plaid jacket you thought you liked when you were in college. But here, to your good fortune, it is staring you in the face. Better yet, it is "priced to go." A similar motivation may underlie the behavior of some January participants, who may be more casual observers of equities than active investors in small caps. When markets become turbulent and a selloff appears too severe, these contrarian bargain-hunter investors may come to the forefront.

In another argument that supports this rebound effect, professors Werner de Bondt and Richard Thaler[12] set forth an "overreaction" hypothesis to explain why the market is less than efficient. They argue that investors perennially overreact to both good and bad news. If a firm releases incremental news of positive business developments, the market is likely to chase its shares to an excessive level. Conversely, companies that experience unexpected bumps in the road are more likely to face an excessive selloff. As noted by de Bondt and Thaler, shares with very strong price trends tend to correct in the weeks or months that follow. According to their argument, evidence that share prices almost always weaken after a dramatic rally is proof of market overreaction. If the market were priced efficiently, this counterswing in prices would not exist.

The majority of rebounds in share prices occur in the month of January. Although some have argued that the January effect is simply a market anomaly reflecting a less efficiently priced market, de Bondt and Thaler creatively assert that investor overreaction drives prices to extremes and therefore promotes a counterreaction.

An oddity of the rebound effect is the tendency for an absence of a seasonal spike after a relatively good year. In theory, momentum investors, who look for developing positive trends, should drive superior results in January after a year in which the market has taken a strong upward trend. After a good year, momentum investors presumably would continue snatching up shares to ride the wave. Yet the data on January returns indicate that the rebound effect is more significant after a poor year. Nonetheless, the January effect is also noticeable when the small-cap market offers return levels north of 10 percent. January returns are above 2.0 percent when the prior year's return for the small-cap market remained above 10 percent, as illustrated in Figure 10.3.

Other factors may account for this result. As noted, investors may simply be buying back shares after selling off their tax losses in a poor year, or they may be responding to the flood of positive information that tends to be released early in the year. Because of these factors, rebounding contrarian buyers are likely to outweigh the trend-following momentum investors at the start of a new year. Simply put, there are just as many "bottom fishers" as there are trend followers.

This rebound strategy has not met unconditional success, however. In 1998, emerging markets, fixed-income strategies, and well-known hedge funds all lost ground in an incredibly turbulent year. The U.S. secondary market fell by approximately 40 percent in six months. Surely, if a January effect were to occur, January 1999 should have represented a market ripe for the taking. In yet another example of how market swings can humble the experts, however, there were only muted signs of a seasonal recovery at the start of 1999. In a less than stellar month for small caps, large-cap stocks continued to roll over the secondary market for the fifth straight year. The Russell 2000, a measure of small-cap stocks, gained 1.2 percent in January 1999, while the Standard & Poor's 500 index gained a strong 4.1 percent in the same period.

Extenuating circumstances in the latter half of 1998 may have minimized the results of the upcoming January. The small-cap rebound began in October. Starting in late April, the small-cap market had begun to weaken severely over a few short months. In hindsight, conditions had been ripe for a small-cap rebound—an asset class that corrects by over 35 percent in a few months should rebound. Although the rate of growth for the overall economy was slowing, economic growth was nonetheless good. Despite the furor over the affair between President Bill Clinton and White House intern Monica Lewinsky, the political environment was relatively benign. Economic growth had not collapsed, however, nor were there inflationary bursts to threaten the wealth of long-term investors. The risks to the U.S. equity market were limited compared to those of many emerging markets that experienced corrections similar to those of the U.S. small-cap market.

Faced by reeling emerging markets in Asia and Russia and the prospective failure of the Long-Term Capital Management hedge fund, the Federal Reserve was forced to ease its policy. The chance that investors had overreacted on concerns and the collapsing small-cap market began to find a floor. Small stocks rebounded by 28.2 from October 9,

1998, to the end of November of that year. It is possible that this occurred because market participants were taking steps to arbitrage a sure-fire end-of-year effect that was only a few weeks away. Investors did not observe a traditional January effect in 1999 because market participants had aggressively bid-up the small-cap market only weeks prior.

SMALL-CAP REBOUND AND LARGE-CAP MARKET

Is the January bounce for small caps more predictable within the context of the large-cap market? Could the rebound effect be tied to the fortunes of the large-cap market? In fact, a closer look at the January results for small caps shows that they are not dependent on the swings of big-cap stocks.

Figure 10.4 presents January small-cap returns in the context of large-cap market performance. Small-cap January returns are sampled according to how severely the small-cap market underperformed the large-cap market in the prior year. A similar dispersion of returns, or extreme polar results found in Figure 10.3 should become evident if the January effect is tied to the swings of the large-cap market. The small-cap market should register a pronounced seasonal gain if it severely lags the large-cap market in the face of a blue chip rally or if it performs relatively poorer than large caps in a big-cap downturn.

The high correlation of returns (i.e., the strong relationship between small and large company returns) should increase the likelihood of a January effect. To some extent, small companies may become more recognized or noticeable if their returns begin to diverge significantly from their large-cap brethren. For example, if the entire market were to weaken, the contrarian buyer would likely to be more interested in the correcting large-cap shares than the hurting fledgling issues. The weak secondary market could be displaced in the midst of the angst being suffered by large-cap bettors. The flurry of large-cap buying activity would, in theory, account for more of a bounce for large caps than small stocks.

Similarly, a more severe correction for small stocks than large stocks might imply more aggressive tax-selling strategies among the secondary stocks. Not only could the tax-selling strategy spur a seasonal rebound, it could spur a rebound with a significant size bias.

Yet dispersion of returns data, such as in Figure 10.4, yield little evidence of a more pronounced seasonal bias among the small caps within the context of the large-cap market. The chart lists the January small-cap

Average January Returns

1.0%	2.9%	4.7%	1.7%	2.6%
−8.1	−2.4			−8.1
−7.4	−2.3	−5.5		−5.3
−6.3	−2.0	−4.6		−4.0
−3.3	−1.2	−2.3		−2.9
−1.2	1.0	0.7		−2.1
0.3	1.1	1.8	−5.2	−1.0
0.7	1.2	2.6	−3.9	1.9
1.2	1.2	3.3	−2.0	2.5
1.4	1.4	3.8	0.8	2.5
1.7	2.5	5.2	2.5	2.6
2.4	4.4	7.2	2.9	2.9
4.4	5.9	7.4	3.3	3.1
6.2	6.3	7.8	3.4	5.1
6.9	7.5	9.1	4.7	7.2
8.1	8.8	11.5	5.9	15.9
9.8	12.8	22.8	6.6	20.7
<−5%	−5..0%	0..5%	5..10%	>10%

(left axis) Actual January Observations (1926–99)

Range of Prior Year's Excess Returns

Figure 10.4   January Returns and Prior Year's Excess Returns

results based on the excess returns of small stocks, or small cap less large cap, in the prior year. The dispersion of returns appears to be almost random. The average January results for small caps are not dramatically stronger when small shares outperform large caps, nor are they dramatically weaker when small caps underperform. As shown in Figure 10.4, the most substantial small-cap January results occur when small-cap stock results are similar to those of large stocks.

OTHER DRIVERS

Another explanation for the January effect relates to the cash flow needs of investors at year-end, which has been referred to as the "Santa Impact."[13] According to this theory, investors need cash at year-end, which forces them to sell off their portfolios. Bargain hunters then repurchase these shares at the start of the year, which causes them to bounce. Although this sounds intuitive, selling stocks to raise cash is an expensive form of financing. After all, because investors face the tax consequence of selling shares they are unlikely to simply sell stocks to convert them to cash unless they are in dire need to raise cash.

Another explanation for the January effect relates to the "window dressing" that money managers perform at year-end. In this instance, issues that are less popular or that have collapsed are more likely to be sold off. According to this theory, active managers prefer to enter their year-end reviews with more winners in their holdings than losers. If this theory indeed accounts for the January effect, one would expect to see evidence of consistent price weakness at or near year-end each year. This is not the case, however.

Confluence of Factors Leading to January Effect

Although many factors partially account for a seasonal bounce, no one single factor provides a complete explanation. And some theories that explain the January effect raise other conflicting issues.

The behavioral theory discussed previously in this chapter nicely accounts for the individual and corporate motivations behind the seasonal anomaly. As an argument based on psychological factors, however, it is difficult to validate. The neglect theory offers a reasonable accounting for the more impressive returns among small-cap shares, but it, too, raises some questions. According to this theory, the release of a spate of information on generally neglected stocks at year-end spurs positive gains. But if lags exist in the release of financial statements at year-end, and to some extent they do, this implies the surge of information being released may have less of an impact on share prices. Some seasonal research suggests that the excess returns are found largely in the first few trading sessions of the new year.[14] If so, seasonality of returns might be due to factors other than neglect.

The tax-selling effect provides a compelling explanation for the January effect. It offers a direct financial motivation for the increased selling pressure that occurs at year-end. But the lack of consistently weak year-end results is confounding.

The January effect may represent a combination of several theories. A confluence of events results in a surge of share prices at the start of the year. This effect is driven by the behavioral tendency of investors to formulate and make decisions at the turn of the year. This behavioral tendency, coupled with companies releasing new and mostly positive information, forces stock prices to jump in January.

The robustness of this effect may depend on the prior year's volatility; an especially weak year forces the hand of opportunistic sellers. The motivation of investors to aggressively sell or overreact may also be driven by existent tax codes—an individual with a sizable tax loss credit may be tempted to sell before the year's end. Finally, evidence of an overzealous seller may be a catalyst for the value hunter. If shares fall below most reasonable measures of intrinsic value, the opportunistic buyer is more likely to enter the market and aggressively acquire assets. The aggressiveness of value hunters may ultimately dictate the robustness of the January effect.

Based on these theories, the January effect may continue to confound efficient market theorists. At its heart, this unpredictable effect may continue to exist because it is driven by the innate behavioral tendencies of investors. These age-old tendencies suggest that such pricing anomalies are likely to persist. For investment managers, the issue is how to manage a portfolio when share prices are driven, at least temporarily, by factors outside stock fundamentals.

The January effect puzzle may not be completely solved in the near future, but the effect is powerful enough to merit an understanding of its causal factors. Any investor would prefer to start off the year by inheriting a seasonal windfall. The competitiveness of money management dictates that investors need to understand better the nuances of the seasonal bias to gain an edge on the competition. More important, if the seasonal bounce favors the investor's peers, it is paramount for the investor to understand this dastardly market sidewinder. Lagging one's peer group by several hundred basis points at the start of the year can have a debilitating impact on the psyche. Because performance results reflect a more pronounced bias toward small and microcapitalized issues, investors of smaller stocks need to be especially aware of seasonal swings.

January Effect as a Value Effect

Seasonal research tends to refer to the January effect as a small-cap phenomenon. But a close look at its underlying causes suggests that the January effect is not simply a small-cap effect but rather a small-cap value effect.[15] That is, value stocks exhibit more of a seasonal bounce than growth stocks.

If the January effect is a value-based phenomenon, small-cap managers need to be aware that their investment style, whether value- or growth-oriented, may affect their January results (see Chapter 9 for a detailed discussion of investment styles). A value-based January effect implies that small-cap growth investors may experience a more difficult start of the year than value investors.

Factors discussed earlier in this chapter, such as the lack of coverage for small caps and the rebound effect, may contribute to this value-based calendar effect. The neglect of small stocks is even more extreme for small-cap value ideas. As discussed in Chapter 9, value shares tend to be terribly underfollowed compared to their small-cap growth counterparts.

The rebound theory argues that stocks tend to bounce after they have corrected, because contrarian buyers enter the picture as the market overreacts or as investors punish shares to extremes. It is not unreasonable that a value-based seasonal effect would occur given the tendencies of the market to overreact and to neglect certain stocks.

The least recognized ideas in the small-cap universe are the "fallen angels" or deep value situations. These forgotten equity ideas are most likely to bounce when information becomes more available on these stocks, and their potential audience is perhaps greater than usual.

To confirm the seasonal value hypothesis, Figure 10.5 presents the relative performance of several simple value measures, namely, price to book value, price to sales, price to earnings, and price to cash flow versus

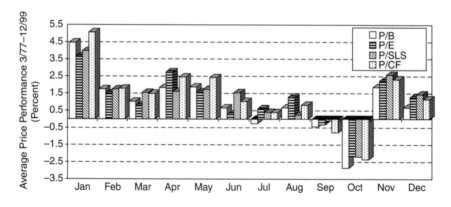

Figure 10.5   Seasonal Bias in Small Value Investing

the small-cap index. Each bar represents the price return on a monthly basis for a separate value measure. For instance, the first bar measures monthly returns for cheap small-cap stocks on a price-to-book value basis. On a price-to-book value basis, the cheapest 10 percent of the small-cap universe handily outpaces the average small-cap returns in the month of January by 1.4 percent. The excess January returns for the value proxy are notable because of the higher hurdle they must meet in that month.

These results do not appear by happenstance. The value bias in January is evidenced in other simple value measures including price-to-earnings, price-to-sales, and price-to-cash flow ratios. The value hypothesis is confirmed not only by these simple value measures, but also by the results of active managers. As discussed in Chapter 9, simple style proxies do a poor job of modeling the results of active growth and value investors. Figure 10.6 represents the actual results of small-cap value funds and small-cap growth funds. Theses results are striking—it appears as though value fund managers generally better small-cap benchmarks and outperform growth managers at the start of the year.

Given the favorable bias toward value investors, growth investors need to tread carefully at the start of the year. Higher-multiple strategies play a supporting role at the start of the year, as the market swoons over out-of-favor strategies. Nonetheless, these results suggest that some of the credit typically accorded to value investing may actually be more the result of the January effect. Even though the results are positive, value investors may need to account for excess returns by excluding anomalous factors such as seasonal variations.

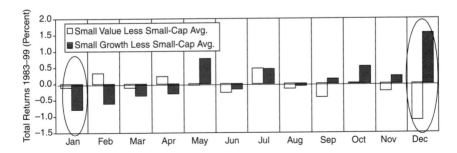

Figure 10.6   Emerging Growth vs. Small Value

December Effect for Growth Stocks

More recently, financial market participants have claimed that the so-called January effect has shifted to December. Not only do the data support a style bias toward small-cap value stocks in January, they suggest that growth stocks experience a surge as the year closes.

To some extent, the end-of-year effect, or December effect, may result from the attempt of investors to exploit the seasonal January effect by getting an early jump on small-cap ideas. Ironically, the attempt to arbitrage a January effect has created a separate and unique seasonal bias. Over the 1990s, small-cap growth stocks have significantly outpaced the small-cap market in December. Figure 10.6 illustrates these results. The results in December 1999 were especially dramatic: small-cap growth stocks jumped 17.0 percent as small-cap stocks gained 12.2 percent followed by a paltry 5.4 percent gain among value stocks.

A December effect also falls in line with the neglect theory discussed previously. To take advantage of the year-end effect, investors generally base their decisions on investment ideas that have exhibited a change in status. Much of this depends on whether firms have released information on their condition. Because emerging growth stocks are more likely to have a stronger information flow, it is reasonable to assume that investors looking for year-end ideas are more likely to gravitate toward growth-oriented companies. The data in Figure 10.6 support a December effect for emerging growth stocks. The rate of return for growth stock managers is above average and well eclipses that of their value counterparts.

Capitalizing on the Seasonal Bias

Although the performance results support the existence of a seasonal bias in stock returns, this can be a fleeting and complex effect. Moreover, like most anomalies, the January effect is not a stable year-after-year event.

Not all experts support the existence of a small-cap January effect. For example, Josef Lakonishok and Seymour Smidt (1984)[16] suggest that the measurement techniques and research methodologies developed for large stocks may be inappropriate for small stocks because of the relative illiquidity of small stocks. Furthermore, a January size bias may simply represent a liquidity mirage, or small-cap returns may appear pronounced because they are thinly traded. Although the results suggest that the high returns for very small and illiquid issues should be viewed critically, the size bias appears to operate on the margin. January results suggest that just as midcap stocks outperform large stocks, small-cap shares beat out midcaps, and so on; size, and not simply liquidity, may be a driving force.

If the illiquidity argument holds, active manager results should not exhibit a traceable performance bias. After all, the more transactions they undertake, the greater the trading costs. At the end of the day, the bounce in the stocks should be offset by the illiquidity of the stock, which results in greater trading costs. Yet the small-cap fund results appear to reflect a seasonal bounce.

Nonetheless, attempting to "game" or arbitrage this effect can lead to mixed results. Although the average small-cap manager may not or should not rely on a seasonal bounce as the sole focus of an investment strategy, the differing performance results for growth and value investing styles at the turn of the year suggest that managers should at least have some level of awareness of the size and style effect at the turn of the year.

The style bias suggests that value managers may want to establish their bets before the start of the year. If the January effect then appears, a well-positioned value list is more likely to reap the full rewards of a value bounce. Similarly, growth managers may want to offset their holdings, especially broken or correcting growth stocks, at the close of the month. If arbitrageurs attempt to capture a seasonal bounce, they are more likely to chase after correcting growth stocks.

Here are additional suggestions for implementing a seasonal strategy.

Covered Call Writing

To enhance performance value, investors could write covered calls on vulnerable value stocks during December, whereas growth investors could write covered calls on vulnerable growth stocks, or stocks with especially sharp gains the prior month, during January. Covered calls represent writing a call option on a stock one holds. Because the stock is held in one's portfolio, it is considered "covered." The risk of this strategy is that if the stock rises above the strike price by expiration, it will be called away; the buyer is likely to exercise the call option. The gain in the trade results from the initial premium received when the investor writes the options.

Opportunistic Tax Rebalancing

Portfolio managers can screen their holdings for vulnerable names. Going into year-end, a manager could sell stocks that are especially weak and have unrecognized losses for the year. By recognizing the losses, managers could realize tax benefits, depending on the tax status of the investor. Taxable investors can take recognized losses three years back and five years forward. This allows one to fully capture the tax benefits of the losses by offsetting them against gains over several years.

Relative Performance Basket

Investors can take a relative performance position, either long or short, to gain from the year-end effect. A relative performance position can take the form of a basket of deep-value small stocks at the start of the year relative to the small-cap index. If the value effect materializes, then the investor benefits from the jump in value stocks above the small-cap index. The investor can benefit even if the January effect fails to materialize. Because the value results appear to be more robust, one is more likely to capture the seasonal value bounce in excess of the seasonal small-cap bounce. However, given trading costs, this trade needs to be carefully implemented.

NOTES

ONE: Small Stocks and the Relevance of Size

1. Satya Pradhuman and Mohamed Chbani, "Size and the Domino Principle," *Small Cap Perspective,* March 9th, 1999.
2. Satya Pradhuman and Mohamed Chbani, "Size and Other People's Money," *Small Cap Perspective,* November 1998.

Recommended Reading:
Geoffrey A. Moor, Paul Johnson, and Tom Kippola. *The Gorilla Game.* New York: Harper Business, 1998.

TWO: The Small-Cap Backdrop

1. For a discussion, see Satya Pradhuman and Richard Bernstein, *Small Cap Perspective,* March 4, 1994.
2. Rolf W. Banz, "The Relationship Between Return and Market Value of Common Stocks," *Journal of Financial Economics,* 9, March 1981. Submitted June 1979.
3. Marc R. Reinganum, "Misspecification of Capital Asset Pricing: Empirical Anomalies Based on Earnings' Yields and Market Values," *Journal of Financial Economics,* 9, March 1981. Submitted December 1979.
4. Steve Kim and Silvio Lotufo, *Portfolio Trading Strategy,* April 21, 1998.

THREE: Major Small-Cap and Large-Cap Cycles

Sources:
"The American Experience/The Presidents." Internet. Available: http://web-cr05.pbs .org/wgbh/pages/amex/presidents. August 6, 1999.
Barron's: National Business and Financial Weekly. New York: Dow Jones & Co., Inc.
Board of Governors of the Federal Reserve System. *Banking and Monetary Statistics: 1941–1970.* Washington, DC: 1976.
————. *Banking and Monetary Statistics: 1914–1941.* Washington, DC: 1943.
Bond, Frederic Drew. *Stock Movements and Speculation,* 2nd Ed. New York: D. Appleton and Company, 1930.

Buck, James, Ed. *The New York Stock Exchange: The First 200 Years.* Greenwich, CT: Greenwich Publishing Group, Inc., 1992.

"Dow Industrials: 1939–1942 Bear Market." Internet. Available: http://www.fiendbear .com/bear1939.htm. July 2, 1999.

"Fidelity: Market Recap." Internet. Available: http://www.fidelityatwork.com/401k/mfp /fundtalk/fidpuritan1.htm. June 30, 1999.

Fridson, Martin. *It Was a Very Good Year: Extraordinary Moments in Stock Market History.* New York: John Wiley & Sons, Inc., 1998.

Hoisington, Harland. *Wall Street 1920–1970: Five Fabulous Decades.* New York: Vantage Press, 1972.

Homer, Sidney, and Sylla, Richard. *A History of Interest Rates,* 3rd Ed. NJ: Rutgers University Press, 1991.

Ibbotson Associates. *Stocks, Bonds, Bills, and Inflation: 1984 Yearbook.* IL: Ibbotson Associates, Inc., 1984.

———. *Stocks, Bonds, Bills, and Inflation: 1994 Yearbook.* IL: Ibbotson Associates, Inc., 1994.

———. *Stocks, Bonds, Bills, and Inflation: 1988 Yearbook.* IL: Ibbotson Associates, Inc., 1999.

Miller, A.T. "Stock Market Outlook for Early '33," *The Magazine of Wall Street,* January 7, 1933.

———. The Market Outlook for 1935," *The Magazine of Wall Street,* January 5, 1935.

———. "The Forces Behind the Market," *The Magazine of Wall Street,* January 7, 1933.

———. "Bear Market Sequence Broken," *The Magazine of Wall Street,* December 24, 1932.

———. "Stock Market Trend for Early 1937," *The Magazine of Wall Street,* December 19, 1936.

Murphy, Thomas, Ed. *The New York Stock Exchange Fact Book.* New York: The New York Stock Exchange, Inc. (1967–1979, 12th Ed.–24th Ed.)

New York Stock Exchange Annual Report: 1954–1956.

Seligman, Joel. *The Transformation of Wall Street: A History of the Securities and Exchange Commission and Modern Corporate Finance.* Boston: Houghton Mifflin Company, 1982.

Sobel, Robert. *The Big Board: A History of the New York Stock Market.* New York: The Free Press, 1965.

———. *Great Bull Market: Wall Street in the 1920's.* New York: W.W. Norton & Company Inc., 1968.

"Stock Market History Since 1928." *Standard & Poor's Current Outlook,* January 27, 1999.

United States Senate Committee on Banking and Currency. *Factors Affecting the Stock Market.* 84th Congress, 1st Session. Washington, DC: 1955.

The Wall Street Journal. New York: Dow Jones & Co., Inc.

Wyckoff, Peter. *Wall Street and the Stock Markets: A Chronology (1644–1971).* Philadelphia: Chilton Book Company, 1972.

FIVE: Asset Allocation and Small Caps

1. "EAFE and World Perspective," Morgan Stanley Capital International, fourth quarter, 1999.

SIX: Driver of Secondary Stocks

1. William Fouse, "The 'Small Stocks' Hoax," *Financial Analyst Journal.* July–August 1989.
2. Jeremy J. Siegel, *Stocks for the Long Run.* New York: McGraw-Hill, 1998, pp. 94–95.
3. Satya Pradhuman, "The Fervor to Favor Large Caps," *Small Cap Update,* February 13, 1997.
4. David C. McCourt, "Resist the Urge to Merge," *The New York Times,* August 27, 1998. Op-Ed pages.
5. Mark Sirower, *The Synergy Trap.* The Free Press, 1997, pp. 18–19.
6. Rex A. Sinquefield, "Are Small-Stock Returns Achievable?" *Financial Analyst Journal,* January–February 1991, pp. 45–50.
7. Elroy Dimson and Paul Marsh, "Murphy's Law and Market Anomalies," *Journal of Portfolio Management,* Winter 1999, p. 59.
8. Jonathan Berk, "Does Size Really Matter? No." Working Paper, University of British Columbia, August 1996, p. 2.
9. Tests such as z-scores allow one to transform sets of data with different means and standard deviations, such as the small- and large-cap returns, to comparable units. After this conversion, one can determine, for example, whether smaller stocks will outperform large stocks, given some change in a factor, such as industrial production, and whether the relationship is statistically significant.
10. Arturo Estrella and Frederic Mishkin, "Predicting U.S. Recessions: Financial Variables as Leading Indicators," *NBER Working Paper* No. 5379, December 1995.
11. Thomas Sargent and Neil Wallace, "Rational Expectations and the Theory of Economic Policy," *Journal of Monetary Economics,* April 1976.

SEVEN: Market Timing Small Stocks

1. The t-statistic for changes over a 3-month basis was a significant −3.26. Additional regression tests also indicate that relative small stocks results are inversely related to changes of aggregate earnings estimates. The changes in aggregate estimate over a 3-month basis is negative (−0.16 coefficient) and statistically significant (a t-statistic of −3.71).
2. Josef Lakonishok and Immoo Lee, "Are Insiders' Traded Informative?" *Working Paper Series* #6656, National Bureau of Economic Research, Inc. Cambridge, MA, July 1998.
3. Ibid.
4. Ibid.

5. An ordinary least squares regression between IPO trend and small-cap performance indicates a positive relationship, a coefficient of 0.023, that is statistically significant (a t-statistic of 3.89).

6. For instance, the regression results between the change in IPO data and the subsequent 6-month small-cap returns are positive, reflecting a coefficient of 0.038 which is statistically significant (a t-statistic of 7.18). The analysis focuses on companies that are considered small stocks on the basis of their issuing market capitalization.

7. Regression results of SEO and the small-cap market are similarly positive with a coefficient of 0.036 that is statistically significant (t-statistic is 3.89). The changes in SEO and subsequent 6-month small-cap returns are positive (a coefficient 0.039) and are statistically significant (a t-statistic of 6.06). The analysis focuses on companies that are considered small stocks on the basis of their existing market capitalization.

EIGHT: Stock Selection Models

1. Richard Bernstein and Satya D. Pradhuman, "The Anatomy of a Model," *Quantitative Viewpoint*, October 2, 1995.

2. Satya D. Pradhuman, "Small Cap Relative Strength Model," *Small Cap Perspective*, November 1995.

3. William O'Neil, *How to Make Money in Stocks.* New York: McGraw Hill, 1988.

4. Narasimhan Jegadeesh. "Evidence of Predictable Behavior of Security Returns," *Journal of Finance*, July 1990: 881–898.

5. Satya Pradhuman. "Estimate Revision Models Add Value," *Small Cap Perspective*, April 1995.

6. Satya D. Pradhuman and Suzanne M. Crosby, "The Presence of Value in Small-Cap Equities," *Equity Style Management*, Eds. Robert A. Klein and Jess Lederman. Irwin Professional Publishing, 1995, pp. 235–248.

NINE: Style Investing

1. Pradhuman and Crosby argue that factors such as neglect and lack of financing cause the style bias to be more amplified in the small-cap market. Satya Pradhuman and Sue Crosby, *Equity Style Management*, Robert A. Klein and Jess Lederman, Irwin, 1992. Chapter 10.

2. Peter Bernstein, "Growth Companies vs. Growth Stocks," *Harvard Business Review*, 1956.

3. Richard Bernstein, *Style Investing.* New York: John Wiley & Sons, 1995.

4. The regression results between a change in industrial production and the relative performance of growth versus value yields a coefficient of −1.90. The R-squared is a solid 0.19 with a t-statistic of −6.75.

5. The coefficient for a change in forecast earnings is −0.70. The R-squared is 0.14 with a t-statistic of −5.61.

6. The coefficient of the relationship is −0.19 with an R-square of 0.09 and a t-statistic of −4.17.

7. Michael Wolff, *Burn Rate*. New York: Simon & Schuster, 1998.

8. The coefficient of one-year change in short-term rates and the style cycle is −0.14. The R-squared in this relationship is 0.06 with a t-statistic of −3.68.

9. The regression statistics for the price-to-sales 12-month lead test exhibits a negative coefficient of −0.31. The R-square is 0.13 with a t-statistic of −5.19.

10. The regression statistics for the one-year lead relative strength risk indicator (RSRI) tests are a negative coefficient of −0.21, with an R-square of 0.18 and a t-statistic of −6.30.

11. Carl Jung, *Psychological Types—The Collected Works of C.G. Jung*. Princeton, NJ: Princeton University Press, 1990.

12. Stephen Stumpf and Thomas P. Mullen, *Taking Charge, Strategic Leadership in the Middle Game*. Englewood Cliffs, NJ: Prentice Hall, 1992.

13. Satya Pradhuman and Sue Crosby, *Equity Style Management*, Chapter 10.

TEN: The January Effect: A Seasonal Premium

1. Donald Keim, "Size-Related Anomalies and Stock Return Seasonality: Further Empirical Evidence," Graduate Business School, University of Chicago, October 1980.

2. Martin S. Fridson, M. Christopher Garman, and Kathryn Okashima, "January Is Superior in the Long Run, Too," *This Week in High Yield*, December 10, 1999, pp. 11–13.

3. Satya D. Pradhuman, "The January Effect: Potential Style Bias at the Turn of the Year," *The Journal of Investing* (Winter 1996, Vol. 5, no. 4).

4. Satya D. Pradhuman and Mohamed Chbani, "Seasonal Bounce Points to Secondary Shares," *Small Cap Perspective*, November 1998, pp. 1–6.

5. Avner Arbel and Paul Strebel, "The Neglected and Small Firm Effects," *The Financial Review*, 17(4), 1982, pp. 201–218.

6. Avner Arbel and Paul Strebel, "Pay Attention to Neglected Firms!" *Journal of Portfolio Management*, 9(2), 1983, pp. 37–42.

7. Avner Arbel, "Generic Stocks: An Old Product in a New Package," *Journal of Portfolio Management*, 11, 1985, pp. 136–145.

8. Dan Givoly and Arie Ovadia, "Year-End Tax-Induced Sales and Stock Market Seasonality," *Journal of Finance*, 38(1), 1983, pp. 171–186.

9. Marc R. Reinganum, "Misspecification of Capital Asset Pricing: Empirical Tests for Tax-Loss Selling Effects," *Journal of Financial Economics*, 9, 1983, pp. 89–104.

10. Josef Lakonishok and Seymour Smidt, "Volume and Turn-of-the-Year Behavior," *Journal of Financial Economics*, 13, 1984, pp. 435–455.

11. Seha Tinic and Giovanni Barone-Adesi, "Seasonality in Stock Prices: A Test of the Tax-loss Selling Hypothesis," University of Alberta, Edmonton, 1983.

12. Werner F.M. de Bondt and Richard Thaler, "Does the Stock Market Overreact?" *Journal of Finance*, July 1985, pp. 793–805.

13. Avner Arbel, "Generic Stocks: An Old Product in a New Package," *Journal of Portfolio Management, 11,* 1985, p. 142.
14. Donald Keim, "Size-Related Anomalies and Stock Return Seasonality: Further Empirical Evidence," *Journal of Financial Economics, 12,* 1983, pp. 13–32.
15. Satya D. Pradhuman and Richard Bernstein, "The "January Effect," *Small Cap Perspective,* November 7, 1994, pp. 3–6.
16. Josef Lakonishok and Seymour Smidt, "Volume and Turn-of-the-Year Behavior," *Journal of Financial Economics, 13,* 1984, pp. 435–455.

INDEX

ABOUT BLOOMBERG

For in-depth market information and news, visit Bloomberg.com which draws proprietary content from the BLOOMBERG PROFESSIONAL™ service and Bloomberg's host of media products to provide high-quality news and information in multiple languages on stocks, bonds, currencies, and commodities—at **www.bloomberg.com.**

Bloomberg L.P., founded in 1981, is a global information services, news, and media company. Headquartered in New York, the company has nine sales offices, two data centers, and 80 news bureaus worldwide.

Bloomberg Financial Markets, serving customers in 100 countries around the world, holds a unique position within the financial services industry by providing an unparalleled combination of news, information, and analytic tools in a single package known as the BLOOMBERG PROFESSIONAL™ service. Corporations, banks, money management firms, financial exchanges, insurance companies, and many other entities and organizations rely on Bloomberg as their primary source of information.

BLOOMBERG NEWS^{SM}, founded in 1990, offers worldwide coverage of economies, companies, industries, governments, financial markets, politics, and sports. The news service is the main content provider for Bloomberg's broadcast media, which include BLOOMBERG TELEVISION®—the 24-hour cable and satellite television network available in ten languages worldwide—and BLOOMBERG RADIO™—an international radio network anchored by flagship station BLOOMBERG® RADIO AM 1130 in New York.

In addition to the BLOOMBERG PRESS® line of books, Bloomberg publishes BLOOMBERG® Magazine, BLOOMBERG PERSONAL FINANCE™, and BLOOMBERG® WEALTH MANAGER. To learn more about Bloomberg, call a sales representative at:

Frankfurt:	49-69-920-410	San Francisco:	1-415-912-2960
Hong Kong:	852-977-6000	São Paulo:	5511-3048-4500
London:	44-171-330-7500	Singapore:	65-438-8585
New York:	1-212-318-2000	Sydney:	61-29-777-8686
Princeton:	1-609-279-3000	Tokyo:	81-3-3201-8900

ABOUT THE AUTHOR

Satya Dev Pradhuman is director of small-cap research at Merrill Lynch. He has also served as quantitative strategist focusing on small- and mid-cap equities and equity derivatives at Merrill Lynch and has held positions in the research departments at E.F. Hutton and Lehman Brothers. Repeatedly named as a top ranking analyst by *Institutional Investor* and Reuters Group, Mr. Pradhuman is a sought-after speaker at professional conferences worldwide. He is widely quoted in the financial press and is a frequent guest on Bloomberg Television and Radio, CNBC, CNN, and MSNBC. He lives outside Manhattan with his wife Mary and their two children.